The Collected Courses of the Academy of European Law
Series Editors: Professor Philip Alston,
Professor Gráinne de Búrca, and
Professor Bruno de Witte
European University Institute,
Florence

VOLUME XII/1
The Enlargement of the European Union

The Collected Courses of the Academy of European Law
Edited by Professor Philip Alston, Professor Gráinne de Búrca, and Professor Bruno de Witte

This series brings together the Collected Courses of the Academy of European Law in Florence. The Academy's mission is to produce scholarly analyses which are at the cutting edge of the two fields in which it works: European Union law and human rights law. A 'general course' is given each year in each field, by a distinguished scholar and/or practitioner, who either examines the field as a whole through a particular thematic, conceptual or philosophical lens, or who looks at a particular theme in the context of the overall body of law in the field. The Academy also publishes each year a volume of collected essays with a specific theme in each of the two fields.

The Enlargement of the European Union

Edited by

MARISE CREMONA

Academy of European Law
European University Institute

OXFORD
UNIVERSITY PRESS

OXFORD

UNIVERSITY PRESS

Great Clarendon Street, Oxford OX2 6DP

Oxford University Press is a department of the University of Oxford.
It furthers the University's objective of excellence in research, scholarship,
and education by publishing worldwide in

Oxford New York

Auckland Bangkok Buenos Aires Cape Town Chennai
Dar es Salaam Delhi Hong Kong Istanbul Karachi Kolkata
Kuala Lumpur Madrid Melbourne Mexico City Mumbai Nairobi
São Paulo Shanghai Taipei Tokyo Toronto

Oxford is a registered trade mark of Oxford University Press
in the UK and in certain other countries

Published in the United States
by Oxford University Press Inc., New York

British Library Cataloguing in Publication Data

Data available

Library of Congress Cataloging in Publication Data

Data available

ISBN 0–19–926093–1
ISBN 0–19–926094–X (pbk.)

1 3 5 7 9 10 8 6 4 2

Typeset by Kolam Information Services Pvt. Ltd, Pondicherry, India
Printed in Great Britain on acid-free paper by
Biddles Ltd., Guildford and King's Lynn

Contents

Table of Cases

Table of Treaties and Legislation

Decisions

Directives

Regulations

United Kingdom

List of Tables

List of Figures

Notes on Contributors

Marise Cremona is Professor of European Commercial Law and Deputy Director of the Centre for Commercial Law Studies, Queen Mary, University of London. Her research interests include the European Internal Market, the EU's regulatory policy, and the external policy of the EU. She is particularly interested in legal integration within the wider dimension of the EU's external relations, the foundational constitutional dimension to EU commercial policy, and the position of the EU as a regulatory body within the wider global context, including relations with the WTO and other international organizations and states, especially the countries of central and eastern Europe and developing countries. She has organized and contributed to training programmes for lawyers from central and eastern Europe, and has acted as consultant on European integration for several governments. Her major publications are in the field of EU external policy, including 'External Relations and External Competence: The Emergence of an Integrated External Policy for The European Union', in P. Craig and G. de Búrca (eds), *EU Law: An Evolutionary Perspective* (Oxford University Press, 1999); 'Creating the New Europe: The Stability Pact for South-Eastern Europe in the Context of EU–SEE Relations', *Cambridge Yearbook of European Legal Studies* Volume II 1999; Cremona, Fletcher, and Mistelis (eds), *Foundations and Perspectives of International Trade Law* (Sweet & Maxwell, 2001); 'Rhetoric and Reticence: EU External Commercial Policy in a Multilateral Context', 38 *Common Market Law Review* (2001).

Bruno de Witte is Professor of European Union Law at the European University Institute in Florence, and Co-director of its Academy of European Law. He is on long-term leave from the University of Maastricht, where he taught EU law from 1989 until 2000. In recent years, he has written on a number of topics of EU constitutional law, including the protection of fundamental rights, the division of competences between the EU and its Member States, the relation between EU law and national law, the reorganization of the European treaties, and the mechanisms for their revision. He has also published on minority protection and cultural and language policies in Europe, with special reference to the forthcoming enlargement of the European Union.

András Inotai has been Director General of the Institute for World Economics of the Hungarian Academy of Sciences since 1991. He has twice held the position of Head of the Strategic Task Force on European Integration (1995–1998 and since July 2002), and was a staff member of the World

Bank, Washington D.C. (1989–1991). He has held posts as Visiting Professor at the College of Europe, Bruges (since 1993) and Natolin (since 1994) and was a Guest Professor at Columbia University, New York (autumn 2002). His key research and teaching areas include development trends in the world economy, European integration, with special reference to eastern enlargement, Hungary's preparation for accession to the EU, and transformation economics in a regional comparative perspective. He has authored or edited several books and innumerable articles in various professional journals in Europe, the United States and Asia, and is a member of the scientific advisory board for various research institutes and of the editorial board of several professional journals in Hungary and abroad.

Marc Maresceau studied at the University of Ghent, the Johns Hopkins University, Bologna, and at the Institut Universitaire de Hautes Etudes Internationales, Geneva. He has been Leverhulme Fellow at the University of Edinburgh and Visiting Professor at various universities. He teaches European law and Institutions at the Universities of Ghent and Brussels, and is the Director of the European Institute at the University of Ghent, where he also holds a Jean Monnet Chair. Many of his publications concentrate on the external relations of the European Union, in particular relations between the European Union and central and eastern Europe.

Phedon Nicolaides is a Professor at the European Institute of Public Administration, Maastricht. He has held academic positions at the London Business School and the Royal Institute of International Affairs, London. He has also served as Minister Plenipotentiary in the Ministry of Foreign Affairs of Cyprus. He is currently advisor to the Chief Negotiator of Cyprus for accession to the EU and consultant to the Cyprus Competition Commission and the Cyprus State Aid Monitoring Authority. He is also a member of the Academic Advisory Group on State Aid of DG Competition of the European Commission. His research and publications are in the fields of competition policy, economic integration, the enlargement of the European Union, and, in particular, the development of effective regulatory systems in the candidate countries.

Karen E. Smith is Lecturer in International Relations at the London School of Economics. She earned her PhD in 1996 from the LSE, and was a Jean Monnet Fellow at the European University Institute in Florence, in 1996–1997. Her publications include: K. E. Smith and M. Light (eds), *Ethics and Foreign Policy* (Cambridge University Press, 2001); K. E. Smith and C. Hill (eds), *European Foreign Policy: Key Documents* (Routledge, 2000); and *The Making of EU Foreign Policy: The Case of Eastern Europe* (Macmillan, 1999).

Milada Anna Vachudova is Assistant Professor of Political Science at the University of North Carolina Chapel Hill. She has held fellowships at the European University Institute in Florence, the Center for European Studies at Harvard University, the European Union Center of New York City at Columbia University, the Center for International Studies at Princeton University, the Belfer Center for Science and International Affairs at Harvard University, and the National Science Foundation. Her research focuses on the impact of international institutions on domestic politics, the enlargement of the European Union, and the democratization of post-communist Europe. She has published on the reform trajectories of post-communist states; on the enlargement of the European Union; on the EU's evolving immigration and security policies; and on the ability of international institutions to promote political and economic reform. Her book *Revolution, Democracy, and Integration* is forthcoming by Oxford University Press.

1

Introduction

MARISE CREMONA

1. AN UNPRECEDENTED ENLARGEMENT

The fifth enlargement of the European Union, projected to take place in 2004, will be unlike any other. In part this results from its sheer scale: there are currently 13 candidate states, with 12 of which negotiations are in process, and the European Council has indicated that, 'if the present rate of progress of the negotiations and reforms in the candidate States is maintained', ten countries may be ready to accede in time to take part as Member States in the 2004 European Parliament elections.[1]

It is also the culmination of a pre-accession process of unprecedented length and complexity, whether we date its start from Turkey's application in 1987, the beginning of normalization of relations with the central and eastern European states in 1990, or the historic decision taken at Copenhagen in June 1993 that 'the associated countries in central and eastern Europe that so desire shall become members of the European Union'.[2] For the first time, specific political, economic, and legal conditions have been applied, regular Progress Reports have been produced, a pre-accession strategy has been developed, founded on bilateral treaty commitments but also incorporating 'Accession Partnerships', technical assistance and participation by the candidate states in Community programmes. 'Pre-accession', as demonstrated by Marc Maresceau in Chapter Two, is more than merely an adjective, descriptive of a strategy or a process: it has become an experience of change and adaptation by the European Union as well as by the candidate states. Nor is it an experience that will come to an end with a 'big bang' enlargement in 2004. Even assuming all ten states do join at once, the remaining three candidate

[1] Conclusions of the European Council, Laeken, 14–15 Dec. 2001, para. 8. See also Commission Strategy Paper, 'Making a Success of Enlargement', Nov. 2001, and Commission Strategy Paper, 'Towards the Enlarged Union', Oct. 2002. The ten countries mentioned were Cyprus, Estonia, Hungary, Latvia, Lithuania, Malta, Poland, the Slovak Republic, the Czech Republic, and Slovenia.

[2] Conclusions of the European Council, Copenhagen, June 1993.

countries (Bulgaria, Romania, Turkey) are likely to be joined by other applicants during the course of the next five years; this enlargement is therefore also the start of an ongoing process that will fundamentally change the character of the European Union.

This enlargement has also been perceived as something other than a 'joining of the club' by a few (or even many) more members. It has immense political and even psychological significance as a 'return to Europe' by the central and eastern European states, a reunification of Europe following the end of the divisions of the Cold War, and with the significant (problematic) potential for redrawing the boundaries of—and within—Europe. It thus has a significance beyond its boundaries, particularly for those states within Europe that may aspire to membership, and for the states on the periphery of Europe for which the EU is a major trading partner and the interests of which are profoundly affected by the stability and security of the region as a whole.

This collection of essays is not intended to provide a comprehensive survey of every aspect of the fifth enlargement of the EU, or EU enlargement in general. In keeping with the policy of this series, it seeks to open up to discussion a number of specific features of this enlargement, in particular those features which are distinctive or which have a wider significance. As we have seen, these include the nature of 'pre-accession' and the political, legal, and economic adjustments required of the candidate states, the application of explicit membership conditionality, the constitutional implications of enlargement, and the implications of the enlargement for the external trade and foreign policy of the Union. Not surprisingly, however, a number of key themes emerge from these various dimensions of enlargement, themes which are reflected through the different perspectives of several academic disciplines but which provide a framework for the subject as a whole.

2. THE INSTITUTIONAL AND CONSTITUTIONAL DIMENSION

The first of these themes emphasizes that enlargement is not just about political will and effective negotiation. The pre-accession process itself—pre-accession instruments and strategies, including screening, Accession Partnerships, and the ability to manage the EU accession-related funds and technical assistance—requires management and an effective institutional structure on both sides. Participation in an enlarged Union imposes institutional demands on both the candidate states and the organization itself. For the candidate states, there is an institutional dimension to each of the three initial 'Copenhagen criteria', established in 1993[3] and discussed here in

---

[3] *Supra* note 2.

Chapter Five. The first, political, criterion (stability of institutions guaranteeing democracy, the rule of law, human rights, and the protection of minorities) is explicit as to the need for an institutional underpinning of constitutional values. Both the ability to fulfil the economic criteria (a functioning market economy with the capacity to withstand competitive pressures within the EU) and the ability to take on the obligations of membership are dependent on an effective legal and institutional infrastructure including but not limited to the institutions of government.

Chapter Three builds on the examination of the pre-accession process in Chapter Two by focusing in more detail on one of its aspects: exactly what is involved in effective implementation of the *acquis*? Phedon Nicolaides points out that in emphasizing the need for effective implementation, the EU is 'both clarifying and toughening' the entry requirements. He argues that the building of appropriate institutional structures is the only way to ensure effective implementation of the Union *acquis* and develops an analysis of the necessary characteristics of such institutions. The institutional capacity of the accession states is important not only for their own ability to manage the demands of membership but also for the Union itself as the new members begin to play a part in policy- and decision-making at Union level.

But the demands of enlargement are not all on one side. Both the pre-accession process and membership conditionality also impose demands on the EU itself and its institutions. In 1993, the European Council recognized that 'the Union's capacity to absorb new members, while maintaining the momentum of European integration, is also an important consideration in the general interest of both the Union and the candidate countries'.[4] As Marc Maresceau points out, it is this 'fourth Copenhagen condition' which has proved to be the weak spot of the Union's pre-accession strategy. The threat to the Union's decisional capacity posed by the dramatic expansion of the Union and the cumulative effects of several enlargements has been recognized but not defused. The candidates may fall short of meeting the membership criteria, but the EU itself has not really responded to the challenge of enlargement in terms of institutional development.

The discussion of these issues by Bruno de Witte in Chapter Eight reveals the link between the institutional reform which is necessary for enlargement (in the sense of a precondition) and the broader questions of constitutional development discussed by the European Council at Laeken,[5] and within the Constitutional Convention.[6] Although these aspects of constitutional reform

[4] *Supra* note 2.
[5] Laeken Declaration on the Future of the European Union, Annex I to the Conclusions of the Laeken European Council, 14 and 15 Dec. 2001.
[6] Established by the European Council at Laeken, the Convention on the future of the Union is charged with the preparation for the Intergovernmental Conference (IGC) planned for 2004.

are not perceived as a pre-condition for enlargement,[7] this enlargement in particular will profoundly influence the constitutional development of the Union. Partly, of course, this will be the result of the input from ten or more new Member States, with their various histories, interests, and objectives. But it is also true that a development of the Union is taking place which moves us on from the widening versus deepening debate; a recognition that the constitutional shape of the Union affects not only its immediate members, but also putative or potential members, other near neighbours, and indeed the wider global community.

This is not to suggest a process of smooth and fully conscious development. The Union has always been better at putting the big questions ('The Union needs to become more democratic, more transparent and more efficient. It also has to resolve three basic challenges: how to bring citizens, and primarily the young, closer to the European design and the European institutions, how to organise politics and the European political area in an enlarged Union and how to develop the Union into a stabilising factor and a model in the new, multipolar world.'[8]) than at answering them. These are questions to which the answers by their nature will change over time, as the future constitutional character of the enlarged EU emerges. Even the process of constructing answers poses questions about the involvement and engagement of the candidate, and potential candidate, states. The candidate states have been accepted as participants in the European Convention on the same basis as Member States, but will only take part in the Intergovernmental Conference (IGC) planned for 2004 if they have concluded a Treaty of Accession by that date. This suggests a possible new role for the European Conference, the creation of the European Council in December 1997 in an unsuccessful attempt to finesse the exclusion of Turkey from decisions on the opening of negotiations and on pre-accession strategy. It has since been extended to include the countries of the Stabilization and Association Process (Albania, Bosnia-Herzegovina, Croatia, Yugoslavia, and the Former Yugoslav Republic of Macedonia), the EFTA states, and most recently Russia, Moldova, and Ukraine. The sensitive debate about which countries should be included (or excluded) as a state eligible for EU membership, as a candidate or potential candidate state, as a participant in these various initiatives (the European Conference, the Convention on the future of Europe) brings us to a second theme which can be identified as a feature of the fifth enlargement.

---

[7] See Declaration No. 23 on the future of the Union, attached to the Treaty of Nice, Dec. 2000, at para. 8.

[8] Laeken Declaration on the Future of the European Union, *supra* note 5.

3. INCLUSION AND EXCLUSION

The Spanish Presidency, in a recent report, referred to 'the inclusiveness of this enlargement process'.[9] Indeed, the nature and scope of this inclusiveness, and its implications, are a fundamental issue of this enlargement. The question of inclusiveness arises at a number of levels: in the opening of accession negotiations with applicant states; in the application of member-ship conditionality criteria; in the timing of the accession process ('big bang' or step by step); in the involvement of candidate states in Union pro-grammes, policies, and constitutional debate; and in the extension of the enlargement process to other potential candidates.

The tension that exists between the desire to extend EU membership, in particular to the economically and politically vulnerable countries of central, eastern, and south-eastern Europe, and the difficulties that such an extensive enlargement will create for the operation of the European Union is a recurring theme in the following chapters. The development of membership criteria, as Karen Smith argues in Chapter Five, has provided a partial solution to the 'widening versus deepening' dilemma. It is significant that the European Council at Copenhagen in 1993 both accepted that 'the associated countries in central and eastern Europe that so desire shall become members of the European Union', and established explicit membership criteria. Out of this declaration has developed a perception that the European Union should play a key role in the reunification or even the recreation of Europe, and the gradual growth of an assumption, now fully-fledged, that the European Union could, and even should, be open to the inclusion of the whole of Europe. The point here is not that all European states *should* eventually join the EU; the point is that the EU accepts at a fundamental level that membership should be an option for all European states and the consequent obligation to assist in the fulfilment of the essential criteria for accession. Further, if enlargement is to be used as an instrument of Union policy, designed to stabilize and restructure Europe,[10] then conditionality is a key to its success. In particular, in a Union which cannot function without a high degree of mutual trust, heavy demands will be made on incoming Members. The need to establish trust, and not least to establish the

---

[9] Presidency Report on Enlargement, presented to European Council, Seville, 21–22 June 2002 (Doc.9765/02). This phrasing reflects that of the European Council Conclusions in Helsinki, Dec. 1999, para. 4.

[10] At Madrid in Dec. 1995 the European Council declared that enlargement 'will ensure the stability and security of the continent and will thus offer both the applicant states and the current members of the Union new prospects for economic growth and general well-being'. See also Commission, Agenda 2000, Vol. I 'For A Stronger and Wider Union', Part One, section IV 'The Union in the World' COM(1997)2000; Commission's Progress Report of 8 Nov. 2000, sect I, 'The Overall Context'.

institutional mechanisms which are the foundation for mutual trust, is one objective of the different elements of the pre-accession process. The institutional dimension to this process is discussed by Phedon Nicolaides in Chapter Three; it is also present in the pre-accession legal harmonization programme and in pre-accession alignment of foreign policy-making within the Common Foreign and Security Policy (CFSP) discussed in Chapter Seven, both in different ways creating the beginning of a track record for the accession states. If the Union is to develop the flexibility it needs to cope with new international agendas and ambitious integration policies while maintaining a position of openness to possible new members, it needs to ensure at least a minimum degree of convergence between its existing and future membership.[11]

To agree these principles does not of course resolve all the dilemmas. To mention just two of these: how is it possible to avoid accusations of double standards and unfairness in the application of membership conditionality where the criteria are inherently 'soft' and the process inevitably highly politicized? And how should the accepted principles of conditionality and differentiation be reconciled with an inclusive approach to enlargement? The two questions are connected: as the critical decisions are taken on how many of the candidate states should proceed to accession in the 'first wave' in 2004, it appears that the benefits of a broader enlargement will be given greater weight, an approach which in itself raises issues of credibility and fairness. The European Council at Helsinki in December 1999, following the recommendations of the Commission and 'in the light of recent developments' (a reference to the Kosovo crisis), decided to open negotiations with all remaining candidate states except Turkey, seeing this as 'a positive contribution to security and stability on the European continent'.[12] In Laeken in December 2001 the European Council likewise decided that 'up to ten' of the candidate states might be ready to conclude negotiations by the end of 2002 so as to be able to accede by 2004.

Differentiation—whereby the candidate countries' progress towards accession will depend on their individual progress in meeting the membership criteria—has been a fundamental principle of pre-accession, reflected in the individual Commission opinions, progress reports, Accession Partnerships with their targets, and negotiations. In Chapter Four, András Inotai examines the implications in this context of the similarities and the differences between the central and eastern European candidate countries in terms of history, geography, and political and economic development. A further distinctive characteristic of this enlargement is the fact that the majority of the candidate

---

[11] See further Cremona, 'Accession to the European Union: Membership Conditionality and Accession Criteria', 25 *Polish Yearbook of International Law* (2001) 220, at 240.
[12] Conclusions of the European Council, Helsinki, Dec. 1999, para. 10.

states are transition economies which are also in the process of renewing their political institutions and legal infrastructure. The Copenhagen criteria reflect the implications of these characteristics for EU membership, and the unprecedented pre-accession process is intended to assist in the transition. As András Inotai points out, the solution lies neither in ignoring the differences between the candidates nor in perpetuating them. The challenge is to create the conditions for sustainable convergence both economically and politically. This use of conditionality will remain an important part of Union strategy for many years after the fifth enlargement, both for the new Member States and in the development of integration policies with other potential candidate states, especially those of the Balkans.

4. THE EXTERNAL DIMENSION OF ENLARGEMENT

Every enlargement has an external dimension. In fact, of course, enlargement is itself an instrument of the Union's foreign policy, affecting not only those candidate states immediately involved in the process but other states in the region and further afield. As Maresceau points out in the context of a discussion of the European Conference, the majority of important cross-border issues (including security policy, regional cooperation, international crime and terrorism, immigration and border policies) go beyond the relationship between the EU and the candidate states. In this too it is significant that 'enlargement' is not a single event; it is a process which has been evolving for at least the past decade, and it will continue over a period of years after the accessions planned for 2004.

Policies which have developed and matured during this enlargement, such as conditionality, also have effects on regions and states which are outside the current enlargement process, but which are 'potential candidates'.[13] In Chapter Five this aspect of conditionality is considered by Karen Smith: as well as forming a key part of the Union's enlargement strategy, conditionality has become a successful element of the Union's foreign policy, as it uses the promise of technical and financial assistance, association agreements, and ultimately membership to influence the conduct of non-member (and non-candidate) countries. Of particular importance here are the Balkans; the impact of the current enlargement on the future of EU relations with these countries is discussed by Milada Vachudova in Chapter Six. Together with Russia and Ukraine, the western Balkans are critical to the success of enlargement as a contribution to security and stability for the EU and Europe as a whole. This geopolitical objective has been identified by both European

---

[13] Conclusions of the European Council at Feira, June 2001, para. 67. See also the Preambles to the Stabilization and Association Agreements concluded with Macedonia (FYROM) and Croatia.

Council and Commission as a primary effect of enlargement in the wider context.[14] It will certainly be a major challenge, as the newly enlarged EU develops its policies in geopolitical regions which encompass Member and non-Member States: the 'Northern Dimension' and Baltic Sea region, the Balkans, and the Black Sea region for example.

However, as Chapter Seven demonstrates, the external aspect of enlargement is as much about trade as about foreign policy. A greatly enlarged EU has implications for the EU's trading partners and for its role within the WTO. Unlike some other aspects of the *acquis* which they are having to adopt as part of the pre-accession process, the external trade *acquis* is not in itself particularly controversial or problematic for the candidate states. The questions arise rather in attempting to predict what effect enlargement will have on external trade policy. Will the EU become more protectionist? Will the new Member States divert trade and investment from the developing countries? How will enlargement affect the simultaneous post-Doha negotiations on agricultural trade? Wider questions can be posed about the continuing commitment of the EU to multilateral liberalization and the development of multilateral governance as a response to globalization. Of course, any answers to these questions have to remain extremely tentative at this stage. It is undeniable, however, that the relative consensus with respect to world trade issues within the EU (admittedly somewhat fragile and not always complete) will come under more strain. This is not because the candidate states are less committed to a liberal trade agenda than the existing Member States. It is rather that building a coherent policy and identification of the common interest will be more difficult in a larger and more economically diverse Union.

This brings us back to the institutional dimension of enlargement. The conclusion of the following chapters is that, while enlargement poses huge challenges for the Union's institutional structure and development, it also makes it all the more necessary to resolve them. There is a risk that the internal constitutional debate will dissipate the energy needed if the Union is to take on a leadership role in global issues and in building relations with its neighbours so that its future borders do not become a new dividing line.[15] The Commission called its autumn 2001 strategy paper on enlargement 'Making a Success of Enlargement'. A successful enlargement will be crucial for the credibility of the EU both internationally and at home—its international identity, its developing identity as a Union—and for the future of Europe.

---

[14] Conclusions of the European Council at Madrid, Dec. 1995. See also Avery, 'Special Report: Endgame for EU Enlargement', *Prospect*, July 2002, 54 at 57.

[15] Commission's Strategy Paper, 'Making a Success of Enlargement', Nov. 2001, at 7.

2

Pre-accession

MARC MARESCEAU

1. INTRODUCTION[1]

Writing on EU enlargement, and in particular the legal aspects of EU pre-accession strategies, is an almost impossible task. The topic evolves very rapidly, prospective analysis very quickly becomes purely speculative, and, perhaps most difficult of all, an interdisciplinary approach is becoming increasingly indispensable. Of course, it is possible to focus on the legal dimension of the pre-accession instruments, but even then the political and economic context can and should never be far away. This is further amplified by the fact that for one or other strange reason, only very few EU law academic experts have been concentrating on EU enlargement. Certainly, it is a fancy topic as a chapter in an institutions course or seminar but, apparently, it is much less popular for in-depth research among EU lawyers. This explains why, in a 'legal contribution' such as this, many of the sources are necessarily political science and economics oriented. But in the author's opinion this is, because of the very nature of the topic, not necessarily a drawback.

The expression 'pre-accession', formally appearing for the first time in the Conclusions of the Essen European Council of December 1994, is now firmly established in the terminological practice of the EU enlargement discourse, and is generally used as an adjective and occasionally even as a noun. Since 1994 'pre-accession strategies', 'pre-accession instruments', '*enhanced* pre-accession strategies', and so on and so forth have been developed. In the current EU enlargement scenario 'pre-accession' policies indeed play a much more predominant role than in previous enlargements of the European Community. In past enlargement practice, pre-accession strategies, as such, were virtually or even completely lacking. The indispensable adaptations that candidate states had to make were very often accomplished during

---

[1] This Chapter is part of a GOA research project of the University of Ghent on 'The External Relations of the European Union: the Legal and Political Framework'.

transitional periods *after* the entry into force of the relevant treaty of accession. To give one illustration of such a post-accession adaptation: one of the most difficult adjustments to the *acquis communautaire* when the UK joined the EC concerned agriculture. In the early 1960s application for membership by the UK led to an unrealistic demand for derogations from the fundamental principles of the common agricultural policy,[2] and it was only in the accession negotiations at the beginning of the 1970s that a compromise could be reached allowing for an orderly adjustment of the UK's national agriculture policy during a transitional period *after* accession.[3] That being said, in past enlargements it was sometimes also the case that important legislative activity in candidate states appeared to be indispensable *before* accession to the EC. This was usually achieved in the, sometimes long, accession negotiation phase and it was not part of a preconceived strategy of the EC. A striking example—but there are others—is again that of the UK where existing domestic constitutional law practice required fundamental adjustments. This was done through the 1972 European Communities Act creating an extremely subtle legal construction allowing existing and future EC law to be applied in the UK at the moment of entry to the EC. This Act, and in particular its masterpiece, Section 2(1), indeed achieved, as very properly formulated by Professor Dashwood, 'a great deal with very few words'.[4] Basically, it had as a consequence that British constitutional law concepts, at first sight irreconcilable with basic EC law principles such as supremacy and direct effect of European Community law, rather unexpectedly, could be smoothly integrated into the British legal order and judicial practice.[5]

The current enlargement debate is of a totally different calibre and it is not easy to give a precise legal definition of the notion 'pre-accession strategies'. Of course, in general the expression refers to EU initiatives whereby candidate countries for EU membership are brought closer to the EU in political, economic, and legal terms so that, in the end, accession is not too abrupt for both the candidate countries *and* the EU to absorb. Clearly, pre-accession strategies seem particularly relevant and absolutely necessary where countries applying for EU membership need to make preliminary

---

[2] See on this point Ludlow, 'British Agriculture and the Brussels Negotiations: A Problem of Trust', in G. Wilkes (ed.), *Britain's Failure to Enter the European Community 1961–1963* (1997) 108, at 117.

[3] See C. Preston, *Enlargement and Integration in the European Union* (1997), at 34–35.

[4] Dashwood, 'The British Way: The Cohabiting with Community Law', in A. E. Kellerman *et al.* (eds), *EU Enlargement. The Constitutional Impact at EU and National Level* (2001) 81, at 82; see also Jacobs, 'The Constitutional Impact of the Forthcoming Enlargement of the EU: What can be Learnt from the Experience of the Existing Member States?', in *ibid.*, at 186.

[5] See Newman, 'Legal Problems for British Accession', in Wilkes (ed.), *supra* note 2, at 120–132; also Dashwood, *supra* note 4, at 82–83.

political, economic, and legal adaptations before accession can seriously be contemplated. This is precisely the case for the applications for EU membership of the Countries from Central and Eastern Europe (CEECs): that is to say Poland, Hungary, the Czech Republic, Romania, Bulgaria, Lithuania, Latvia, Estonia, and Slovenia.[6] Moreover, accession to today's EU is also much more complex than at the time of previous enlargements to the European Community (EC). The sheer volume and extreme complexity of the present *acquis communautaire*—including also the EU *acquis* with its Second and Third Pillars[7]—make enlargement a particularly daring operation for the candidates and implies for them a solid basis of EU know-how before they can function properly in such an enlarged EU. Last but not least, there is also the EU itself which domestically, to put it euphemistically, is not yet fully prepared institutionally speaking, nor even, if one may say so, mentally speaking, to absorb such an overwhelming accession scenario, including not only the ten CEECs already mentioned but also Cyprus, Malta, and Turkey, the latter three candidates having applied for membership in 1990 and 1987. Moreover, it is certain that EU enlargement will not be completed even with these 13 candidate countries, and others are still in the waiting-room.[8] Consequently, in the end, pre-accession is not only a preparatory process for accession by the candidates but also very much so for the EU itself. In reality, this aspect of pre-accession proves to be a very difficult, if not the most difficult, aspect of the enlargement process as a whole.

2. ORIGIN OF THE 'PRE-ACCESSION STRATEGY' CONCEPT

It was the 1994 Essen European Council that constituted the formal departure of the 'real' pre-accession strategy, but it took root long before then. In a

---

[6] On the other hand if Switzerland or Norway should want to become an EU member pre-accession strategies would be unnecessary since they 'already meet all of the membership criteria': see European Commission, 1999 Composite Paper. Reports on progress towards accession by each of the candidate countries, COM(1999)500 final, 13 Oct. 1999, at 2.

[7] The expression '*acquis communautaire*' in the *EU* enlargement terminology is not always used in a strict legal way since it often implies also Second and Third Pillar *acquis*. From a strict legal point of view it is better therefore to use the expression '*EU acquis*'. The problem, however, is that in many official documents the expression *acquis communautaire* continues to be used to refer also to the Second and Third Pillar. For an analysis of the notion *acquis communautaire*, see Delcourt, 'The *Acquis Communautaire*: Has the Concept had its Day?', 38 *CMLRev.* (2001), at 829–870.

[8] The countries with which Stabilization and Association Agreements are signed or envisaged are qualified as 'potential candidates' in the preambles to these agreements. So far such agreements have been signed with the Former Yugoslav Republic of Macedonia (1 June 2001) and Croatia (29 October 2001).

way, every EC initiative to promote political and economic transition in Central and Eastern Europe since 1989, even in the absence of any accession prospect originally, has at a later stage been able to be turned into a pre-accession instrument. The conditions *sine qua non* for such a qualitative change are, on the one hand, the willingness of the country concerned to become a member of the EU and, on the other, the commitment of the EU to be willing to enlarge to embrace that country.

It was at the 1993 Copenhagen European Council that the Heads of State and Government of the EU agreed that those associated countries of Central and Eastern Europe so desiring could become members of the European Union. Accession could take place once the candidates were able to assume the obligations of membership. This implied that they would have to satisfy a number of political and economic conditions, as enumerated in the Copenhagen Conclusions.[9] Included among the political conditions were the need to achieve stability of institutions guaranteeing democracy, the rule of law, human rights, and respect for and protection of minorities. These broadly formulated requirements, as such, were not revolutionary as political conditions for EU membership and would, in principle, not pose insurmountable problems in most cases,[10] since all candidates as PHARE beneficiaries had already qualified for a 'democracy test', a political pre-condition to obtaining financial support under this programme. In fact, and although this was not mentioned explicitly in the relevant basic Community Regulations,[11] the application and extension of the PHARE Programme had been made conditional on organizing free elections, establishing a multiparty system, respect for human rights, and introducing a market economy,[12] and the same pre-conditions were also 'reaffirmed' in the preamble to the

[9] See Smith, 'The Evolution and Application of EU Membership Conditionality', in this vol. For a legal analysis of these conditions see Müller-Graff, 'East Central Europe and the European Union: From Europe Agreements to a Member Status', in P.-C. Müller-Graff (ed.), *East Central Europe and the European Union: From Europe Agreements to Member Status* (1997) 9, at 17–22; same author, 'Legal Framework for Relations Between the European Union and Central and Eastern Europe: General Aspects', in M. Maresceau (ed.), *Enlarging the European Union. Relations Between the EU and Central and Eastern Europe* (1997) 27, at 34–37.

[10] When on 15 July 1997 the Commission gave its opinions on the ten CEECs' applications for EU membership, only Slovakia did not satisfy the Copenhagen political conditions: see further *infra*.

[11] See for the first basic PHARE Regulations: Council Regulation 3906/89 of 18 Dec. 1989, OJ 1989 L 375/11 and Council Regulation 2698/90 of 17 Sept. 1990, OJ 1990 L 257/11.The first regulation applied to Poland and Hungary and is the origin of the acronym 'PHARE' (Poland–Hungary Action for Reform).

[12] This explains why originally only Poland and Hungary benefited from PHARE: they were the first COMECON countries to have initiated political and economic reforms. The aid granted was 'primarily to support the process of reform in Poland and Hungary, in particular by financing or participating in financing of projects aimed at economic restructuring': see Art. 3, Regulation 3906/89.

Europe Agreements.[13] These PHARE prerequisites found their origin in the initiatives developed in various multilateral frameworks of industrialized countries. The G7 meeting in Paris on 15 July 1989 in particular was instrumental in this respect. At this meeting it had been noted that leaders in some countries of Central and Eastern Europe '[were] aware of the positive contributions that greater freedom and democracy [could] make to the modernization of their countries and [were] starting to make changes to their laws, practices and institutions'. This process of reform needed to be supported, and the EC Commission was asked to coordinate this support and to associate other interested parties to this initiative. The G24 was rapidly involved but the main work was, and continued to be, performed by the EC and the Commission in particular. It was also the Commission that was the first to refine the pre-conditions for PHARE support.[14] In a Commission Communication to the Council and European Parliament of 1 February 1990 on 'the development of the Community's relations with the countries of central and eastern Europe',[15] the Commission observed that coordinated assistance was intended 'to facilitate political reform and economic liberalisation'. It would, according to the Commission, 'not be reasonable to require the demonstration of success in implementing reform as an initial condition for participation in assistance programmes' but 'it is, however, necessary to require commitments to democratic elections and economic liberalisation, preferably within a specified time-table'.[16] Consequently, countries seeking access to assistance had to provide clear commitments regarding the rule of law, respect for human rights, establishment of a multiparty system, the holding of free and fair elections, and economic liberalization with a view to introducing a market economy. These prerequisites and later the Copenhagen Conditions were, as is easily seen, to a large extent comparable, the most novel element of the Copenhagen Conditions being that of protection of minorities. Of course, democracy is never perfect and qualitative improvements can always be made, but once a certain level in the democratization

---

[13] 'Social justice' was also mentioned in the preamble, and furthermore in the Europe Agreements of the Second Round (from 1993 onwards) 'protection of minorities' was explicitly added.

[14] See *Agence Europe*, 15 Feb. 1990. On the political preconditions for PHARE see in particular Lequesne, 'Commerce et aide économique: les instruments d'une politique', in F. de La Serre, C. Lequesne, and J. Rupnik (eds), *L'Union européenne: ouverture à l'Est?* (1994) 43, at 50–51; K.E. Smith, *The Making of EU Foreign Policy. The Case of Eastern Europe* (1999), at 70–72; De Smijter, 'Constitutionele beoordeling van de relaties tussen de Europese Unie en landen van Centraal en Oost-Europa', in De Meyere *et al.* (eds), *Oost-Europa in Europa. Huldeboek aangeboden aan Frits Gorlé* (1996), 153 at 156. Only once PHARE became part of the 'enhanced pre-accession strategy' was conditionality clearly formally and procedurally consolidated (see further *infra*).

[15] SEC(90)196 final.

[16] *Ibid.*, at 2–3.

process is reached, the matter of assessing whether the Copenhagen Conditions are met or not becomes less of a 'yes or no', 'black or white' question, but more one of degree and intensity. As will be demonstrated further, the pre-accession strategies have developed specific procedures and instruments to assess, monitor, and accompany compliance with these broadly formulated conditions. Besides political conditions, economic ones and conditions related to the administrative capacities of the candidate countries have been formulated. Following the Copenhagen Conditions candidate countries must have 'a functioning market economy' and 'the capacity to cope with competitive pressures and market forces within the Union'. Moreover, membership 'presupposes the candidate's ability to take on the obligations of membership including adherence to the aims of political, economic and monetary union'. The 1995 Madrid European Council Conclusions placed strong emphasis on the need to adjust administrative structures, while it soon became clear that judicial capacity in the candidate countries also needed to be upgraded drastically. It is further worthwhile noting that the Copenhagen Conclusions stipulated 'that the future co-operation with the associated countries had to be geared to the objective of membership' and that they already indicated the direction in which initiatives could be developed. Basically, this included organizing structured relationships with institutions of the Union within the framework of a multilateral dialogue, accelerating trade liberalization, appropriating the necessary financial resources, in particular through PHARE, in order to support the ongoing or planned transformation, participating in Community programmes, and, last but not least, the need to support the necessary approximation of laws in the associated countries to those applicable in the Community. These were precisely the elements that would later become the main points of reference for the formal EU pre-accession strategy.

3. EUROPE AGREEMENTS BECOMING A KEY COMPONENT OF THE EU PRE-ACCESSION STRATEGY

At the 1994 Corfu European Council it was recalled that the Copenhagen Conclusions *and* the Europe Agreements constituted the framework for deepening relations with the associated countries and for creating a context to enable these countries to meet the Copenhagen Conditions. Furthermore, the Presidency and the European Commission were asked to report 'on the strategy to be followed with a view to preparing for accession' and on the progress made in the process of alignment undertaken by the associated countries. Europe Agreements indeed provide a framework for organizing the bilateral relations between the European Communities and the Member States on the one hand and the countries of Central and Eastern Europe on the other. This is not the proper place to analyse these agreements in detail[17] and it may suffice to recall that ten such agreements have been signed. The first were signed in December 1991 with Poland, Hungary, and the Czech and Slovak Federal Republic (still one country at the time), that is to say *before* the political reorientation of the EU policy *vis-à-vis* the countries of Central and Eastern Europe at the 1993 Copenhagen European Council. The Europe Agreements signed between 1993 and 1996, thus *after* the 1993 Copenhagen Summit, remained largely unaffected as regards their structure, content, and wording by the new policy orientation of the EU on the question of enlargement. This may be surprising at first glance since, originally, Europe Agreements were perceived by the EU more as an alternative to, rather than a preparatory instrument for, accession.[18] The first Europe Agreements contained only one short explicit reference to accession formulated in the preamble in a very subtle way, precluding any political or legal commitment by the EU to enlargement. In this formulation the parties recognized that the associated country's 'ultimate objective is to become a member of the European Union and that association through this Agreement will, in the view of the parties help [the associated country] to achieve this objective'. Professor Müller-Graff has provided the most comprehensive and accurate legal interpretation of this formulation. According to him, this means 'that (1) one partner is aware of the intention of the other, but (2) does not incur any corresponding contractual commitment, and (3) that both partners only assess the agreement as being helpful for the achievement of the objective of one partner'.[19] Notwithstanding this preamble, Europe Agreements would gradually assume a more important role in the pre-accession strategy.[20] It is interesting to note, and this confirms the above, that neither the preamble nor the provisions of the Europe Agreements with Poland, Hungary, Romania, Bulgaria, the Czech Republic, and Slovakia are fundamentally different from those of the agreements concluded later with the Baltic states and Slovenia. The 'accession phrase' in the preamble in the first Europe Agreements quoted above remained intact in the subsequent Europe Agreements. This is logical for the Europe Agreements with Romania, signed

---

[17] A piece of very useful and original research on the historical and political background of the Europe Agreements is that by J.I. Torreblanca, *The Reuniting of Europe. Promises, Negotiations and Compromises* (2001). For a comprehensive study of the Europe Agreements see: Müller-Graff (ed.), *East Central Europe, supra* note 9. For a synthetic analysis, see M. Maresceau, 'Europe Agreements: A New Form of Cooperation Between the European Community and Central and Eastern Europe', in P.-C. Müller-Graff (ed.), *East Central European States and the European Communities: Legal Adaptations to the Market Economy* (1993), at 209–233.

[18] See also Müller-Graff, 'Legal Framework' *supra* note 9, 27, at 33–34.

[19] Müller-Graff, 'East Central Europe', *supra* note 9, at 16.

[20] On this reorientation see in particular Inglis, 'The Europe Agreements Compared in the Light of their Pre-accession Reorientation', 37 *CMLRev.* (2000) 1173.

in February 1993, and with Bulgaria, signed in March 1993—*before* the June 1993 Copenhagen European Council. But the reference to accession in the preamble to the Europe Agreements signed with the Czech and Slovak Republics in October 1993, *after* the Copenhagen European Council, also remained unchanged as compared to its formulation in the Agreement with the Czech and Slovak Federal Republic in December 1991. After the dissolution of the Czech and Slovak Federal Republic, the EC did impose a renegotiation on the two newly established states, basically with one purpose: to incorporate an explicit reference in the preamble as well as in the provisions of the Agreements not only to the respect for the rule of law and human rights, as was done in the Agreement with the Czech and Slovak Federal Republic of 1991, but also referring to the respect for 'the rights of persons belonging to minorities'. Failure to respect this provision could lead to unilateral suspension of the agreements.[21] This suspension clause has also been incorporated in the Europe Agreements that were signed thereafter with the three Baltic states and Slovenia. In these four agreements, the only difference worth mentioning in any comparison with the earlier agreements is that, after the 'classical' accession reference in the preamble, a recital has been added stipulating that the Contracting Parties '[take] into account the accession preparation strategy, adopted by the Essen European Council of December 1994, which is being politically implemented by the creation, between the associated states and the Institutions of the European Union, of structured relations which encourage mutual trust and will provide a framework for addressing topics of common interest'. It is not very clear how this recital should be interpreted legally. The 'addendum' in question is to be found only in the four Europe Agreements mentioned. However, the wording of the reference to the pre-accession strategies in the preamble is such that it does not appear to be sufficient to transform the Europe Agreements, from a legal point of view, into pre-accession agreements. In addition, it appears totally unacceptable that some Europe Agreements can be considered to be pre-accession agreements while others do not have this quality. Whatever the case may be, it is undeniable that indeed many of the substantive law objectives of these agreements, such as those on the creation of a free-trade area, the provisions on workers, establishment, services, as well as those providing a general basis for the approximation of laws in their implementation, have acquired a true pre-accession dimension as a result of the 1993 Copenhagen European Council as well as the applications for EU membership by the associated countries between 1994 and 1996. This

---

[21] See Pollet, 'Human Rights Clauses in Agreements between the European Union and Central and Eastern European Countries', 7 *Revue des affaires européennes* (1997) 290; also King, 'The European Community and Human Rights in Eastern Europe', 2 *Legal Issues of European Integration* (1996) 93.

strange legal metamorphosis took place without the renegotiation or amendment of any Europe Agreements. In other words, it was the political and legal
context in which these agreements were to be implemented that had fundamentally changed and continued to change. This phenomenon also explains
why, without any hesitation, the various institutional frameworks established
under the Europe Agreements, such as the Association Councils (ministerial
level), Association Committees (high-level civil service), and in particular the
technical sub-committees which provide for regular in-depth technical discussions of the various areas of the Agreements, have increasingly been used
directly or indirectly for pre-accession activities. This tendency became even
more accentuated after the establishment of Accession Partnerships (see
further below). Be that as it may, the institutions created under the Europe
Agreements have been obliged to adapt and reorient their agendas better to
monitor the implementation of the pre-accession strategy and the integration
of the candidate country into the EU.[22] The Europe Agreements, by the
simple fact of their existence, provided a ready-made channel for communication, so to speak, on various pre-accession questions. This also explains why
the European Commission could later easily qualify Europe Agreements as
'a key element of the pre-accession strategy'.[23]

4. THE 1994 ESSEN EUROPEAN COUNCIL: THE PRE-
ACCESSION STRATEGY LAUNCHED

The request of the Corfu European Council to reflect on an EU strategy
'preparing for accession' resulted in a Council policy paper,[24] which took the
form of an Annex to the 1994 Essen European Council Conclusions. In this
Annex, for the first time—be it somewhat hidden in the paragraph on
'Preparing to extend the Internal Market'—the expression 'pre-accession
strategy' was used (Annex IV to the Conclusions). In this document the
need to develop 'structured relations' aimed at encouraging mutual trust and
offering a framework for addressing topics of common interest was strongly

---

[22] See also European Commission, *supra* note 6, at 5.

[23] Ibid.

[24] As a matter of fact the Council's report was very much the result of two preparatory
studies of the Commission taking the form of Communications to the Council: 'The Europe
Agreements and Beyond: A Strategy to Prepare the Countries of Central and Eastern Europe
for Accession', COM(94)320 final, 13 July 1994, and a Follow up to this Communication,
COM(94)361 final, 27 July 1994. The latter, which set out specific proposals for implementing the strategy to prepare for accession, covered the following areas: the framework to deepen
the relationships with the CEECs, the creation of the appropriate legal and institutional
environment for economic development and integration, the increase of trade opportunities,
the macro-economic and structural changes, and the Community assistance to integration
and reform.

emphasized, even if some Member States remained rather cool about the idea as such.[25] But, no doubt, one of the priority actions of the pre-accession policy was the integration of the associated countries into the Internal Market of the EU. This necessarily implied the gradual adoption of the Internal Market *acquis* by the associated CEECs.[26] In doing so, the associated countries would move forward to take on the obligations resulting from EU membership, and at the same time they would develop their capacity to cope with the competitive pressures and market forces in the Union. In order to achieve these goals, short- as well as medium-term objectives were suggested. While the first objectives concentrated heavily on trade matters, the medium-term measures focused on the necessary legislative adaptations in the CEECs. With this aim in mind, the Commission was asked to prepare a White Paper on approximation of national laws related to the Internal Market, outlining the measures which these countries were supposed to adopt. In particular, special attention was to be devoted to the measures necessary for setting up the legislative infrastructure needed to apply the EC competition policy, including the rules on state-aid control. It is also worthwhile observing that it was the same Essen European Council which added as a new political condition for EU membership to the Copenhagen requirements that of '*bon voisinage*' since 'for the success of the [pre-accession] strategy, intra-regional co-operation between the associated countries themselves and their immediate neighbours is of particular importance.'[27]

In the Essen Conclusions on enlargement the CEECs are not the only addressees of the pre-accession strategy. The EU also was urged to do its homework. This apparent parallelism between widening and deepening was perfectly in line with the Copenhagen Conclusions, mentioned above, in which conditions were not only formulated for the associated countries but where also an explicit condition for further enlargement was imposed on the EU itself and its Member States. As a matter of fact it was the duty of the EU and the Member States to guarantee that the enlarged EU had the capacity to absorb new members 'while maintaining the momentum of European integration'. The Annex to the Essen Conclusions elaborates this very sensitive aspect of the Copenhagen Conditions by insisting that, on the European Union side, the institutional conditions for ensuring the proper functioning

[25] See Sedelmeier and Wallace, 'Eastern Enlargement. Strategy or Second Thoughts?', in H. Wallace and W. Wallace (eds), *Policy-Making in the European Union* (2000), 4th edition, 427, at 443.

[26] See also A. Mayhew, *Recreating Europe. The European Union's Policy Towards Central and Eastern Europe* (1998), at 165.

[27] On this condition see Smith, 'The Conditional Offer of Membership as an Instrument of EU Foreign Policy: Reshaping Europe in the EU's Image', 8 *Marmara Journal of European Studies* (2000) 33, at 36; see in particular her comments on Cyprus's and Turkey's applications for EU membership, at 41–44.

of the Union be created at the 1996 Intergovernmental Conference (IGC), 'which *for that reason* must take place *before* accession negotiations begin'.[28] The wording used by the European Council unequivocally means that the necessary institutional adaptations in the EU had to be accomplished *before* accession negotiations were opened.[29] However, the reality would prove to be different: accession negotiations were opened *after* the 1996 IGC leading to the Treaty of Amsterdam, notwithstanding the fact that the IGC had been unable to achieve the objectives set by the Essen Conclusions. As a matter of fact, the final outcome was such that the Treaty of Amsterdam did not create 'the institutional conditions for ensuring the proper functioning of the Union'. Consequently, with regard to the issue of enlargement, the Treaty of Amsterdam is to be regarded as a complete failure. The sole 'result' was a particularly obscure and even mysteriously[30] formulated *Protocol on the institutions with the prospect of enlargement of the European Union.* While Article 1 of that Protocol seemed to imply that a political compromise on an adapted EU institutional structure was indispensable to further enlargement, Article 2 of the same Protocol held that an enlargement not exceeding a membership of more than twenty was possible without a comprehensive review of the provisions on the composition and functioning of the institutions. . . . [31] The only thing that was certain after Amsterdam was that another IGC would be indispensable to the making of institutional progress on the enlargement agenda.

5. THE FIRST PRE-ACCESSION INITIATIVES

After the Essen European Council the first initiatives to be developed within the pre-accession strategy were the organization of the 'Structured Dialogue' which, as a matter of fact, had already been initiated under the German Presidency itself. This was symbolized by the first meeting of the members of the European Council with the Heads of State and Government of the CEECs who had been invited, at the initiative of Chancellor Kohl, to the

[28] Emphasis added.
[29] See also Cameron, 'The European Union and the Challenge of Enlargement', in Maresceau (ed.), *supra* note 9, 241–251, at 250: 'in plain language this meant that the institutional question had to be tackled successfully *before* enlargement'.
[30] This expression is from A. Duff, *The Treaty of Amsterdam. Text and Comments* (1997), at 134. Even the President of the European Commission seems to have trouble in interpreting it: see *infra* note 80.
[31] For a critical analysis of the wording of this Protocol see Gaudissart, 'Le protocol sur les institutions dans la perspective de l'élargissement de l'Union européenne: vers un élargissement sans perspectives pour l'Union?', in Y. Lejeune (ed.), *Le traité d'Amsterdam. Espoirs et déceptions* (1998), 411–429; Maresceau, 'EU-Central and Eastern Europe Relations at a Turning-point', 7 *Revue des affaires européennes* (1997), 263–264.

Essen Summit dinner.[32] At the same time it also symbolized the leading role that the reunified Germany intended to play in the 'New Europe'. Another initiative which would assume an ever increasing importance in the pre-accession policy was situated in the legal sphere and concerned the development of an impressive programme on approximation of laws. This objective, already suggested in the Copenhagen European Conclusions, was to become one of the cornerstones of the pre-accession strategy. The Essen European Council, also as part of the pre-accession strategy, further proposed that existing European Community programmes and agencies be opened to participation by candidate countries.

A. Structured Dialogue

One of the eye-catching achievements of the 1994 German EU Presidency and the Essen European Council was the setting up of the so-called 'Structured Dialogue' between the EU and the CEECs, aimed at allowing the candidate countries to become progressively familiar with the various activities of the three pillars of the EU. In practice, this meant that joint meetings were established at different levels, particularly ministerial level. Of course, these meetings had themselves no legislative capacity and could not replace the formal EC institutions in the decision-making process.[33] Although called 'Structured Dialogue' they were not always examples of well-structured meetings and were often of a general nature. Already in the first year of the ministerial Structured Dialogue (1995),[34] it became clear that such meetings did not always live up to the expectations of the various parties. They were organized on the margins of formal EU Council of Ministers' meetings, frequently lacked preparation, were under strong time constraints, and, more often than not, there was a lack of coordination and not really any dialogue as such.[35] On the whole the direct and concrete results of this form of pre-accession activity were limited. Some of these meetings were

---

[32] Not all Member States were enthusiastic about this initiative and strong negotiating skills of the German Presidency were necessary to convince some of the reluctant Member States: see Sedelmeier and Wallace, 'Policies Towards Central and Eastern Europe', in H. Wallace and W. Wallace (eds.), *Policy-making in the European Union* (1996), 353, at 380. The first edition of Wallace and Wallace is on this point more detailed than Wallace and Wallace (2000), 4th edition, 426, at 443.

[33] In Annex II to the 1993 Copenhagen Conclusions it was stipulated that the Structured Dialogue meetings 'will be of an advisory nature' and that 'no decisions would be taken'.

[34] For an inventory of these meetings see 1995 Cannes European Council Conclusions, Part B and 1995 Madrid European Council Conclusions, Annex 6.

[35] For a comprehensive study of the Structured Dialogue as a pre-accession instrument see Lippert and Becker, 'Structured Dialogue Revisited: the EU's Politics of Inclusion and Exclusion', 3 *European Foreign Affairs Review* (1998) 341; on the shortcomings of the Structured Dialogue, see in particular at 349–350.

no doubt fruitful, but others, on the contrary, were perceived purely as a waste of time. Anyhow, because of political and legal obstacles and limitations there was no perspective for these meetings ever becoming joint decision-making bodies.[36] In the end one of the main contributions of the Structured Dialogue was probably that this forum created useful contacts between EU ministers and officials and their candidate country counterparts. With the introduction of the *enhanced pre-accession strategy* (see further below) the multilateral 'structured dialogue' as originally conceived was deemed no longer appropriate: for accession issues contacts could best be organized on a country-by-country basis. However, the idea of maintaining a multilateral framework aimed at discussing transnational issues was not totally dropped and re-emerged somehow with the idea of launching the *European Conference* at the 1997 Luxembourg European Council (see further below).

B. Approximation of Laws

An important early pre-accession activity was the 1995 Commission's White Paper on the Preparation of the Associated Countries of Central and Eastern Europe for Integration into the Internal Market of the Union, laying down a detailed programme of approximation of laws for the CEECs. In this document, legal integration of the *acquis communautaire* relating to the Internal Market was presented as a fundamental objective for a successful accession policy.[37] The 1995 Cannes European Council referred to the economic connotation of legislative approximation in the pre-accession process where it stated that 'the gradual alignment of the associated countries on Community policies for the construction of the internal market will strengthen the competitiveness of their economies and increase the benefits of their economic reforms'. Originally the programme of approximation was not seen as a legal condition for accession and, hence, it was supposed not to prejudice the result of the negotiations on accession. Yet it was obvious that the process of

---

[36] This has been very clearly formulated by Lippert and Becker, *supra* note 35, at 358: 'The first hopes of the CEECs of becoming involved into the EU policy cycles, of becoming "pre-members" or "almost members" were necessarily disappointed. The EU never intended and never attempted to cross the institutional and legal boundaries of granting some kind of membership in the club. There were no second-class membership options, no attempt to develop flexible options for integrating the associated candidate countries into the internal policy processes at a level lower than the threshold of membership'. Mayhew, for his part, also had mixed feelings about this initiative but nevertheless was more positive in his approach and evaluation since the structured dialogue must be assessed 'as going very far towards the wishes of the associated countries and being a very important part of the strategy for accession': *supra* note 26, at 171–172.

[37] For a thorough analysis, see Gaudissart and Sinnaeve, 'The Role of the White Paper in the Preparation of the Eastern Enlargement', in Maresceau (ed.), *supra* note 9, 41–71.

approximation of laws contributed in a fundamental way to the creation of an irreversible legal framework for integration. The 'learning process' here is neither the most pleasant nor necessarily the most stimulating. Indeed, seen in this context, the expression 'approximation of laws' was, as it is now often, nothing more than a soft formulation of a stringent requirement for the associated countries to adapt their laws and practices to those of the EU. One of the main problems that the associated countries were facing was perhaps not only the size and complexity of EU law itself but also the fact that those human resources familiar with the specificity of the EU legal system were limited. Important areas of Community law where approximation was and remains necessary include, in particular, competition rules and state aid, intellectual property, and transport legislation. It should be noted that the approximation effort necessarily implies, on the one hand, the establishment of control mechanisms ensuring compatibility of new domestic legislation in the associated countries with that of the Community and, on the other, appropriate inter-ministerial coordination units.

Now that for many candidates the last and most difficult phases of the accession negotiations are approaching, it is easy to see how crucial this approximation of law exercise has been and continues to be. Some of the hard nuts to crack in the negotiations were previously, and still are, found where approximation has hardly or only very slowly been working. Of course, the interaction between the need to accomplish the legal adjustments and the dynamics of the accession negotiations is evident. Coherence is necessary between positions taken in the pre-accession strategy on the one hand and in the negotiations on the other. The enhanced pre-accession strategy, with its screening and regular evaluation of the progress made by the candidates (see further below), goes in parallel with the accession negotiations and, naturally, puts great pressure on the pace of the candidate's programme of approximation. This close interaction is also clearly demonstrated by the fact that since the October 2000 Progress Reports of the European Commission, the progress achieved by the candidates has been analysed and presented with the same subdivisions as are used for the negotiating chapters. One seems far away indeed from the time when the White Paper was launched. It should be the rule in accession negotiations that the closing of chapters is in the first place determined by whether the candidate has accomplished the required approximation process or, if not, whether at least each approximation is likely to be expected after accession through the granting of transitional periods. In comparison with negotiations in some previous enlargements—negotiations with Spain, for example, took seven years—the pace of the present negotiations seems to be particularly rapid, especially if one considers that for some candidates negotiations started only in February 2000. Undoubtedly, political pressure on the negotiations is very high and the timetable of the Road map for the negotiations may explain why recently sensitive substantive chapters such as, for example, environment protection were closed with so many candidates.[38] One last general observation on approximation: candidate countries as well as Member States experience approximation as not just a matter of legislative formulation but also of introducing new legislation and amending existing rules. It involves permanent training and retraining at various levels, including at administrative, judicial, university, etc. levels. In other words it is not enough to have the proper legislation on paper—implementation and application must be ensured. It will probably also be necessary to organize post-accession support programmes to make it possible for European Community law to be properly and uniformly applied in the enlarged EU.

C. Opening of European Community Programmes and Agencies

Another initiative within the framework of pre-accession strategy is the participation of candidates in the wide variety of European Community programmes and agencies.[39] The opening of these programmes and agencies

[38] Knowing the enormous distance between the EC environment law standards and those of the candidate countries, one is astonished to see the ease with which the EC has been willing to close the negotiating chapter on environment, be it with considerable transitional periods, with nine of the candidates in 2001 (Slovenia, *Uniting Europe*, 2 Apr. 2001; the Czech Republic, Hungary, Estonia, *Uniting Europe*, 11 June 2001; Lithuania, *Uniting Europe*, 2 July 2001; Cyprus, *Uniting Europe*, 2 Aug. 2001; Poland, *Uniting Europe*, 31 Oct. 2001; Latvia, *Uniting Europe*, 3 Dec. 2001, and Slovakia, *Uniting Europe*, 20 Dec. 2001). It is very doubtful whether the majority of the enumerated candidates are really capable in terms of human resources, know-how, and infrastructure of complying with EC environmental law. It is also true that the present Member States are not always examples of diligent and smooth application of EC environmental law, but the environmental reality in the candidate countries is still very different from that of the Member States. On this matter, it is interesting to note the Commission's view in the 1999 Composite Paper, quoted *supra* at note 6, at 23, where it was observed that 'none of the candidate countries are [*sic*] very far advanced in the transposition of environment laws' and 'all countries will face serious difficulties to achieve significant progress with the environment acquis in the near future'. One year later the Commission observed that 'in contrast to the last year, the transposition of environment acquis has started to progress faster in a number of countries' but that still 'much remains to be done...for both acquis alignment and implementation capacity': 2000 Enlargement Strategy Paper, Report on progress towards accession by each of the candidate countries, COM(2000)700 final, 8 Nov. 2000, at 23. In the 2001 Strategy Paper. Making a Success of Enlargement. Report on the progress towards accession by each of the candidate countries, COM(2001)700 final, 13 Nov. 2001, at 20 'the need to further strengthen administrative monitoring and enforcement capacity, in particular in the field of waste, water and chemicals' is mentioned. One cannot escape the impression that the 'negotiation dynamics' may at times side-slip into 'easy successes' on paper but which may prove particularly difficult to achieve afterwards.

[39] The first CEECs' participation in a Community Agency is that in the European Environmental Agency (Copenhagen). Details and modalities of this participation are included in bilateral agreements signed with the 13 candidate countries: see OJ 2001

was already agreed in principle at the Copenhagen European Council, and was integrated into the pre-accession strategy as formulated at the Essen European Council. However, concrete implementation decisions were taken only from 1997 onwards.[40] The aim of this policy is to help the candidate countries familiarize themselves with Community policies or working methods and to demonstrate how these policies work in practice. At first sight, such participation is not so evident since, in principle, Community programmes, agencies, and committees aim to promote cooperation *between EU Member States* in specific fields of EU policy such as research, education, vocational training, the audio-visual sector, youth, energy, social policy, information society, public health, etc., and are financed through a specific allocation of the EU budget. As far as the CEECs' participation in these programmes is concerned, the candidate must apply to participate and conditions of participation are negotiated with the European Commission in the framework of the Europe Agreements (financial contribution of the candidate, place of candidate in institutional structure of the programme concerned, etc.). Formally, the terms and conditions of participation in a programme are incorporated in a decision of the relevant association council. 'Popular' Community Programmes are Socrates,[41] Youth Culture, the Fifth EC Framework Programme on R&D (1998–2002), in which all the CEECs together with Malta and Cyprus already participate. The financial repercussions of such participation are co-financed by PHARE, but it is expected that the candidates will gradually increase their own financial input. For Cyprus, Malta, and Turkey the existing association agreements do not offer a legal basis for such participation, which implies that for those countries to participate, specific bilateral arrangements are necessary. Although participation in certain Community programmes by third countries is not necessarily limited to accession candidates, it is undeniable that the growing number of Community programmes in which the candidates participate and the intensity of their participation will contribute to the development of a European strategy that is favourable to the objectives of pre-accession.

L213/1–119. For other Community Agencies see e.g. European Centre for the Development of Vocational Training (Thessaloniki), European Foundations for the Improvement of Living and Working Conditions (Dublin), etc. Various CEECs have applied for participation in agencies, for some negotiations with the Commission are under way, sometimes implementing preparatory measures are being taken: for more details see Overview regarding candidate countries' participation in Community Agencies, European Commission, DG Enlargement-D-3.

[40] For more details see European Commission, Participation of candidate countries in Community programmes, agencies and committees, COM(1999)710 final, 20 Dec. 1999.

[41] e.g. in 1998–1999 more than 16,000 students from the applicant countries participated in the Socrates Programme: European Commission, 2000 Enlargement Strategy Paper, Report on progress towards accession by each of the candidate countries, COM(2000)700 final, 13 Nov. 2000, at 13.

6. CONSOLIDATION AND INTENSIFICATION OF PRE-ACCESSION STRATEGIES

A. Background

Between 1994 and 1996 the associated countries of Central and Eastern Europe all applied for EU membership. Following Article O of the EU Treaty (now Article 49) the European Commission had to express its opinion on each of these applications for membership. This was recalled at the 1995 Madrid European Council where the European Commission was asked to submit its opinions on each application as soon as possible after the 1996 IGC. In order to prepare its assessment the Commission asked the candidates to answer a very detailed questionnaire. A strong emphasis was laid on the legal and administrative capacity to adapt the national laws to that of the EU.[42] Also, information about the human resources available was requested. On 15 July 1997 the European Commission published an elaborated strategy paper on enlargement under the title *Agenda 2000*, together with ten individual opinions on the applications for membership. In *Agenda 2000* the Commission offered a general perspective for the development of the European Union and presented its views on the impact of enlargement on the EU as a whole. *Agenda 2000* also outlined a financial framework incorporating the prospect of an enlarged EU, which would be refined and politically endorsed at the 1999 Berlin European Council. In ten individual opinions the Commission assessed each application for EU membership. The result of this exercise was that, according to the Commission, accession negotiations could be opened with five CEECs: Poland, Hungary, the Czech Republic, Slovenia, and Estonia. Not that any one of these countries was immediately ready for EU membership, but at least the political situation in each of these countries was such that the Copenhagen Conditions did not constitute an obstacle to the negotiations. However, that did not mean that in these countries everything was perfect. To give one example, improvements in the field of minority protection in Estonia had still to be made, but it was expected that these could take place during the necessary long negotiation process. Also, the 'selected' candidates all had to improve their administrative and judicial infrastructure and capacity in order to be able to cope with the requirements of membership. And, of course, fundamental progress from all candidates was still needed in order to be able to claim that they had a 'functioning market economy'. Four of the non-selected candidates (Bulgaria, Romania, Latvia, and Lithuania) had failed the admissibility test on economic grounds and/or reasons related to their administrative capacity,

---

[42] For more details see G. Avery and F. Cameron, *The Enlargement of the European Union* (1998), at 37–39.

while Slovakia, for its part, was not selected for political reasons (its treatment of minorities and the disrespect of the Meciar Government for democratic principles). The Commission not only suggested that negotiations be opened with the five selected CEECs but also suggested that Cyprus be included in the category of applicants with which negotiations could be started, thereby confirming its 1993 Opinion on the Cypriot application for membership of 1990. Malta was not included in the 'first group' of candidate countries, notwithstanding that the Commission's 1993 Opinion on its application for membership was positive, since it had itself 'frozen' its application in 1996. Malta was to resume its position in the accession process only in 1998 after a new government had come to power.

The Commission's Opinion in the enlargement procedure is an important step, but the decision whether to open accession negotiations is, above all, a political one decided at the highest political level of the EU. Therefore, the European Council which followed the publication of the Commission Opinions was expected to be of crucial importance, as was indeed demonstrated by the Luxembourg European Council of December 1997. The Luxembourg European Council, on the one hand, confirmed the selection made by the Commission of with whom negotiations could be started but, on the other, it was not immune to the strong negative reactions by some of the non-selected applicants to the Commission's choice. But the most vigorous reaction was that of Turkey which had been largely ignored in the Commission's enlargement policy. Turkey had applied for membership in 1987 but the Commission had expressed a negative opinion in 1989, while in 1993, as already mentioned, it had given positive opinions on Malta's and Cyprus's applications. Although this had not led to a quick decision to open negotiations with these two countries, now that Cyprus was included in the group of countries with which negotiations could be opened relations between Turkey and the EU naturally became particularly sensitive. Turkey's extremely bitter reaction towards its exclusion from the enlargement process[43] would eventually considerably affect the enhanced pre-accession strategy as conceived by the Luxembourg European Council.

Besides the confirmation of the opening of accession negotiations, the Luxembourg European Council also defined enlargement as 'a comprehensive, inclusive and ongoing process' taking place in stages in which each of the applicant countries proceeds at its own rate, depending on its degree of preparedness to become a member of the EU. Rather ambiguously the European Council mentioned in its Conclusions, immediately under the heading, 'European Union Enlargement' but even before the section

[43] Also on 15 July 1997 the European Commission published a 'Communication on the Further Development of Relations with Turkey', COM(97)394 final in which it reiterated Turkey's *eligibility* for EU membership but totally disconnected Turkey from the pre-accession process.

dealing with 'the process of accession and negotiation', the establishment of the *European Conference*. Obviously—and there can be no doubt about it—this new initiative was seen as a prominent achievement of the European Council. In fact, however, the real, hard core of the Luxembourg Conclusions was the formal launching of the *enhanced pre-accession strategy*. This new strategy was to be applied to *all* CEEC applicants irrespective of whether they had received a positive opinion from the Commission. Later, in the year 2000, the enhanced pre-accession strategy was extended to Cyprus and Malta. Moreover, as a result of the 1999 Helsinki European Council, Turkey was also to be incorporated in this strategy although, for the moment, accession negotiations have not yet been opened with the latter.

B. The European Conference

The main objective of the European Conference, as conceived in the Luxembourg Conclusions, was, as it remains today, to offer a multilateral forum for political consultation on issues of common concern to its participants. Issues of common concern were understood as issues with a cross-border dimension, such as for example justice and home affairs—particularly crime and drugs—security policy, regional cooperation, and, of course, in the context of the year 2001, international terrorism. The Conference, chaired by the Member State holding the Presidency, was to be a very high level meeting. The Luxembourg Conclusions stipulated that European Conferences were to be composed of Heads of State and Government (and the President of the Commission) meeting once a year but they could also be organized at ministerial level (Ministers for Foreign Affairs).

The question of which countries could participate was a more delicate matter. The Luxembourg Conclusions indicated that the members of the Conference were expected '[to] share a common commitment to peace, security and good neighbourliness, respect for other countries' sovereignty, the principles upon which the European Union is founded, the integrity and inviolability of external borders and a commitment to the settlement of territorial disputes by peaceful means, in particular through the jurisdiction of the International Court of Justice in the Hague'. They further stipulated that 'countries which endorse these principles and respect the right of any European country fulfilling the required criteria to accede to the European Union and sharing the Union's commitment to building a Europe free of the divisions and difficulties of the past will be invited to take part in the Conference'. European States which accepted these criteria and principles would be invited to take part in the Conference, but initially these invitations would be extended only to the applicant CEECs, Cyprus, and Turkey. The various non-EU-member countries invited to the Conference were seen as

European States '*aspiring*[44] to accede to [the EU] and sharing its values and internal and external objectives'. The expression '*aspiring* to accede' was, unfortunately, not defined any further and is therefore not without its ambiguity. Aspiring to become a member of the EU is something which, in the first place, depends on the country concerned, but accepting a country as a participant in the Conference also necessarily implies that the Member States of the EU are willing to grant such status to that country. It was easy to understand that this expression was used deliberately to include Turkey since that country was explicitly mentioned as one of the countries that would be welcome to the first European Conference. It has to be said, however, that the quoted 'general requirements' for Conference participation seemed to have been drafted—not without considerable input from Greece—aiming at 'conditioning' Turkey for such participation. In fact, Greece had been strongly opposed to inviting Turkey to the Conference and the wording of this 'conditionality' was the price to pay for Greek approval.[45] Furthermore, it is interesting to note that the Conference Conditions as formulated in the Luxembourg Conclusions were later to be incorporated to a very large extent in the 1999 Helsinki European Council Conclusions on the 'general' values and objectives that *all* applicants must share in order to become members of the EU. Although these values and objectives are equally relevant to all the candidates, it was again understood at the Helsinki European Council (see further below) that in reality they were meant to be addressed to Turkey. It is true that in the past Turkey's *eligibility* for EU membership had already been confirmed on various occasions,[46] but participation in the European Conference did not necessarily imply that Turkey had obtained the formal status of 'candidate state', a qualification that the Luxembourg European Council did not grant that country. The tribulations around the London European Conference of February 1998 have been examined in detail elsewhere[47] and will not be discussed again here. To make a long story short, Turkey refused to play the game and, in the end, did not participate in the first European Conference. On the face of it, this attitude could easily be understood. Turkey was bluntly denied access to the real accession process and enhanced pre-accession strategy and, consequently, was placed entirely outside this strategy. Therefore, participation in the Conference could by no means offer a valid alternative to Turkey's European

---

[44] Emphasis added.

[45] See *Agence Europe* of 24 and 29 Nov. 1997.

[46] See e.g. *Agenda 2000*, Vol 1, 15; also Commission Communication on the Further Development of Relations with Turkey, COM(97)394 final, 15 July 1997. In other words the quality of 'eligibility' could more easily be attributed than that of 'candidate country'.

[47] See the author's study 'The EU Pre-Accession Strategies: a Political and Legal Analysis', in M. Maresceau and E. Lannon (eds), *The EU's Enlargement and Mediterranean Strategies. A Comparative Analysis* (2001) 3, at 6–7.

ambitions. At the same time Turkey's absence meant the failure of the first European Conference and so its 'results' can be quickly forgotten. The same holds true for the subsequent Luxembourg European Conference of 6 October 1998, organized this time at the level of Ministers of Foreign Affairs. In 1999, probably because of the Turkish boycott, no European Conferences were organized. However, after the official recognition of Turkey as 'candidate country' at the 1999 Helsinki European Council and its later inclusion in the pre-accession strategy, Turkey participated at the ministerial European Conference of Sochaux of 23 November 2000 as well as at the Nice European Conference of 7 December 2000 at the level of Heads of State and Government, which dealt with the future of the EU's institutional framework. At the time of writing, the last European Conference was that which was held at ministerial level on 20 October 2001 under the Belgian Presidency on—what else could it have been?—the fight against international terrorism. But again, very little substance can be found in the declaration that resulted from this almost totally unnoticed meeting. Besides a number of general statements and references to Security Council Resolutions taken in the aftermath of the terrorist attacks of 11 September 2001, nothing innovative or concrete was proposed. The only really innovative and interesting characteristic of the European Conference of 20 October 2001 was that it was organized in an enlarged format composed of the countries of the European Conference which included, besides the EU Member States, the 13 candidates, and for the first time the EFTA countries (Switzerland,[48] Norway, Iceland, and Liechtenstein) as well as the countries of ex-Yugoslavia (Bosnia, Former Yugoslav Republic of Macedonia, Croatia, Federal Republic of Yugoslavia) and Albania.[49] Even more interestingly, the Belgian Presidency had also taken the initiative to invite Ukraine, Moldova,[50] and Russia, although the latter three countries were not (yet) qualified as 'countries of the European Conference'. This explains why officially the meeting was called 'enlarged European Conference'. The invitation to Ukraine, Moldova, and Russia, indeed, can be seen as a positive signal for the Conference's future, or rather it is probably the Conference's only way to survive. It is easy to understand that the majority, if not all, of the real cross-border issues go beyond the EU-candidate states' relationships. Therefore, it appears that the Commission's official position that the Conference is instrumental 'to provide the overarching framework for the enlargement exercise' and that it is 'necessary to reserve participation in the Conference for *Member States and*

[48] Switzerland had already participated as a 'designated member' in the 2000 Nice European Conference.

[49] The 2000 Nice European Council had further suggested the incorporation of the countries covered by the Stabilization and Association Process as well as the EFTA countries.

[50] The 2001 Göteborg European Council suggested that Ukraine and Moldova should be invited (Russia was not mentioned).

candidate countries only'[51] has become, or is becoming, obsolete and needs to be fundamentally revised. The Commission too at last seems to be aware that the Conference's working methods need to be reviewed, but nevertheless continues to be of the opinion that the Conference should remain a framework for discussing the future of the Union with 'the candidate countries'.[52] However, in the future, there will be a pressing need to disconnect the European Conference from the present accession process as such.[53] The Conference must be capable of offering a forum to tackle the real pan-European issues, otherwise the very reasons for its existence are difficult to comprehend.

C. Enhanced Pre-accession Strategy

The idea of an 'enhanced pre-accession strategy' was formally launched at the 1997 Luxembourg European Council and set in motion on 30 March 1998. The aim of this strategy was then, as it is today, to enable *all* the CEEC applicants to become members of the EU. In order to facilitate this accession process the ten CEECs are encouraged to align themselves with the EU *acquis* prior to accession. The three new key components of the enhanced pre-accession strategy are *Accession Partnerships, annual assessment of the progress achieved by the candidate country,* and *increased pre-accession aid.*[54] Later Cyprus, Malta, and Turkey were also incorporated in the enhanced pre-accession strategy. The accession negotiations with Hungary, Poland, the Czech Republic, Estonia, Slovenia, and Cyprus were formally opened with the bilateral intergovernmental conference of 31 March 1998. In April 1998 the *screening* or analytical examination of the *acquis* with each of the candidate countries, whether accession negotiations were opened or not, took place. This technique helped to identify and also to anticipate some of the problems faced or to be faced in the negotiations. After the initial screening operation updates are necessary, the more so since the *acquis* itself is not something static.

[51] Composite Paper. Reports on the progress towards accession by each of the candidate countries, 4 Nov. 1998, at 21, emphasis added.

[52] See European Commission, 2000 Enlargement Strategy Paper, *supra* note 41, at 14.

[53] It remains even at the moment of writing (end of 2001) the official position of the European Commission that the European Conference continues to be part of the pre-accession strategy. In the 2001 Strategy Paper. Making a Success of Enlargement, *supra* note 38, the European Conference is somewhat hidden in Annex 3 but the title of this annex is 'the pre-accession strategy'.

[54] For a legal appraisal of these components, building on the bodies and achievements of the Europe Agreements so far, see Inglis, 'The Accession Partnerships', in A. Ott and K. Inglis (eds.), *Handbook on European Enlargement* (2002) forthcoming.

1. Accession Partnership

The main idea behind the new concept of 'Accession Partnership' is that the priorities for each candidate country are set out and all the various forms of EU assistance are brought within one single framework. The 'Accession Partnerships' are the key legal instruments in the administrative and political matrix of policy instruments that underpin the pre-accession strategy, which builds on the bilateral structures and achievements so far under the Europe Agreements.[55] The concrete implementation of the Accession Partnerships is monitored through the various Europe Agreements' institutions. Accession Partnerships are the result of intensive consultations with the candidate states and, from a legal point of view, they are not agreements but unilateral acts.[56] The basic legal act establishing Accession Partnerships is Regulation 622/98 of 16 March 1998, while on 30 March 1998 specific decisions for each CEEC candidate were taken, defining the general conditions of each Accession Partnership and setting out the principles, as well as spelling out the priorities to be observed for adopting the EU *acquis*, particularly the short-term priorities as well as the medium-term objectives. Taking into account the respective developments in the various candidate countries, they were updated on 6 December 1999.[57] These updates are a reaction to the Commission's findings in the Regular Reports and, of course, are also a consequence of the assessment in the Europe Agreement bodies of the progress made in adopting the *acquis*. At the moment of writing Accession Partnerships are again being reviewed and their priorities and intermediate objectives refined. This permanent adaptation is the price to pay for the proper functioning of pre-accession strategy as organized by the EU. In 2000 and 2001 Accession Partnerships were also adopted for Cyprus, Malta, and Turkey (see further below). The Accession Partnerships are thus clearly individualized country by country and now apply to the 13 candidate countries. For their part, the candidate countries have had to adopt their National Programmes for the Adoption of the Acquis (NPAA). These programmes indicate how they will implement the priorities as defined in the Accession Partnerships, specifying the laws and regulations, institutional and administrative adaptations, data about the human and budgetary resources, administrative infrastructure, and timetable needed to address their individual pre-accession targets. Moreover, NPAAs are also gradually being adapted and updated. Such intervention may be needed, for example, as a result of the assessment of the Commission of the progress

[55] Ibid.

[56] See also Inglis, 'The Europe Agreements Compared in the Light of their Pre-accession Reorientation', 37 *CMLRev.* (2000) 1173, at 1184.

[57] Ten Council decisions country by country concerning the updating were taken: OJ 1999 L 335.

made by each candidate in the fulfilment of the Copenhagen Criteria and alignment with Internal Market rules.[58]

2. Annual Progress Reports

An important feature of the enhanced pre-accession strategy concept is the annual review by the European Commission of the candidate's progress towards accession. This review procedure was explicitly requested by the Luxembourg European Council. The idea was that these regular reports would 'serve as a basis for taking, in the Council context, the necessary decisions on the conduct of the accession negotiations or their extension to other applicants'. In a way one could say that the first assessment reports, made on a country-by-country basis, were the Opinions of the Commission of 15 July 1997 in which a synthesis and evaluation were provided of the progress made by the applicant CEECs towards the fulfilment of the Copenhagen Conditions. However, the first *real* 'Progress Reports' were those presented in 1998 after the Luxembourg Summit. Since then, this exercise has been repeated every year in October/November. The last reports used for this contribution are those published on 13 November 2001. The country reports cover the 13 candidate countries, thus including Turkey from the beginning,[59] and they are published together with a 'Composite Paper', which since the 2000 review has been called 'Strategy Paper'. The Composite or Strategy Papers contain a synthesis of the various country reports as well as a series of recommendations. They also give data about the state of affairs in the accession negotiations and the pre-accession strategy. The Progress Reports concentrate mainly on what has concretely been achieved for the transposition of the *acquis* in the candidate country and what progress has been made in building up administrative and judicial capacity to implement and apply the *acquis*. In particular they, as their title indicates, highlight the legal measures taken since the previous report. The systematic reporting in an enhanced pre-accession framework while, simultaneously, accession negotiations are being held puts enormous pressure on the candidates. Acceleration, or at least maintenance of the rhythm, of reform is the wish and objective of all the candidates. The publication of progress reports, or even the simple fact

[58] For a recent example of such an operation in a candidate country see the *National Programme for the Accession of Romania to the European Union* (2001). This impressive two-volume document of the Romanian Government is a particularly detailed updating of the previous programme, focusing on fulfilling the objectives of the Accession Partnership, and it also aims at 'correcting the deficiencies pointed out in the European Commission's Regular Report of November 2000': Vol I, at 7.

[59] The 1998 Cardiff European Council had requested the Commission to include Turkey in the first Regular Reports on the basis of the Conclusions of the Luxembourg European Council and of Art. 28 of the 1963 Association Agreement with Turkey which refers to 'the possibility of the accession of Turkey to the Community'.

that such reports are anticipated, creates an atmosphere of permanent follow-up and contributes considerably to the enhancement in the candidate countries of an awareness that the necessary measures must be taken for the credibility of the enlargement process as such and to move forward in the accession negotiations. The overall impression is that the pre-accession and enhanced pre-accession strategies coupled with these yearly evaluations have contributed substantially to consolidating and developing democracy, respect for the rule of law, and human rights, and the situation of minorities in certain candidate countries has also improved. In the 2001 Regular Report the Commission notes that most of the candidate countries now have a functioning market economy. Only three candidates do not yet qualify: Bulgaria needs to make some further efforts but is close to it, Romania has made serious progress but does not yet meet the objective, and Turkey, given its deep economic and financial crisis, is not a properly functioning market economy although regarding certain economic chapters of the *acquis*, as a result of its customs union with the EC, it is as advanced as, if not more so than, many of the CEECs. One of the most important difficulties, on which pre-accession strategies have been concentrating and need to continue to do so, particularly in the present crucial phase of the accession negotiations, concerns the administrative and judicial capacity of the candidates. Certainly, considerable progress has already been achieved but, as is also demonstrated in the 2001 Progress Report, much still needs to be done, and these efforts need to be deployed in many of the important negotiation chapters.[60] This explains why, in 2002, the Commission intends to launch a special action plan to stimulate further improvements of the candidates' administrative and judicial capacity without which it is difficult to imagine how they will function properly in an enlarged EU.[61]

It is impossible here to make a detailed critical analysis of the Commission's Progress Reports, Composite and Strategy Papers. Some of the positive aspects have just been mentioned but in certain chapters a more balanced approach would be welcomed. The leading source of information for the drafting of the reports is clearly the government of the relevant candidate country itself, and the Commission Delegation in the country concerned is also instrumental in providing information. Of course, information can also be contained in reports from other EU institutions or from international organizations. However, the fact that the candidate country remains by far the main source of information is not necessarily always the best assurance of

---

[60] The Report enumerates the following areas where action is needed in most of the candidate countries: internal market, competition, transport, energy, telecommunications, culture and audio-visual policy, environment, social policy, justice and home affairs, customs, taxation, agriculture, structural policy, and financial control, *supra* note 38, at 19–21.

[61] This action plan was announced in the 2001 Progress Report, *supra* note 38, at 25–26. See further Chap. 3.

objectivity, and sometimes the Commission's reporting on particular issues gives the impression of being 'coloured'. It is difficult to understand why on certain sensitive political issues the Commission seems unable to perform its reporting function in a truly objective and independent manner. One such area is, for example, minority protection. Often the Commission's description of the situation is particularly meagre and incomplete if not with a strong intonation of complacency about the authorities of the candidate country.[62] It is disquieting to see that reports on minority treatment prepared by other institutions are often much more reliable than those produced by the Commission and present a rather different picture.[63] It is unfortunate that for this type of activity the Commission has not been able to (or perhaps it has simply been unwilling to) rely much more on independent research centres or experts to do the job.

3. Enhanced Pre-accession Aid

It has already been mentioned that Accession Partnerships aim to bring the various forms of EU support together within a single framework but the Luxembourg European Council also added that financial assistance would be linked to the progress made by the applicants. In other words compliance by the candidates with the implementation of the set programme for the adoption of the *acquis* would constitute a condition of obtaining financial support. Besides the adoption and implementation of the *acquis*, PHARE is also to be used for the reinforcement of administrative and judicial capacities. Seen in this way, the Accession Partnerships constitute a single programming framework for channelling EU assistance to the candidate countries as they prepare themselves to become EU members. The clearly accession-oriented pre-accession support is granted with respect for the principle of equal treatment, regardless of whether accession negotiations have been opened or not with the applicant state and taking into consideration the candidates' greatest needs. It is impossible here to go into the technical details of the new pre-accession financial framework, but it may be useful to say a few words about the financial instruments organizing the increased pre-accession aid. Secondly, and this is also interesting from a legal point of view, for the first time in the pre-accession process an explicit legal framework organizing the element of conditionality has been set up.

---

[62] See our criticism of the Commission's assessment of the treatment of the Russian minority in Estonia and Latvia, *supra* note 47, at 17–19.

[63] e.g., the country reports of the privately sponsored Open Society Institute are not only often more detailed than but also sometimes contradict at least in part the Commission's view as formulated in its Regular reports; See *Monitoring the EU Accession Process: Minority Protection* (2001).

(a) Financial Instruments

For the moment there are three financial instruments assisting the applicant countries in the enhanced pre-accession phase: PHARE, ISPA (Pre-Accession Structural Instrument),[64] and SAPARD (Structural Adjustment Programme for Agriculture and Rural Development).[65] At the 1999 Berlin European Council the political decision was taken to offer a financial perspective for the period 2000–2006 and the necessary budgetary measures were suggested. The three financial pre-accession instruments are all clearly accession-oriented[66] and the financial support is coordinated by the European Commission which, therefore, logically, plays the leading role in the financing of the enhanced pre-accession strategy.[67] The first—PHARE—is an 'old' and well known financial instrument. Originally, PHARE was the main instrument for financial and technical support to the CEECs. It was later extended to Albania and the countries of ex-Yugoslavia, but in 2000 a specific financial instrument called CARDS (Community Assistance for Reconstruction, Development, and Stabilization) was set up for these countries.[68] Consequently, PHARE is now again exclusively applicable to the CEECs included in the pre-accession process and totally refocused on the accession priorities. The two other instruments, ISPA and SAPARD, are new and have been operational since 2000. For financial support to the CEECs the annual budget was fixed at the Berlin European Council at 3,120 million euros: 1,560 million euros for PHARE, 1,040 million euros for ISPA, and 520 million euros for SAPARD. The three forms of pre-accession aid are all non-refundable. Pre-accession financial assistance for Cyprus, Malta, and Turkey is now also foreseen (see further below). It should be noted that pre-accession financial assistance, as its name indicates, is limited to the 'pre-accession' phase. Concretely, that means that the foreseen pre-accession financing can be used only during the pre-accession period. For candidates becoming EU members before the end of 2006—and candidates become EU members only

[64] Council Regulation 1267/99 establishing an instrument for structural policies for pre-accession, OJ 1999 L 161/73.

[65] Council Regulation 1268/99 on Community support for pre-accession measures for agriculture and rural development in the applicant countries of Central and Eastern Europe in the pre-accession period, OJ 1999 L 161/87.

[66] The European Commission calls PHARE 'an accession driven instrument', in 1999 Composite Paper, *supra* note 6, at 5. For a recent analytical study of these financial instruments see Guggenbühl and Theelen, 'The Financial Assistance of the European Union to Its Eastern and Southern Neighbours: A Comparative Analysis', in Maresceau and Lannon (eds), *supra* note 47, at 217–254.

[67] See Regulation 1266/99 on co-ordinating aid to the applicant countries in the framework of the pre-accession strategy and amending Regulation 3906/89, OJ 1999 L 161/68.

[68] See Council Regulation 2666/2000 of 5 Dec. 2000 on assistance for Albania, Bosnia and Herzegovina, Croatia, the Federal Republic of Yugoslavia and the Former Yugoslav Republic of Macedonia, OJ 2000 L 306/1.

once the ratification process has been completed and their treaty of accession has entered into force—the pre-accession funds made available but not used will be re-allocated to the remaining candidate countries.

The PHARE Programme finances institution-building measures in various fields of the *acquis* and provides investment support helping to meet the EU norms and standards. Institution-building support means in the first place helping to strengthen the democratic institutions and public administration in charge of implementing and enforcing EU law, in particular the judiciary. In other words the main objective is strengthening the administrative and judicial capacity of the candidate country, and this also includes training and equipping of administrations as well as organizing twinning programmes.[69] PHARE also focuses on investment support, in particular in those areas where important investment is needed by the candidate country in order to adapt enterprises and particularly infrastructure to meet EU norms and standards. This is obviously the case, for example, in areas such as nuclear safety, transport, and safety control of production processes. Finally, PHARE also supports economic and social cohesion. One of the main objectives here as well as with investment support is to help to prepare the field in the candidate countries so that they become sufficiently equipped technically but also mentally to implement structural funds after accession.

ISPA is a financial instrument for structural pre-accession policies providing support for important environmental and transport infrastructure. ISPA projects include rail and road improvements, waste-water treatment, waste management, etc. SAPARD focuses on financing sustainable agricultural and rural development. SAPARD implementation is decentralized, and in each candidate country an agency is responsible for the management of SAPARD locally and for the payments. Criteria applied for the allocation of financial assistance under the programme are agricultural population, agricultural land surface, gross domestic product in purchasing power parity, and the specificity of the territory.

(b) Conditionality
The legal cornerstone of the enhanced pre-accession strategy is financial conditionality. This conditionality works in two directions that may be intertwined. First, financial assistance will be granted only if certain conditions are satisfied. These conditions are determined by the priorities of the Accession Partnerships. Experience shows that sometimes candidates face difficulties in matching these priorities or that simply their 'absorption capacity' cannot cope with the foreseen assistance.[70] The second type of

---

[69] Twinning involves secondment of officials from the Member States to officials from the candidate countries to encourage the transfer of technical and administrative know-how in priority areas of the *acquis communautaire*.

[70] For more details see Guggenbuhl and Theelen, *supra* note 66, at 226–227.

conditionality establishes a form of sanction. Accession Partnership Regulation 622/98 indeed contains a conditionality clause which reads as follows: 'where an element that is essential for continuing to grant pre-accession assistance is lacking, in particular when the commitments contained in the Europe Agreement are not respected and/or progress towards fulfilment of the Copenhagen criteria is insufficient, the Council, acting by a qualified majority on a proposal from the Commission, may take appropriate steps with regard to any pre-accession assistance granted to an applicant State'. It is interesting to note that insufficient progress towards meeting the Copenhagen Criteria and/or implementing the Europe Agreement obligations are explicitly mentioned as possible grounds for application of the conditionality clause. Through the annual Commission progress reports, achievements as well as shortcomings can be assessed rather swiftly but, so far, there has been no need to use this clause. Where shortcomings do occur, the objectives in question can be closely monitored and the simple knowledge that a progress report will follow seems to have put sufficient pressure in practice on the candidate country to conform to the EU requirements. From a legal point of view it has very properly been noted that Regulation 622/98 'upgrades the Copenhagen Criteria from political preconditions of the European Council to legally binding conditions, subject to sanctions alongside the conditions contained in the [Europe Agreements]'.[71]

4. Enhanced Pre-accession Applied to Cyprus, Malta, and Turkey

The enhanced pre-accession strategy launched at the 1997 Luxembourg Summit was clearly intended to enable all the CEECs to align themselves as far as possible with the EU *acquis* prior to accession. For Cyprus, a specific pre-accession strategy distinct from that for the CEECs was suggested originally, since that country was economically far more advanced than the CEECs, and it by no means faced the type of transition problems experienced by the CEECs. Of course, Cyprus had its own very serious political problem resulting from the *de facto* division of the island in 1974 but this was not the object of the specific pre-accession strategy for that country. It was intended to concentrate on certain aspects of justice and home affairs and on judicial and administrative capacity to cope with the EU *acquis*. Also, participation in Community programmes and agencies was foreseen as well as certain forms of technical assistance. However, on 13 March 2000 the EC

---

[71] See Lannon, Inglis, and Haenebalcke, 'The Many Faces of EU Conditionality in Pan-Euro-Mediterranean Relations', in Maresceau and Lannon (eds), *supra* note 47, 97–138, at 111; see also Inglis, *supra* note 56, at 1187 who calls this 'the additional legal stick' which Regulation 622/98 has provided to the EU in the handling of its pre-accession policy.

decided to extend the Accession Partnership to Cyprus as well as to Malta.[72] After the reactivation of Malta's application for EU membership (see above) the European Commission presented an update of the 1993 Opinion on Malta's application for EU membership in 1999. The Commission concluded that, owing to Malta's decision to freeze its application, there was a considerable backlog regarding the adoption and implementation of the *acquis* in comparison to those of other candidates. Malta was urged to take the indispensable measures as soon as possible in order to join the candidate countries with which negotiations were already underway. Consequently, this new situation led to the adoption of an Accession Partnership for Malta.

Turkey is a special case in the enhanced pre-accession strategy. Before the end of 1999 Turkey was declared only as being 'eligible' for EU membership in the official EU statements but was not incorporated into the pre-accession strategy. At the 1997 Luxembourg European Council it became clear that by placing Turkey under a 'specific' strategy called 'European Strategy for Turkey', Turkey was in reality excluded from the enhanced pre-accession process. As a reaction Turkey suspended the political dialogue with the EU and threats on the Cyprus issue became more and more outspoken. The 1999 Helsinki European Council brought a fundamental reorientation of the EU approach towards Turkey in which it qualified Turkey 'as a candidate state destined to join the Union on the basis of the same criteria as applied to other candidate States'. However, this important qualitative improvement did not yet mean that accession negotiations could be opened with that country. Turkey had first to take considerable steps towards meeting the Copenhagen political criteria, something which she appears to be prepared to do. In the light of this process constitutional and legislative initiatives are expected in the course of 2002 and the years to come. Anyhow, for that country, the pre-accession road will be lengthy and difficult. Interestingly enough, Turkey was the subject of a second and, perhaps in real terms, bigger qualitative upgrade than its candidate status implied. Indeed, the Helsinki Conclusions also stipulated that 'Turkey, like other States, will benefit from a pre-accession strategy to stimulate and support its reforms'. A close reading of these Conclusions even revealed that the European Council meant to say that Turkey would be covered by the '*enhanced* pre-accession strategy' in the same way as the other 12 candidates. This implied, among other things, the adoption of an Accession Partnership for Turkey, the adoption by Turkey of a National Programme for the Adoption of the Acquis, as well as enhanced political dialogue between Turkey and the EU. The first two main legislative

---

[72] See Council Regulation of 13 Mar. 2000 on the implementation of operations in the framework of the pre-accession strategy for the Republic of Cyprus and the Republic of Malta, OJ 2000 L 68/3; for implementing measures see Council Decision on the principles, priorities, intermediate objectives, and conditions contained in the Accession Partnership with the Republic of Cyprus, OJ 2000 L 78/10 and for Malta, OJ 2000 L 78/17.

measures to formalize this new approach were Council Regulation 390/2001 of 26 February 2001 on assistance to Turkey in the framework of the pre-accession strategy, and in particular on the establishment of an Accession Partnership,[73] and Council Decision of 8 March 2001 on the principles, priorities, intermediate objectives and conditions contained in the Accession Partnership.[74] These legal instruments follow exactly the same pattern as that followed for other candidates.

Consequently, from the point of view of legal methodology on enhanced pre-accession, there is no longer a differentiation between Turkey and the other candidates. Of course, priorities are not the same among the various candidates. For Turkey, for instance, the enhanced political dialogue and political criteria are, in accordance with what had been stipulated in the Helsinki Conclusions, very visible in the short-term priorities as well as in the medium-term objectives of the Accession Partnership. Respect for human rights is prominently present in this enumeration. It is true that the incorporation of Turkey in the enhanced pre-accession strategy constitutes a challenge for both the EU and Turkey. But for political, economic, but also historical and human reasons it is certainly worth the effort. If the enlargement process in the end manages to grant Turkey its proper and secured place in Europe then this may be one of its most important and initially unexpected achievements. It must also be said that the EU's option for a large and global, all-inclusive enlargement with so many countries has facilitated the move towards the inclusion of Turkey in the enhanced pre-accession strategy. Seen in this context the recent rapid 'promotion', whereby Turkey makes a qualitative jump in the EU pre-accession strategy from nowhere, even without passing through the first stages of the pre-accession strategy, immediately to '*enhanced* pre-accession' is not in itself surprising. Of course, it remains paradoxical that the inclusion of Turkey in the enhanced pre-accession strategy is also in part based on the 'European Strategy for Turkey', a strategy which Turkey itself had so sharply condemned and rejected after the Luxembourg Summit. On the other hand, however, it was also obvious that the decision of the Helsinki European Summit could turn out as it did only because there had already been a very intense and long-standing relationship between the EC and Turkey, *inter alia* through the 1963 Association Agreement and the 1996 customs union. Among the candidates, Turkey is not only the second most important trading partner of the EU after Poland but there is also great potential for further trade development. It is also interesting to note that the application of the enhanced pre-accession policy to Turkey took place without a formal revision of the 1989 negative Opinion of the Commission on Turkey's application for membership and thus without the publication of any formal new opinion. Of course, there is still a long way to

[73] OJ 2001 L 58/1.   [74] OJ 2001 L 85/13.

go before Turkey can be a member but, as was observed in the 2001 Laeken European Council Conclusions, there has undoubtedly been evolution in this matter. The Conclusions indeed recognize that 'Turkey has made progress towards complying with the political criteria established for accession, in particular through the recent amendments of its constitution'. This has brought forward 'the prospect of the opening of accession negotiations with Turkey'. Turkey is encouraged to continue its progress in meeting the Copenhagen Criteria, 'notably with regard to human rights'. And, also important enough to mention, 'the pre-accession strategy for Turkey should mark a new stage in analysing its preparedness for alignment on the acquis'.

The inclusion of Cyprus, Malta, and Turkey also implied that specific pre-accession assistance has been made available for these countries. For Cyprus and Malta, 95 million euros has been provided for the period from 2000. The main focus is approximation of laws. For Cyprus, projects having a bi-communal impact also receive special attention. For the financial dimension of the pre-accession strategy for Turkey Council Regulation 2500/2001 of 17 December 2001 is instrumental.[75] Grants for a total of 177 million euros a year are committed to Turkey,[76] while various loan facilities under MEDA also remain open. Pre-accession financial assistance is pre-accession-oriented and should be directed towards structural reforms, approximation of laws, institution building, and investment in the *acquis*.

7. 'WHILE MAINTAINING THE MOMENTUM OF EUROPEAN INTEGRATION'

Simultaneously with the fundamental reorientation of the EU's policy to-wards Central and Eastern Europe, it was stated that enlarging necessarily required measures to be taken to adapt the EU's existing institutional framework, and its decision-making process in particular. As already men-tioned above, the 1993 Copenhagen and 1994 Essen European Council Conclusions have explicit provisions in this respect—the last of which even suggests that such measures needed to be taken before accession negotiations were opened. Also, the 1997 Luxembourg European Conclusions reiterated that 'as a prerequisite for enlargement of the Union, the operation of the institutions must be strengthened and improved in keeping with the insti-tutional provisions of the Amsterdam Treaty'.

---

[75] OJ 2001 L 342/1.
[76] This is still a very modest offer (for example in 1999 under the national PHARE programmes 231 million Euro were allocated to Poland, 167 million euros to Romania, 103 million euros to Hungary).

A great deal was expected from the Nice Treaty. However, only one part of the institutional objectives was accomplished in Nice.[77] In a prospective approach, that of successfully concluding the accession negotiations, the EU Member States managed to assess the position of every candidate country with which accession negotiations were underway—an elegant way to avoid incorporating Turkey in this exercise—in the enlarged EU institutional framework. This delicate and difficult task was performed well so that the weight and place of each applicant in the various EU institutions could be fixed. But this activity, as such, has nothing to do with the indispensable institutional adaptation needing to be made in order to have an EU capable of functioning properly with 20, 25 or potentially even more Member States. Seen in this context the statement by the European Commission that 'the European Council of Nice has defined the framework for the institutional reform necessary for enlargement'[78] is astounding. As Gautron rightly observes: '*le traité de Nice ne garantit pas le bon fonctionnement de l'Union européenne après l'élargissement*'.[79] The stated need for parallelism between moving towards enlargement and the necessary modernization of the EU institutional structures seems gradually but surely to give way to what is now called the credibility of the EU's enlargement policy towards the candidate countries. This goes so far that it has even been suggested that, from a legal point of view, the ratification of the Treaty of Nice is not indispensable to going ahead with EU enlargement.[80] Certainly, the pre-accession process, later the enhanced pre-accession process, and the accession negotiations have all moved forward. For the candidates which are beginning to find themselves at the end of the pre-accession road further waiting until the EU has completed its domestic institutional reforms is no doubt very, if not unbearably, disillusioning. The European Commission has properly expressed these

---

[77] For an analysis see Dehousse, 'The Treaty of Nice: A Watershed in the History of European Integration', LIII *Studia Diplomatica* (2000) 19.

[78] Making a Success of Enlargement. 2001 Strategy Paper, *supra* note 38, at 4.

[79] Gautron, 'Le traité de Nice satisfait-il aux exigences de l'élargissement?', 10 *Revue des affaires européennes* (2000) 343, at 353.

[80] See R. Prodi, President of the European Commission in the *Irish Times*, 21 June 2001: 'Legally, ratification of the Nice Treaty is not necessary for enlargement. It is without any problem up to 20 members, and those beyond 20 members have only to put in the accession agreement some notes of change, some clause. But legally, it is not necessary.' The legal argument to which Mr. Prodi refers is no doubt Art. 2 of the Amsterdam Protocol on Institutions after enlargement but this implies overlooking Art. 1 of the same Protocol. However, President Prodi does not seem to be totally convinced by his statement since he later declared that 'without ratification we will put Europe on hold. ... We should have a paralysis. The Nice Treaty is a political condition for enlargement', quoted from BBC News, http://news.bbc.co.uk/1/hi/world/europe/1400187.stm. It is also difficult to conceive legally that without the global institutional arrangements and rearrangements made via the Nice Protocol on the enlargement of the European Union amending the basic Treaties, the same can be achieved directly through the Accession Treaty and Act of Accession.

feelings in the following terms: 'over the last ten years society in the candidate countries of Central and Eastern Europe has been placed under enormous strain. These societies have had to make the transition from communist rule and centrally planned economies to democracy and the market, while at the same time gearing themselves up to the sophisticated machinery of European integration. The resultant social stresses cannot be ignored. It is perfectly understandable that people now want to see the light at the end of the tunnel. The appetite for further efforts and reforms might well diminish if these countries start to feel that the goal of EU membership will never be in reach. To prevent a possible surge of doubt and frustration, determination and leadership is needed from the EU'.[81] But the EU's mission is not only to enlarge, however important and necessary this may be in itself. There are not many opportunities left to the EU to tune the indispensable institutional reforms to the realities of the ongoing accession process. The Member States but also the various EU institutions bear their own enormous responsibilities. So far the Member States and the European Council have not been able to give the impetus necessary for adequate domestic reforms. And the European Commission's responsibility is colossal, given that it has presented and pushed the pre-accession strategy forward very strongly, unfortunately with little or no vision as regards the implications of enlargement on domestic institutional structures and the decision-making process. Over the years the European Commission, and in particular its Commissioner for enlargement, have become the strongest advocates for enlargement—almost the spokesmen for the candidates—while the Commission's role in and influence on the institutional debate in the EU are virtually nil. The Commission simply lacks strength domestically but in the meantime it organizes, structures, evaluates, etc. the accession process in the field. Seen in this context the role and task of the Convention on the Future of Europe which is, to use the terminology of the 2001 Laeken Declaration, 'to pave the way for the next Intergovernmental Conference' is crucial. First and foremost the Convention and afterwards the 2004 IGC will have to provide the answer to the question how the EU can continue to function after enlargement. At the same time everybody is aware that an adequate answer can be given only when there is sufficient readiness among the Member States to accept the institutional reforms and adaptations. It is in nobody's interest—except for those who are opposed to the European integration construction as such—and certainly not in the interests of the candidates to lead the pre-accession process not only to EU enlargement but also to an impotent EU. An enlargement where widening is victorious over deepening would be a bad enlargement, bad for the EU and bad for Europe as a whole.

---

[81] European Commission, 2000 Enlargement Strategy Paper, *supra* note 38, at 5.

3

Preparing for Accession to the European Union: How to Establish Capacity for Effective and Credible Application of EU Rules

PHEDON NICOLAIDES*

1. INTRODUCTION AND SUMMARY

The countries that have applied for membership of the European Union are currently preoccupied with the huge task of the adoption, application, and enforcement of EU law, policies, and practices, otherwise known as the *'acquis communautaire'*. Although, the implementation[1] of the *acquis* is largely seen as a technical issue and has not so far received much public attention, one of the objectives of this Chapter is to explain why it is likely to become more prominent in the next 12 months as the accession negotiations between the EU and the front-runner candidate countries near their end.

When one looks more carefully there are implementation-related problems in most of the bilateral relations between the EU and the candidates. For example, at the time of writing this Chapter (May 2001), the EU suspended its aid to Slovakia because of irregularities in its disbursement within the country. During the same period, agriculture Commissioner Franz Fischler, speaking at a conference in Warsaw, contended that the SAPARD programme had not yet started, despite long delays, because the candidates had not established the paying agencies required by the EU's agricultural rules.

This Chapter is developed along a series of questions exploring the issue of effective policy implementation, in general, and that of EU rules, in

* I am grateful to San Bilal, Frank Bollen, and Ines Hartwig for their comments and to Anne-Mieke Den Teuling for comments and research assistance in preparing this Chap. Even though their suggestions have enriched the Chap., I am solely responsible for its contents.

[1] The term implementation is used in this Chap. to denote the whole process of legal adoption, application, and enforcement of EU rules. The terms *acquis* and EU rules are also used interchangeably.

particular. The questions and the answers given eventually lead to a proposal on how candidate countries may establish capacity for effective implementation of the *acquis communautaire*.

The recommendations made by the EU to the candidates in this connection and the information provided by the candidates back to the EU have centred on what may be called the 'M&M solution': i.e. it is expected that EU rules will be effectively applied and enforced in the candidates once sufficient and properly qualified staff are hired and adequate amounts of resources are committed to those purposes (hence, the 'money & men' solution).

By contrast, this Chapter advocates an institutional approach to building that kind of capacity. The current preoccupation with the number and quality of staff and the resources they have at their disposal is unlikely to be a successful approach in the longer term. Although I am not rejecting the view that staff and resources are important, one of the main objectives of this Chapter is to explain why the problem of effective implementation goes beyond any count of bodies and Euros.

At the core of integration, in any form, lies the need to establish credible commitments. I argue that it will be easier for the candidate countries to demonstrate to the EU a credible commitment to apply the *acquis communautaire* if they assign the task of implementing EU rules to sufficiently empowered and accountable institutions which will both have considerable decision-making independence and be subject to specific performance obligations.

My reasoning is rather simple. The execution of any task requires three necessary conditions: knowledge, ability, and willingness (incentives). The top officials of the candidate countries have graduated from the best school in which to learn the *acquis*: the screening stage of the accession negotiations. Most of them have also attended numerous seminars and other training programmes within the framework of the EU's technical assistance to the candidates. They do not lack knowledge of EU law and policies, although naturally they still seek advice on the precise implementation methods of those laws and policies. With respect to their ability to apply the *acquis*, the efforts of the candidate countries and of the EU are currently focused on committing resources, hiring extra staff, training them, and getting them acquainted with national practice in the existing EU Member States (for example, through Taiex activities and Twinning programmes).

By contrast, the 'willingness' of those who will apply and enforce the *acquis* (i.e. the structure of incentives within the candidates) has so far been relatively neglected by the EU and, as far as I can ascertain, by the candidates themselves. Perhaps it is natural to give precedence to knowledge acquisition and investment in essential facilities and equipment. Now, however, issues of institutional design deserve more attention because it is they that will determine the success or failure of the effective adoption of the *acquis* in the longer term.

I begin, however, by explaining in the following section why, paradoxically, the progress of the candidates in adopting the *acquis* is likely to be one of the most contentious aspects of the accession negotiations, even though it is not formally a subject under negotiation.

2. WHAT IS THE SIGNIFICANCE OF EFFECTIVE IMPLEMENTATION OF EU RULES?

The issue of effective implementation of EU rules has come to the forefront of the enlargement process only in a gradual way. The conclusions of the Copenhagen European Council (June 1993), which laid down the basic requirements for EU membership, made no mention of implementation or of the need of the then applicant countries to have implementing capacity. The first mention came at the Madrid European Council (December 1995) in a single sentence that merely stated that the candidates should adjust their administrative structures. That statement was made in the context of the broader reform and modernization of the public administrations of the countries that had only recently emerged from many years of central planning, which was a system responsive only to the commands of the planners rather than the needs of the citizens.

More explicit statements about the indispensability of capacity for effective implementation of EU rules have been made only since the decision to start the accession negotiations. The Luxembourg European Council (December 1997), which gave formal approval to the launch of the negotiations, stipulated that 'incorporation of the *acquis* into legislation is necessary, but not in itself sufficient; it will also be necessary to ensure that it is actually applied'. The Helsinki European Council (December 1999), which broadened the negotiations to include the remaining candidate countries (except Turkey), went further by declaring that 'progress in negotiations must go hand in hand with progress in incorporating the *acquis* into legislation and actually implementing and enforcing it'. The most distinct statement about the importance of implementation and enforcement came at the Feira European Council (June 2000) which stated that 'in addition to finding solutions to negotiating issues, progress in the negotiations depends on incorporation by candidate States of the *acquis* in national legislation and especially on their capacity to effectively implement and enforce it'.[2]

---

[2] For a more detailed review of these developments see P. Nicolaides, *Enlargement of the European Union and Effective Implementation of its Rules* (2000) and Nicolaides, 'Effective implementation of EU Rules: An Institutional Solution', 36(1) *Intereconomics* (2001), 14–19.

A question that arises when considering these conclusions of the various European Councils is whether these successive and gradually more explicit and detailed statements represent a mere clarification of the criteria that have to be fulfilled by the candidates or whether they constitute a hardening of the EU position which in effect raises the entry requirements.

I believe that for the reasons outlined below they are both a clarification and a toughening of the entry requirements. First, they must be seen as a clarification because the EU has naturally been learning more about the situation in the candidate countries and their capabilities as they have been trying to apply EU rules. The sources of information have been primarily the initial assessment by the Commission of their suitability for membership, the subsequent updates in the form of the annual reports, the National Plans for the Adoption of the Acquis prepared by the candidates, the documents submitted during the screening stage of the accession negotiations, and the formal position papers. As the EU obtains a more accurate picture of the conditions in the candidates, it elaborates the entry requirements to guide their adaptation process.

Secondly, however, this process of elaboration, precisely because it adds new details and, more importantly, because it is unilateral, creates uncertainty about what degree of preparedness by the candidates would be acceptable to the EU.

Thirdly, the candidates feel that there is indeed an element of arbitrariness and unfairness in the assessment of their preparedness, because the EU does not have explicit criteria for judging whether its Member States have capacity for effective implementation of EU rules and because it does not subject its own members to the same kind of scrutiny of their domestic implementation mechanisms and procedures.

Fourthly, careful reading of the European Council conclusions suggests that the EU has not just been clarifying the entry requirements. It has actually been bringing commitments forward in time. Adoption, application, and enforcement of the *acquis* have to be achieved before actual accession and even before the negotiations are concluded. In fact, the conclusion of the negotiations is contingent on the achievement of an acceptable standard of implementation by the candidates. Since it is not known what that standard might be, it strengthens the negotiating position of the EU because the latter may claim that no acceptable standard has been achieved by the candidates and, as a consequence, demand more concessions, more commitments, or a longer period of preparation before entry can be achieved.

I conclude, therefore, that not only is the issue of implementation of the *acquis* important to the enlargement process, it also has the potential to obstruct it. Politically it would be too difficult for the EU to conclude the negotiations with the candidates on the technical and financial issues of enlargement and suspend their entry process until they improve their implementation record. However, a poor implementation record would give negotiating ammunition to the EU to stall on tough technical and financial issues (e.g. structural funds, direct payments to farmers) where Member States could disagree among themselves, even where the candidates are eager to reach agreement.

3. WHY IS EFFECTIVE IMPLEMENTATION OF EU RULES AN ISSUE IN THE CURRENT ENLARGEMENT OF THE EUROPEAN UNION?

Is the EU justified in insisting that the candidates must demonstrate that they have established capacity for effective implementation and that they actually adopt all EU rules and begin the process of enforcement of those rules before they accede to the Union? In other words, why has the EU made capacity for implementation a pivotal issue in the enlargement process?

This is indeed the first enlargement where the candidates are asked to demonstrate that they have that kind of capacity. Very revealing in this context is a recent publication on Finland's own accession negotiations, which contains no reference at all to any requirement for capacity for implementation.[3] Not only was the EU not concerned about the capacity of the then applicants in 1993–1994, but it even accepted vague commitments from them to establish the requisite implementing procedures to enforce EU rules after they had entered the EU! The reader should not too hastily conclude that the EU was not overly concerned because the then candidates were advanced, democratic economies. Candidates in previous enlargements received exactly the same treatment. So what has prompted the EU to change its attitude towards the present candidate countries?

The first and most obvious answer is that most of the present candidates have emerged from many years of communism, and they have to build institutions which are accountable to citizens and which function in a very different environment from the one that prevailed in those countries in the past. This of course does not explain why Cyprus and Malta are also subject to the same treatment. Annex I summarizes the main administrative requirements of EU membership, classified according to the 30 substantive chapters of the accession negotiations.

Secondly, there are too many candidates. It would be very difficult for the EU to accommodate the largest ever number of candidates if each candidate were to cause just a few problems of its own. These problems could quickly multiply to unmanageable proportions for the EU and its institutions.

---

[3] See A. Kuosmanen, *Finland's Journey to the European Union* (2001).

Thirdly, the process of integration within the EU itself has progressed, and as a result it exposes more easily internal impediments to free trade, movement, and investment caused by administrative weaknesses and incorrect or incomplete implementation of EU rules by the Member States. It is not simply that the deepening of integration raises concerns about effective implementation. Such concerns can exist at any stage of integration. Rather, once the very visible statutory impediments of an outright discriminatory and protectionist nature are removed, administrative weaknesses become more obvious. It is no accident that in recent years the attention of the Commission, which is the Guardian of the Treaties, has turned to issues of incorrect/incomplete implementation of EU rules by the Member States.

Fourth, and related to the previous reason, is the fact that the *acquis* has expanded and there are now, in the area of the internal market alone, close to 1,500 directives. Supervision of the continually increasing number of directives and regulations imposes a heavy administrative burden on the Commission which would not be able to cope and fulfil its task of 'Guardian of the Treaties' in an expanded EU. As the EU admits new members, it becomes more important that both the newcomers and the existing members function more smoothly within the EU.

4. HOW DOES THE EU ENSURE EFFECTIVE IMPLEMENTATION OF ITS RULES?

Given that the issue of effective implementation of EU rules has assumed centre stage in the accession negotiations, the next question which arises is how will the EU judge the performance of the candidates and how should they prepare for that 'judgement'. The second part of this question, which is the main topic of this Chapter, is developed in more detail later on. In this section, I examine the first part of the question and, in particular, how the EU deals with incorrect/incomplete implementation in the case of its current members.

Before continuing further, an important distinction needs to be made. Although the EU, through the Commission, checks whether Member States respect their obligations by transposing and applying correctly EU rules, it has no formal jurisdiction to evaluate the capacity of its members to comply with their obligations. It does not pass judgements, for example, on the performance of their public administrations. I will, however, explain below that in reality the EU has many informal channels through which to evaluate and apply pressure on the public administrations of the Member States. Increasingly it also compares the administrative structures of the Member

States; a fact that indirectly induces Member States to strengthen their national authorities.[4]

It appears possible to distinguish between eight different approaches or methods of checking and encouraging compliance by the Member States:[5]

1. Publication of the national records of transposition of directives;
2. Publication of surveys of business opinions about problems and barriers encountered in each Member State;
3. Encouragement of citizens and businesses to take action against their own national authorities;
4. Inspections carried out by Commission officials or staff of European agencies;
5. Legal proceedings, mostly initiated by the Commission against Member States;
6. Evaluation by the Commission of the state of the internal market;
7. Monitoring and coordination of national policies (e.g. Luxembourg process);
8. Peer review and peer pressure.

The first method centres on the transposition record of each Member State, which is published in the Single Market Scoreboard (latest issue: no. 7 of November 2000). This appears to be a 'name and shame' approach. Although in early issues of the Scoreboard, the Commission would limit itself to presentation of statistics on the transposition and infringement record of each Member State, in more recent issues it also uses more qualitative statements about their performance, such as the slow progress of reform in some Member States.

The second method for encouraging compliance is through a survey of business opinion about the various obstacles encountered by companies in each Member State (see the November 2000 issue of the Scoreboard). Although the answers of the companies surveyed are reported by country, it is not clear whether the perceived barriers and problems corresponded to that country or other countries. Presumably the purpose of this method is to provide more information to Member States about the problems towards which they should focus their efforts.

---

[4] See, e.g., Recommendation on Minimum Criteria for Environmental Inspections in the Member States, 2001/331, OJ 2001 L 118/48 which urges Member States to supply to the Commission data on staffing and other resources of the inspecting authorities, even though there is no legal requirement on Member States concerning levels of staffing (at 45).

[5] For a wider and more detailed review of implementing measures in various policy areas of the *acquis* the reader is directed to the recent series of studies published by EIPA on the general theme of 'capacity building for integration'. More information can be found on EIPA's website at www.eipa.nl/publications.

The third method aims to promote the rights of citizens and business through 'contact points'. As both citizens and businesses obtain more information about the nature of the national measures that prevent them from exercising their rights, they will assert those rights more vigorously through action before national courts and force Member States to respect their obligations. In this way, the Commission hopes to have many allies in its efforts to promote a climate of compliance.

In this respect, it is worth noting that private action against the failure of Member States to transpose or to apply correctly Community law is facilitated by relatively recent judgments of the Court of Justice which have clarified the extent of liability of Member States (see, for example, the famous *Francovich* judgment[6]).

The fourth method refers to enforcement of Community law by EU institutions, mostly the Commission and European agencies. This is relatively rare as the responsibility for application and enforcement largely rests with the Member States and their national authorities. We can distinguish here between two different types of enforcement: that which is related to the application of EU rules by the Commission itself and that which is related to inspection of compliance by national authorities. Prominent examples of the first type are the inspections by Commission competition officials (anti-cartel and anti-abuse of dominance cases) and trade officials (anti-dumping and countervailing duty cases). Prominent examples of the second type are the inspections carried out for the purposes of financial control, prevention of fraud, and for checking health and safety standards.

The fifth method concerns legal compliance. In fact, this is the oldest method. As is well known there is the established procedure of Articles 226 (reasoned opinion and initiation of infringement proceedings), and 228 (failure to comply with a ruling of the Court) EC Treaty. Both are used by the Commission to force Member States to apply correctly primary and secondary legislation. Note that over the past decade or so, proceedings have progressed from non-transposition infringements to non-application infringements.

The sixth method, that of evaluation of the state of the various fields of the internal market, is carried out by various Commission services using their own distinct methodologies. Although this is the least systematic method (because it is not regular and not based on a unified methodology) it is probably the most illuminating instrument for understanding the problems in each policy area in each Member State.[7] It is naturally up to the Member

---

[6] Joined Cases C–6/90 & C–9/90, *Andrea Francovich and Danila Bonifaci and others v Italian Republic*, [1991] ECR I–5357.

[7] See, e.g., the annual reports on the implementation of the telecommunications directives.

States to agree with the findings of the Commission and to adopt its recommendations.

The seventh method is part of the relatively recent process of monitoring and coordination of the employment and economic policies and performance of the Member States. Strictly speaking Member States do not have hard *acquis* to implement here, but they have to manage their economies in such a way as to comply with their other obligations (e.g. the Stability Pact and the requirement to maintain public debt and budget deficits below the ceilings of 60 per cent of GDP and 3 per cent of GDP, respectively).

Lastly, the eighth method which relies on peer review and peer pressure is the least visible to outsiders. The EU is a massive network of committees and working groups. These do not just discuss new legislative proposals. They also consider the state of implementation in the Member States, any remaining barriers, and possible new measures for the removal of those barriers. Participating national officials often have to explain and defend national policies. In the process, they come under pressure to modify them. At the same time they learn from each other by sharing views on less contentious issues of national experience and by identifying best practice. Contact within these committees therefore is conducive to the transfer of ideas for the improvement of national policies on the basis of the experience of other Member States.

It should also be realized that the EU 'forces' its Member States to improve their domestic procedures by continually introducing more details in its legislation. Directives, for example, are no longer confined to identifying the objectives to be achieved by the Member States.[8] They habitually contain specific time targets, implementation procedures, and reporting obligations. Naturally, it has become relatively easier for the Commission to detect and prove non-compliance by the Member States as directives contain so much more information than in the past.

In conclusion, while it is formally true that Member States are free to organize their public administrations as they wish and to adopt implementing measures of their choice, in practice their room for manœuvre is much more limited than in the early years of the Community. This is especially relevant where Community law requires Member States to establish independent authorities to enforce the *acquis* or to assign to particular authorities that task, such as in the case of national regulatory authorities for

---

[8] It is not only directives that leave room for discretion by the Member States. Regulations and decisions that formally require no transposition may also leave to Member States the choice of the precise implementing procedures. Take e.g. the case of the common agricultural policy which is the most developed, detailed, and complex Community policy and which is implemented through regulations. In this policy Member States are required to establish 'paying agencies'. Yet they can choose the form of these agencies, ranging from ministerial departments to independent authorities.

telecommunications, post, and electricity, environmental inspection authorities, standards certification and accreditation bodies, market surveillance authorities, auditing authorities, coordinating bodies for structural operations, etc. See Annex I at the end of this Chapter for a list of principal administrative bodies required in the various sectors of the *acquis*, classified according to the chapters of the accession negotiations.

5. ARE THE CURRENTLY USED METHODS SUFFICIENT TO GUIDE THE CANDIDATE COUNTRIES?

The answer to this question must be partly negative. Although they are certainly useful, they are not enough. The mere fact that the EU has so many different methods is itself an indication that no single method is sufficient. They all have their weaknesses. In this section and in the rest of the Chapter I explain why all eight methods together are not enough for the candidate countries.

Consider, first, the legal approach. Although it is often said that the EU is based on the 'rule of law', the nature of the legal process is such that it does not lend itself to assessment of the structure and performance of national authorities. The main objective of the procedures of Articles 226–228 EC and any resultant Court ruling is to confirm whether there has been a breach of Community law or not. They do not normally contain recommendations on how the Member State or institution found at fault should amend its policies and actions so as to comply with EC law, let alone improve its performance.

In addition, when delivering its opinion on requests for preliminary rulings from national courts, the European Court of Justice habitually refrains from passing judgments on the specific conditions that prevail in each Member State because it, correctly, regards that to be a task for national courts.

Although most of the literature on enforcement of EU rules is legal in nature, the judgments of the Court of First Instance and the Court of Justice contain very little in terms of requirements, criteria, or indicators of how Member States should structure their mechanisms and procedures for policy implementation and enforcement. The closest the Court has come to laying down criteria for enforcement is to stipulate that Member States should apply the same standards and show the same diligence with respect to Community law as they apply with respect to national law. The fact that, as explained in the following section, the Commission is increasingly turning its attention to performance indicators and assessment of the results of the application of EC law is proof that a purely legalistic approach is insufficient, even though it may be an indispensable tool for forcing Member States to comply with their Treaty obligations.

The remaining methods for encouraging effective implementation of EU rules seek, with one exception, to apply pressure on national authorities to improve their performance either indirectly through actions by individuals and companies or directly by measuring that performance and producing rankings of the Member States. These methods do not define the components, the necessary inputs, or the structural/institutional requirements for the establishment of capacity for effective policy implementation and enforcement of Community law. The exception is the reviews of the state of the internal market. There the Commission does express opinions on the capacity of the Member States and includes recommendations on how to improve this. As explained earlier, however, there is no systematic methodology or analysis across the various internal market fields.

Recently, however, a different trend has emerged. Instead, of identifying inputs, it identifies desirable outputs. It focuses on performance indicators and its more popular version of 'benchmarking'. The following section examines the strengths and weaknesses of this trend.

6. WHY IS THERE A SHIFT TOWARDS PERFORMANCE INDICATORS?

One definition of effective implementation of the *acquis* is that Member States apply it and enforce it in such a way as to fulfil not only its letter but also its spirit by creating a truly integrated internal market. Hence, it is not enough to comply formally with EU requirements. It is also necessary to use implementing measures that do not themselves become barriers to the free movement of goods, services, persons, and capital. In this connection, the Commission believes that it has to look at the quality of the results achieved by the Member States rather than restrict itself to checking just their record of transposition.

In particular, the Commission is committed to reinforcing the regular Scoreboard with indicators of the performance of the Member States (see, for example, the background documents submitted to the Stockholm European Council in March 2001). This increasing interest in results and performance is not unusual when considering that there are similar developments in many different areas of public and business affairs in Europe. For example, the Lisbon European Council of March 2000 endorsed the use of a new 'open method' of evaluating the performance of the Member States based on 'benchmarking'.[9]

---

[9] Benchmarking, like many theories and fads that periodically capture the imagination of managers and administrators, is a tool. As such, it has both strengths and weaknesses, and it will soon be realized that it is not a panacea. For a review of the concept see Sisson and Marginson, 'Benchmarking and the Europeanisation of Social and Employment Policy',

At the time of writing, the performance indicators that will be used by the Commission are not yet known but a glimpse of what could be expected was given in the last issue of the Scoreboard (November 2000). These were the criteria used for the business survey whose results were reported in that Scoreboard.

A series of questions was put to various businesses across the EU, whose primary aim was to detect the existence of measures that should not have been used by Member States because they are contrary to EC law. What is interesting is that the survey tries to establish whether national measures also create obstacles that would not normally be illegal, such as the following:

- National specifications resulting in additional costs;
- Unusual testing, certification, or approval procedures;
- Complicated VAT procedures;
- Complicated or slow administrative procedures;
- Complicated appeal procedures;
- Attitude of public authorities;
- Lack of useful information.

We may conclude from the above that true integration cannot be fully achieved solely on the basis of prohibition of barriers to trade, movement, and investment and the elimination of other discriminatory measures. It also requires improvements in national policies, practices, and attitudes that go beyond legal proscriptions. This is another reason why legal standards and methods are a necessary but not sufficient means for ensuring that both the letter and the spirit of the *acquis* are implemented and enforced effectively so as to create a truly integrated internal market.

Also illuminating in this context are the results of Commission inquiries into the state of the internal market in particular policy areas or sectors of the economy. Take, for example, the case of telecommunications. The Commission publishes annual reports on the situation in the telecommunications markets and on the state of implementation of EC law. Naturally, it examines whether Member States have transposed and applied correctly the various telecoms directives. But, what is even more interesting for our purposes is that many of the issues identified by the Commission as being indispensable to effective implementation are not stipulated in the directives, and consequently they do not constitute legal obligations for Member States. It follows, once more, that effective policy implementation goes beyond legally binding concepts and measures.

More specifically in the area of telecommunications the main responsibility for effective implementation of the *acquis* rests with the National

Briefing Note 3/01, Apr. 2001, UK Economic and Social Research Council (*Programme: One Europe or Several?*).

Regulatory Authorities (NRAs). The relevant directives define their regulatory tasks, primarily with respect to prices, licensing, interconnection, provision of universal service, and resolution of disputes, and require that they are
independent from any telecoms operators and structurally separate from any
government department which supervises any state-owned operators.

Yet, starting from the same Community legal base the Member States have
established quite diverse implementing systems. A central problem in telecommunications is to ensure a competitive market structure. The use of
normal competition rules, in addition to the sector-specific rules, is therefore
essential. At the one extreme, there is the UK where the NRA (OFTEL) has
powers to apply competition law in full. At the other extreme there are
countries such as Greece where the NRA (EETT) has no such powers and
the application of competition rules to the telecoms operators is left to the
competition authority. Somewhere in between there are countries like the
Netherlands with an explicit cooperation protocol between the NRA
(OPTA) and the competition authority (NMa), or like Portugal with partial
allocation of certain competition-related tasks to the NRA. With respect to
access to the market, there are also significant differences. The UK, for
example, operates an extensive licensing system that specifies the obligations
of the providers, while, by contrast, the Netherlands has only a very light
system of registration, which allows anyone to enter the market.[10]

In view of this diversity in implementing systems, the question naturally
arises whether they are all equally effective. Perhaps, more importantly for the
candidate countries, it is not easy to identify the right model of implementation to follow. That is why in the next section the Chapter develops basic
elements of capacity for effective policy implementation.

Interestingly, in its periodic reports the Commission has, in addition to the
legally-mandated obligations, identified the following as being essential features of the NRAs for the purpose of effective implementation of the telecoms
acquis (see, for example, the latest annual report published in November 2000):

- Clarity in the assignment of the NRA powers and absence of
  overlapping of regulatory responsibilities with other authorities;
- Regulatory stability that encourages companies to invest in new
  technologies;
- Transparent and speedy decision-making procedures;[11]

---

[10] See Slot and Skudder, 'Common Features of Community Law Regulation in the
Network-Bound Sectors', 38 *CML Rev.* (2001) 87.

[11] Apparently, negotiations for interconnection to the incumbent's network are reported
to vary from a few days (the Netherlands) to six months (UK) to a whole year (Finland,
Portugal). This suggests that NRAs have distinctly different standards about intervention in
the market to force interconnection and resolve disputes between operators. See Slot and
Skudder, *supra* note 10.

- Clear procedures for consultation, coordination, and appeal of their decisions;
- Proactive intervention in the market;
- Sufficient budgetary resources and well-qualified staff.

What is perhaps even more surprising is that the essential features which have been identified by the Commission in the area of telecoms concerning the structure and actions of the NRAs actually have little to do with telecommunications. This observation suggests that some features of capacity for effective policy implementation are generic rather than sector-specific. We may therefore generalize across other authorities, agencies, or organizations responsible for implementing the *acquis*. They should at minimum be:

- Sufficiently empowered, having adequate powers that can be exercised independently without needing further authorization;
- Enforcing regulations and standards which are not overly complex and unusual;
- Mandated to be proactive through constant monitoring and assessment of the market situation;
- Open, transparent, and prompt;
- Coordinating with other authorities and consulting interested parties;
- Accountable and subject to judicial review process.

It must be amply obvious by now that the concept of effective implementation can be interpreted in different ways. It can be defined in terms of the quality of output or policy results or in terms of the 'policy inputs' with respect to the structure, resources, and design of the regulatory system or authority responsible for implementing and enforcing a set of rules or laws. The next section examines this issue in more detail and proposes an 'institutional' definition.

7. SO, WHAT IS EFFECTIVE POLICY IMPLEMENTATION?

The Chapter has so far referred to the concept of implementation without defining it. In place of a formal definition I presume that at the core of capacity for effective policy implementation is the triad of 'knowledge-ability-willingness (incentives)'. All three must exist at the same time for effective implementing capacity to exist. In this section, I analyse in more detail each of the three components, starting with ability.[12]

---

[12] The OECD has been running an extensive research programme on regulation and regulatory reform. Part of this programme has focused on regulatory implementation and compliance. See, in particular, *Reducing the Risk of Policy Failure: Challenges for Regulatory Compliance* (2000). See also A. Ogus, *Regulation: Legal Form and Economic Theory* (1994).

It is almost a truism to say that to achieve something you must be able to identify it. Some policies cannot be implemented because their objectives are not quantifiable or verifiable. For example, it would be impossible to implement effectively a policy aiming to encourage people to have 'nice' thoughts.

Naturally, policies are not always formulated in observable, quantifiable, or verifiable terms. Therefore, the first step in their implementation is to recast them in terms that can be observed or quantified. Make no mistake, often this is easier said than done. The correspondence between general policy objectives (e.g. raising national competitiveness) and the specific actions that can achieve those objectives can be one of the most contentious and difficult aspects of policy-making. Not only can there be many different possible specifications of the overall policy objective (e.g. market share *v* value-added), some of which may be contradictory, but there may also be many different ways of achieving each of the measurable specifications (e.g. subsidizing investments in technology *v* supporting general education).

Therefore, at the heart of effective implementation there is the ability to define specific targets, identify the particular actions needed, measure achieved results, and assess whether they reach those targets. In other words, effective implementation depends on having the right means at one's disposal. But the agency[13] responsible for implementation should also be capable of assessing whether it does its job well. It is not enough to know the *acquis*. It must also get to learn the particular market conditions in which it operates.

In addition to this 'learning' capacity, it is also necessary to have the means to adjust the various policy actions so as to improve policy outcomes, in case the initial actions prove to be ineffective. Hence, learning capacity (observation and verification) must be accompanied by 'adjustment' capacity. It not only means that the required resources are available. It also means that the agency in question is legally empowered to amend its implementing measures. The point here is not that agencies should do as they please. Rather, within the context of their general tasks which are defined by law (e.g. the transposed directives), they should have the flexibility to adjust (or calibrate) the particular implementing measures until they reach the legally-mandated targets. If they are dependent on higher authorities for any slight revision of their implementing measures, as market conditions change they will quickly lose the ability to address market problems effectively.

Particularly in the case of the candidate countries which have little experience in applying EU rules, capacity for learning and adjusting is likely to be

[13] Please note that in the context of this Chap. I regard the terms agency, authority, institution, notified body, etc. as being equivalent. They are intended to cover any public or private organization which is responsible for implementing some part of the *acquis*. Other considerations, such as the political legitimacy and identity of such organizations, are also ignored.

essential to their successful implementation of the *acquis*. It would certainly make good sense if they were to acknowledge from the outset that they are likely to make mistakes, and for this reason to build into their legal frameworks and corresponding institutional structures mandated review, evaluation, and revision procedures at regular intervals.

Our first conclusion must be that whoever is responsible for the implementation of any policy must be vested with the means to learn and adjust. Adjustment here not only means changing those policy measures which are already implemented. Perhaps more importantly, it also means the ability to put into force all the measures which are indispensable for the fulfilment of the various policy objectives. This requires that there are no legal lacunae, that the authority or agency in question has sufficient legal powers, in addition to having enough resources at its disposal.

Even a sufficiently empowered agency may not be able to act if its decisions and actions have to receive prior approval by a higher authority. Such approval may be granted after considerable delay or with strings attached, or it may not be granted at all. Empowerment that can translate into speedy action may require considerable autonomy and decision-making independence. In principle such independence should go as far as the scope of application of the various policy measures. For this purpose too, the authority or agency in question should have discretion to adjust as necessary the measures for which it is responsible.

Yet it may not be possible to define measures with neat boundaries. There may be overlaps or cross-linkages with measures implemented by other authorities or agencies. The decision-making independence or discretion of one authority may impinge on the independence or discretion of another by partly nullifying the latter's decisions. Some kind of coordination may be unavoidable. In an economy with independent authorities and agencies, coordination is a prerequisite of effective overall policy implementation.

Decision-making independence and discretion may cause another problem. They may be abused. It follows that this kind of independence should be granted only when there are safeguards in place against abuse. The policy-implementing authorities and agencies must, therefore, be accountable so as to have strong incentives to perform according to their assigned missions. This brings us to the third component of effective policy implementation, that of 'willingness (incentives)'. This does not mean that responsible authorities somehow become enthusiastic about the prospect of getting to implement EU rules. It only means that they are subject to such constraints that it is in their interest to perform as expected of them. If they are accountable or if they are subject to explicit performance criteria they will indeed have such incentives.

Accountability can take different forms, varying from requirements of openness and transparency, to an obligation to explain decisions adequately, to explicit performance standards. Since in democratic regimes no one is above the law, accountability must at minimum include the possibility of appeal and judicial review of the decisions of those agencies.

The available procedures for appealing administrative decisions are a complicated issue. In particular with respect to the candidate countries, the Commission has warned in its regular reports that they have to improve the speed and efficiency of their judicial systems. This raises the question of how the effectiveness of the implementation of the *acquis* can be safeguarded when judicial processes are very slow and cumbersome. One solution that western European countries have found to avoid slow legal procedures is to provide other means of appeal. For example, the decisions of the newly established Competition Commission of the UK can first be appealed to a specially constituted Panel of Appeals. The same is true of the Dutch competition authority (NMa) and telecommunications regulatory authority (OPTA).

Not only do these specialized panels speed up the processing of contested decisions, they are also equipped to deal with technically complex cases. Another concern expressed by the Commission, in this instance in the context of its reviews of the state of the internal market, is that in some Member States appeals deal with procedural rather than substantive issues. So the courts or the institutions that review administrative decisions appear to ask whether the procedures were followed properly instead of examining the contents of the contested decisions. Naturally, an authority that respects procedural requirements will not necessarily apply EU rules in the spirit in which they are intended.

We can summarize now the main features of the capacity for effective policy implementation. The authority responsible must be sufficiently empowered, must have the means to learn and adjust, must have adequate decision-making independence, and must be accountable. At the same time it must operate in coordination with other authorities. All these features suggest that the core issue of the process of building capacity for effective policy implementation is not just about having plentiful resources (money and equipment). It is about designing institutions with both the means and the incentives to act in such a way that they get as close as possible to their pre-assigned objectives.

Before moving to the next section, a comment is in order. What has been presented above is a very simplified scheme. The precise meaning of empowerment, independence, or accountability would naturally vary from policy sector to policy sector. Since the aim of this Chapter is to be general, some loss of sector-specific relevance is inevitable. Suffice it to say that candidate countries need to be aware that not all of the identified features need to be equally relevant in all policy sectors. There may also be cases where there are trade-offs between them. Nonetheless, the essence of what it is argued here is that all these features must be present in one form or another.

They are the bare minimum of what constitutes capacity for effective policy
implementation.

8. HOW TO ACHIEVE EFFECTIVE AND *EFFICIENT* POLICY IMPLEMENTATION?

Policy-makers often come under pressure to commit money and other
resources to high-profile problems. It is probably presumed that if the
government demonstrates enough commitment through the allocation of
resources, the right solutions will somehow be found. But apart from the fact
that, as argued in the previous section, the design of the regulatory system
may be more significant than the size of personnel or budget, there are never
enough resources around. To put it more precisely, there are too many
competing demands for the same resources. Efficient implementation is as
important as effective implementation.[14]

It has long been recognized that in most situations there is a trade-off
between effectiveness and efficiency. I will not elaborate further on the typical
advice given by economists according to which attempting to extract the last
Euro's worth from a given policy measure may not be worth the cost
incurred. My purpose here is to identify two kinds of efficiency and explore
the implications for the mechanisms of policy implementation. The reason is
that if effectiveness is not to be pursued at all costs, then it is natural to ask
'what kind of costs'? Indeed, as explained below, some of these costs are not
only to be traded off against effectiveness (in the sense that they can be
thought of as the 'price' of effectiveness), but they directly impinge on
effectiveness.

Efficiency is usually defined as achieving a certain objective or amount of
value at the lowest possible cost or achieving the largest possible amount
of value from constant costs. Let us call this 'internal efficiency' because it
minimizes costs or maximizes value-added. Economics has also identified
what may be termed as 'external efficiency'.[15] An efficient policy measure is
that which causes the minimum amount of two other types of costs: negative
side effects or spillovers (or 'externalities') on third parties and compliance
costs.

Once these costs are recognized, it is rather easy to draw two implications
for the mechanisms of policy implementation, although it is much more

---

[14] In this context see the classic paper by George Stigler on 'The Optimum Enforcement
of Laws', 78 *Journal of Political Economy* (1970), 526.
[15] The terms internal and external efficiency are used only for the purposes of this Chap.
I am not adding anything of substance that has not already been identified in the economics
literature.

difficult to identify the right policy response. The first implication is that policy implementation is a task that should involve not just the authority which is directly or primarily responsible for any given task. The views of other affected authorities and parties should be solicited and the potential effects on them should be taken into account during the policy-formulation stage. This does not mean that whatever claims they make should be accepted at face value. They may exaggerate or even lie to protect their interests. Nonetheless, the implementing authority, in addition to exercising judgement and prudence when evaluating such claims, should also consider the information they contain about the impact of its own policies and actions.

The second implication is that policy implementation has a strategic element. If compliance is costly and non-compliance is not easily observed by the authorities, it should be expected that individuals or firms will simply not comply. It should also be expected in those cases where non-compliance is easily observable that individuals and firms will seek to demonstrate formal compliance without necessarily doing what the policy makers intend them to do. Policy-makers, therefore, have to factor these behavioural reactions in the policy design and use appropriate instruments for detection and punishment of evasion precisely in order to discourage evasion.

Policy-makers cannot ignore compliance costs. They cannot say either that these are costs that do not concern them or, at the other extreme, that they will pursue a given policy at all costs. The higher the compliance costs, the stronger the incentive for evasion and the less effective the policy in question. Effectiveness, therefore, is improved either by reducing compliance costs (possibly by choosing among measures that are least costly to industry) and/or strengthening detection procedures and raising the penalties associated with non-compliance.

9. HOW TO ACHIEVE EFFECTIVE AND EFFICIENT POLICY IMPLEMENTATION IN THE CONTEXT OF INTEGRATION PROCESSES?

The concepts outlined in previous sections could apply to any country in the world. The question arises, then, whether anything changes when a country participates in a system of regional integration such as that of the EU. The answer is that nothing significant changes, but that some components of policy implementation need to be emphasized more than others.

Indeed, in the context of integration one aspect of policy implementation stands out: the costs imposed on partner countries by the national implementing measures.[16] There are two types of costs which are relevant here: those caused by direct spillovers (e.g. lax inspection of the safety of exported food) and the extra compliance costs imposed on partner-country products and firms when they enter the national market. It is presumed here that other costs caused, for example, by conflicting policy goals are eliminated at the stage of the formulation of the common policy and that the two kinds of costs just mentioned are those generated at the stage of implementation of the common policy.

The first type of cost is reduced through coordination and consultation among the partner countries. It is not just that the act of talking to each other reduces costs. Rather, consultations raise awareness, lead to the sharing of information, and encourage partner-country authorities to learn from each other. So these cross-border communications mechanisms need to be built into the system of national policy implementation.

The second type of cost is reduced by ensuring that regulatory duplication, unusual regulatory requirements, and, in general, opaque or slow procedures are avoided as much as possible. The reader is reminded that an earlier section of this Chapter has already pointed out that the Commission's sectoral assessments of the application of the relevant *acquis* revealingly stress some non-sector-specific issues such as transparency, openness, regulatory simplification, speedy response to complaints, adequate explanation, etc.[17]

Trade takes place because economies differ. Sometimes it pays to accentuate economic, technological, and regulatory differences. But open economies also gain by not being too different from their partners. If the essence of integration in this context is to look at the problem of implementation through the 'collective eyes' and according to the 'overall interests' of all the partner countries, then effective policy implementation also requires reliance on transparent and well-understood common standards and procedures and avoidance of complex and too idiosyncratic standards and procedures. The implication for the candidate countries is that they should aim for open and simple procedures, and perhaps they should copy what existing Member States appear to do well.

---

[16] There are other costs which appear earlier at the stage of formulation of the common policy. The most prominent of those is caused by the fact that adoption of common policies forces partner countries to deviate from the national optimum. I do not examine such costs in this Chap. because the focus of the Chap. is on the costs which are associated directly with policy application and enforcement.

[17] For a recent example of this tendency towards commonality in implementing measures see the Recommendation on Minimum Criteria for Environmental Inspections in the Member States, 2001/331, OJ 2001 L 118/48.

10. HOW MUCH DETAIL SHOULD THE IMPLEMENTING MEASURES CONTAIN?

A question which is often raised by officials from the candidate countries is how detailed their implementing measures should be. The question itself reveals that they understand that the task of implementing the *acquis* is not simply copying into national law the provisions of directives and then enforcing them. I explain in this section why the ability to enforce the *acquis* very much depends on the quality of the provisions inserted into national law.

As a shortcut to solving this problem the last sentence of the previous section suggested that the candidates could consider imitating the measures adopted by existing Member States. But this is not a panacea. Their methods of transposing EU law and the substantive provisions they incorporate in their statute books reflect their prevailing legal, economic, and administrative systems which are significantly different from those of the candidates. It would be beneficial for the candidates to consider the experience of the existing Member States, without however embarking on simple copying of their legislation.

Let us return now to the main theme of this section. The answer to the question posed at the beginning of this section is that the amount of detail that should be written into the implementing measures depends primarily on two factors: (a) the extent of decision-making discretion which is conferred on the implementing or enforcing authority, and (b) the extent to which individuals and companies can take evasive action to avoid compliance. The wider the decision-making discretion of the authority in question, the more general can be the implementing measures, and vice versa. At the same time, the easier it is for individuals and companies to escape from the scope of those measures the more general they should be. To put it in other words, the more complex the task of the authority the wider its discretion should be and the more general the scope of the measures it should have at its disposal.

But, unfortunately, this is not the end of the story. Wide discretion and general rules make it very difficult for individuals and companies to comply because they cannot know whether or not they actually comply. Discretion and generality inject uncertainty into the regulatory environment, affecting negatively the commercial and investment decisions of companies. As explained earlier, the regulators or enforcers have to take into account the costs of compliance they impose on the market. They can reduce those costs by reducing uncertainty about their actions and about the scope and applicability of the rules. And they reduce that kind of uncertainty by elaborating the rules and explaining how they may apply in different situations.

At the same time, discretion makes authorities vulnerable to political and lobbying pressure. Even if we assume that implementing authorities have benevolent intentions, they may still be vulnerable to 'regulatory capture'. They do not have to be corrupted with bribes in order to be captured. It can happen, for example, when the authorities become dependent on market participants for essential information. To avoid regulatory capture, implementing authorities need to be empowered (so that they escape dependence on market participants) and to be accountable as suggested in previous sections, but at the same time their regulatory/implementing tasks must be such that they can be carried out autonomously by the authorities in question. For instance, the fixing of prices using the formula 'costs plus x% profit' requires much more information from market participants than the formula 'RPI–X'.[18]

Two conclusions of relevance can be drawn. First, the decision-making discretion which was identified in previous sections as being essential to the effectiveness of policy implementation must be accompanied by an explicit obligation on the part of the implementing/enforcing authority to elaborate the rules as necessary. In effect, it has a responsibility to 'educate' and guide market participants.

Secondly, unless it is absolutely clear from the beginning what the policy targets should be, it is a mistake to expect that there is an optimum or sufficient level of detail (or generality) that can be fixed at the outset. Implementing measures need to be adjusted to reflect changes in market conditions or changes in the behaviour of market participants. This is one more reason why the efforts of the candidate countries should not just be confined to the establishment of the implementing system but also to considering how it can change in the future, how that change may be facilitated, and how the authority responsible for managing that change should be accountable for both its actions and inactions.

11. SHOULD THE CANDIDATE COUNTRIES ADOPT THE PROPOSED INSTITUTIONAL APPROACH TO BUILDING CAPACITY FOR EFFECTIVE POLICY IMPLEMENTATION?

The candidate countries should adopt the approach proposed in this Chapter because it will enhance their credibility in the eyes of the EU. Naturally, no one, myself included, can be certain how the EU will eventually assess the capacity of the candidates to apply and enforce the *acquis communautaire*. Therefore, in this penultimate section I explain why an approach to capacity-

---

[18] 'RPI–X' means that the price that may be charged by a regulated company may increase by the rate of inflation as given by the Retail Price Index minus a certain amount 'X' which reflects technological advances that lower costs.

building which emphasizes the right design of the institutions responsible for implementation is more likely to be accepted by the EU.

There are many explanations of the origins and aims of the EU. Irrespective of which explanation one espouses, integration in all its forms means at minimum a kind of reciprocal policy 'disarmament'. Partner countries agree not to formulate and pursue policies unilaterally. Towards that end, they establish common rules, common procedures, and common institutions. But the edifice we call '*acquis communautaire*' does not define in detail all possible policy contingencies and all possible implementing measures. In fact the EU deliberately leaves certain aspects of implementation undefined by allowing its Member States to determine for themselves the precise means through which directives are put into force and the means by which they comply with regulations and decisions. Any system of integration, and in particular the EU system, necessarily relies on trust; that the commitments undertaken by its members will in fact be fulfilled.

Trust reveals expectations about future behaviour. When we say we trust someone, we really mean one of two things: either that a person has no other option but to act in a particular way (i.e. the structure of incentives or costs is such as to make any other option sub-optimal, as when we say, for example, 'I trust he will keep his side of the deal') or that a person has a reputation for acting in a consistent manner and we expect no deviation from the established pattern of behaviour. A reputation for consistent behaviour needs a track record.

The candidate countries have no track record in implementing EU rules. Hence, the only means they have at their disposal to induce the EU to trust them is to make it impossible for themselves to behave in any other way. By establishing properly empowered and accountable institutions they do precisely that. By granting them sufficient decision-making autonomy together with explicit responsibility to apply EU rules, it is as if they tie their own hands behind their backs. Irrespective of what the government of the day wants or the powerful lobbies demand, these institutions will pursue the goals assigned to them and apply the *acquis* not only because that is their remit but more importantly because they will be sanctioned (possibly by private legal action or parliamentary scrutiny) if they do not carry out their tasks properly. In Annex V, a more elaborate explanation of the relationship between integration, credible commitments, and decision-making discretion is set out.

Of course, it is always possible for any sovereign country to change and even abolish whatever domestic institutions it establishes. Of course, a determined government that commands a sufficient majority will succeed in the end in changing any domestic law and institution. However, this is not the real issue because the purpose is not to prevent wholesale reform. The purpose is to prevent low-level and habitual interference in the tasks of institutions entrusted with the application of the *acquis*. If these institutions are explicitly and from the outset fully empowered and accountable it will be politically costly for politicians to influence their everyday decisions. This is also the reason I do not believe that the current emphasis on levels and quality of staffing and the amount of committed resources are any real guarantees that institutions established in the candidate countries will in the end be able to apply EU rules effectively and enforce them rigorously. The next government may simply reassign staff or reallocate resources.

Before concluding this section, there is one more point of advice to the candidate countries worth mentioning here. Officials from the candidates often complain that the EU does not seem to trust them, because it keeps asking for more detailed information on their implementation mechanisms and results. No matter how one may sympathize with their predicament, it is hard to blame the EU when the candidates themselves lack a credible track record. Perhaps the candidates would appear more credible in the eyes of the EU if they were explicitly to assume that they would make mistakes in the application of the *acquis* and as a result were to incorporate in their implementing mechanisms periodic evaluation and revision procedures, if possible involving EU officials as well. It is commitments of this kind that reinforce credibility both domestically and internationally.

Lastly, Annex II at the end of this Chapter summarizes the main features of implementing capacity in different contexts, while Annex III proposes 30 questions as a checklist for detecting the existence (or not) of capacity for effective policy implementation. Annex IV provides information on a recent evaluation of the Dutch regulatory authority for telecommunications, OPTA, that was carried out on behalf of the Ministry of Transport which has the overall political responsibility for the formulation of broad policy objectives in the field of telecommunications.

Two aspects of that evaluation are relevant to this Chapter. First, the evaluation itself was mandated by the law that established OPTA. Although unusual, it is not unheard of to include provisions in the relevant law stipulating evaluation of the performance of the enforcing authorities at some point in the future. Secondly, the criteria used for the evaluation are different and in some respects much wider than the provisions of the relevant *acquis*. Once more we see that effective implementation of the *acquis* does not simply mean compliance with legal requirements.

12. CONCLUSION

This Chapter has been developed along a series of questions exploring the issue of effective policy implementation and leading to a proposal on how candidate countries may establish capacity for effective implementation of the *acquis communautaire*.

The Chapter advocates an institutional approach to building that kind of capacity. The current preoccupation with the number and quality of staff and the resources they have at their disposal is unlikely to be a successful approach in the longer term. Although I am not rejecting the view that staff and resources are important, one of the main objectives of this Chapter is to explain why the problem of effective implementation goes beyond any count of bodies and euros.

The Chapter proposes instead an institutional approach because at the core of integration, in any form, lies the need to establish credible commitments. I argue that it will be easier for the candidate countries to demonstrate to the EU a credible commitment to apply the *acquis communautaire* if they delegate that task to sufficiently empowered and accountable institutions which both have considerable decision-making independence and are subject to specific performance obligations.

ANNEX I: PRINCIPAL ADMINISTRATIVE REQUIREMENTS FOR IMPLEMENTATION OF THE *ACQUIS* (CLASSIFIED BY NEGOTIATING CHAPTER)

Negotiating Chapter	*Administrative Requirements*
1. Free movement of goods	Establishment of standards institute
	Competent authorities for accreditation of (notified) bodies for testing & certification
	Competent authorities for market surveillance
	Responsible body for managing public procurement policy
	Monitoring and review bodies for procurement practices
2. Free movement of persons	Mutual recognition of professional qualifications
3. Freedom to provide services	Existence of supervisory bodies for banking, insurance, and securities
4. Free movement of capital	Establishment of financial intelligence unit (money laundering)
5. Company law	Company register and control of incorporation
6. Competition policy	Competition authority
	State aid monitoring authority
7. Agriculture	Common market organizations
	Intervention systems and supply management

(*continues*)

Annex I: (*continued*)

Negotiating Chapter	Administrative Requirements
	Accredited paying agencies and separate auditing
	Competent authorities for veterinary & plant inspections
	Laboratory testing infrastructure
	Administration of structural actions (rural development)
8. Fisheries	Administration of common marketing standards, quantity control, and information collection
	Administration of structural actions
9. Transport policy	Line ministry issues safety certificates
	Independent slot coordinator (air transport)
	Flag-state and port-state control
	Supervision of classification societies
10. Taxation	Few administrative requirements most of which concern VAT and excise system, information exchange, and cooperation procedures
11. Economic & monetary union	Independent central bank
12. Statistics	National statistical office collect and process data
13. Social policy & employment	Line ministries apply labour law and employment policy
	Health and safety inspectorates
14. Energy	General requirement for regulation and control system in electricity and gas
	Nuclear safety authority
15. Industrial policy	Few administrative requirements
16. SMEs	Few administrative requirements
17. Science & research	Few administrative requirements (national contact point)
18. Education & training	Few administrative requirements, mostly about national agency for programme implementation and contact point
19. Telecommunications & postal services	National regulatory authorities
20. Culture & audiovisual policy	National procedures for licensing, monitoring, and sanctioning broadcasters
21. Regional policy	Inter-ministerial coordinating body and partnership between regional authorities and other participating parties
	Programme managing authorities
	Programme evaluation and monitoring (committees)
	Payment authorities

(*continues*)

Annex I: (*continued*)

Negotiating Chapter	Administrative Requirements
	Financial control and independent auditing
22. Environment	Competent authorities for implementation, assessment, and licensing
	Environmental inspectorates
	Notified bodies for certification separate from inspectorates
23. Consumer & health protection	Designated authority with overall responsibility
	Market surveillance authorities
24. Justice & home affairs	Independent judiciary
	Border control and Schengen information system
	Administration of visas, migration, and asylum
	Reliable police and anti-fraud services
25. Customs union	Customs authorities for checking and collecting revenue
26. External relations	Line ministries
27. CFSP	Ministry of foreign affairs
28. Financial control	Financial management systems
	Internal and external financial audits
29. Financial & budgetary provisions	Financial management systems
30. Institutions	None specified (but it would be necessary to have effective internal coordination of national positions)

ANNEX II: FEATURES OF IMPLEMENTING CAPACITY IN VARIOUS CONTEXTS

Purpose of building implementing capacity ⇒	*Effective policy implementation*	*Efficient policy implementation*	*Policy implementation in regional blocs*	*Policy implementation in the EU*
	Sufficient legal powers and/or decision-making independence	*Previous column plus*	*Previous column plus*	*Previous column plus*
	Sufficient resources	Coordination & consultation	Cross-border coordination & consultation	Periodic reviews involving EU officials

(*continues*)

Annex II: (*continued*)

Main features of implementing capacity ⇒	Market monitoring mechanisms	Cost minimization	Simplified procedures (understood by partners)	
	Rule adjustment mechanisms	Simplified compliance requirements		
	Transparent implementation procedures			
	Accountability & performance standards			
	Appeal procedures			

ANNEX III: A CHECKLIST OF THIRTY QUESTIONS REGARDING CAPACITY FOR EFFECTIVE POLICY IMPLEMENTATION

In square brackets are suggested indicators of compliance with the checklist; most questions are phrased in such a way so that they can be answered with 'yes or no'.

Knowledge

1. Do staff have good knowledge of the relevant *acquis?* [as evidenced by degrees, seminars, internships, secondments, work experience]
2. Are there provisions or requirements for participation in EU conferences or meetings involving peers and where experiences are shared? [yes/no]
3. Do staff have good knowledge of the corresponding situation in their own country? [studies, seminars, secondments, work experience]
4. Are there formal mechanisms for obtaining information from the market? Are they used? [yes/no; studies, data banks, registers]
5. Are there requirements for periodic consultation of market participants and assessment of the situation in the market (economic, technological, etc.)? [yes/no]

Ability

1. Does national legislation contain all aspects of the relevant *acquis?* [yes/no]
2. Is the agency in question legally empowered to apply all aspects of relevant national law? [yes/no]
3. Does it have decision-making autonomy with respect to its tasks? [yes/no]
4. Does its responsibility overlap with that of other agencies? [yes/no]
5. If yes, are there formal coordination mechanisms? [yes/no]
6. Is there a formal mechanism for resolving potential disputes? [yes/no]
7. Can the agency amend the implementing instruments and/or procedures it uses? [yes/no]
8. Can it propose to higher authority amendments to implementing instruments and/or procedures? [yes/no]
9. Can it propose to higher authority amendments of broader policy objectives? [yes/no]
10. How complex and time consuming is the procedure for amending implementing instruments and/or procedures? [description]
11. Are there adequate staff for carrying out the tasks of the agency? [yes/no] How is adequacy determined in this context? [description]
12. Do they have at their disposal adequate resources? [yes/no] How is adequacy determined in this context? [description]
13. Does the budget of the agency need higher approval? Or can it be submitted directly to the national budgetary authority? [yes/no]

Willingness (incentives)

1. Are there any formal performance standards for the agency? [yes/no]
2. If not, is there provision for periodic external assessment of the performance of the agency? [yes/no]
3. Is there a periodic internal procedure for review of staff functions and actual work? [yes/no]
4. Are there potential situations of conflict of interest that could be remedied through separation of tasks? If yes, has such separation been carried out? [yes/no][19]
5. Is the agency under an obligation to monitor developments in other EU Member States, identify, and adopt best practice? [yes/no]

---

[19] Examples of potential conflicts of interest that may require segregation of tasks: accreditation or registration *v* performance evaluation or *ex post* control or accident investigation; project selection or programme approval *v* results assessment; making of payments *v* auditing; investigating a case or complaint *v* deciding a case or complaint; personal or financial relations with chosen contractors or projects.

6. Is it under an obligation to guide and inform market participants about policy objectives, policy changes, and means of achieving compliance? [yes/no]
7. Are its decision-making procedures open to the public? [yes/no]
8. Is it under an obligation to publish and explain its decisions? [yes/no]
9. Does it have an internet site that makes accessible all relevant information and decisions? [yes/no]
10. Does it have to prepare and publish an annual report? [yes/no]
11. Does it have to present its annual report to parliament? [yes/no]
12. What kind of sanctions may be brought to bear on the management and/or staff of the agency and for what reasons? [description]

ANNEX IV: SUMMARY OF CRITERIA AND THE FINDINGS OF AN EVALUATION OF THE PERFORMANCE OF THE DUTCH AUTHORITY FOR THE REGULATION OF TELECOMMUNICATIONS (OPTA)

Main Questions

How did OPTA fulfil the legal tasks assigned to it?
To what extent was the performance of OPTA effective and efficient, given the instruments at its disposal?
What effects did the performance of OPTA have on the telecommunications and postal markets?

Overall Findings

OPTA fulfilled the legal tasks assigned to it *well* (good) (on a five-point scale: bad–moderate–sufficient–good–very good).

Regulation of the Telecommunication Market: *Good*

The assessment is based on action in five categories:

1. The assignment of operators with Significant Market Power (KPN and Libertel).
2. The operationalization of regulatory standards.
3. Arbitration/conflict resolution.
4. Maintaining the fulfilment of obligations.
5. The distribution of phone numbers.

Encouragement of competition and market processes: *good*

1. Views of the consumers of telecommunication services.

2. Views of the sellers of telecommunication services and networks.
3. Respect for the freedom and conduct of business of KPN.
4. Speed and timing of the appearance of OPTA.

Regulation of the postal market: *sufficient*

1. The calculation system of costs and benefits.
2. The investigation of cross-subsidies.

Functioning of its internal organization: *sufficient*

1. The costs of operations of OPTA.
2. The efficacy of OPTA.
3. Quality of the services provided.
4. Quality of the conduct of business.

Relationship with responsible ministry: *moderate*

Relationships with other institutions and organizations: *good*

According to the report, more attention should be paid to the context in which OPTA operates. Present research is too much influenced by specific Dutch considerations.

> Note: Own summary.
> Source: OPTA, report published on 30 March 2001.

ANNEX V: INTEGRATION AS A PROCESS OF INTERNAL COMMITMENTS

The analysis in this Chapter is based on the assumption that effective policy implementation is in the interests of the EU as a whole. In this Annex I will show formally that rules that improve the effectiveness of policy measures also raise the welfare of each partner country.

Integration, at least of the economic kind, is often perceived to be a process of 'external' commitments where independent countries undertake certain obligations towards each other. I want to explain that there is a corresponding process of 'internal' commitments, which is rather illuminating about the direction and success of integration. The reason it is illuminating is that it focuses on domestic factors that facilitate or obstruct integration.

Integration is a process which is supported by those that gain from it and resisted by those that lose out from it. The outcome of that process is determined by these opposing interests. To understand the consequences of

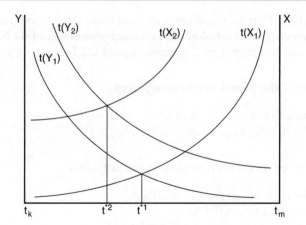

Figure 3.1. *National Policy Formulation Before and After Integration*

the interplay between these interests, we need to understand why at a certain point in time countries abandon unilateral policies and espouse common policies and reciprocal liberalization (integration through unilateral liberalization is very rare). The conception of integration as a set of external commitments does not explain why countries are ready to abandon their pre-integration state. Even the argument that they gain by integrating is not sufficient if it does not consider the benefits from the continuation of the pre-integration status quo and the distribution of those benefits (and costs) within each of the integrating countries.

We must begin, therefore, by identifying what determines the pre-integration state of equilibrium with restricted trade. Please bear in mind that the purpose of this Annex is not to propose a new theory of integration but to elaborate a little more formally the argument in the main text of the Chapter that internal commitments matter to both the initial formation of a customs union, common market, etc., and the continued success of any integrationist project after it is established.

Figure 3.1 shows the pre- and post-integration situation in a given country. There are two groups in this country whose actions determine national trade policy: an export-competing group, X, and an import-competing group, Y. For the sake of simplicity assume that policy is determined solely by the relative expenditure of these two groups in gaining political influence.[20] The functions $t(X)$ and $t(Y)$ show the amounts of money X and Y that

[20] There is a voluminous and rich literature on the political economy of trade protectionism and regional integration. This literature has produced many models of varying levels of complexity and sophistication. The basic assumption of this Annex, that policy makers respond to lobbying by special interest groups and that policies are shaped by these groups, may sound far-fetched but in fact it has been analysed in great depth and extensively tested in

the two groups are willing to expend to avoid the corresponding values of the trade regulation denoted as 't' (t can also indicate any other regulation that directly or indirectly impedes cross-border trade). The relevant axis for group Y is the left one, while that for group X is the right one.

This may look at first glance like a strange formulation, but on further reflection it becomes more obvious that since policy determination does not start from zero, given the fact that always several proposals are made before one is adopted, the two groups identify and rank proposals in terms of their impact on their interests (expected profits or losses) and spend corresponding amounts of money to prevent the outcomes they do not like (through research, lobbying, advertisements, etc.).

In Figure 3.1, the worst outcome for group X is t_m while the worst outcome for group Y is t_k. The outcome that emerges as the policy compromise (or equilibrium) is that at which no group has any incentive to spend any more money to achieve an alternative outcome. In the figure, it is shown as point t^{*1} where $t(X) = t(Y)$. (You may also regard the two functions as indicating the marginal spending of each group in order to obtain a shift to a preferable value of the trade regulation 't'.) In this simplified exposition, the equilibrium regulation is rather mechanistically determined. A more sophisticated analysis would include strategic behaviour such as use of misinformation, threats, etc.

This explains the existence and level of trade impediments before integration begins. The next question is to ask why and how would this country reduce or eliminate its trade restrictions with respect to products from another country. The reason is that the corresponding reduction in the partner country's restrictions raises the profit opportunities of the export-competing group, X. In other words, X becomes 'an advocate of integration' and is willing to spend more money to induce a shift away from the status quo of unilateral trade protection and towards reciprocal trade liberalization. This is shown by the leftward shift of $t(X_1)$ to $t(X_2)$. The function $t(Y)$ also shifts because relaxation of regulation t results in market liberalization which increases imports into the domestic market.

Whether markets in the end become more integrated through increased trade depends on the new equilibrium value of t. If it shifts to the left then there will be more trade and greater integration. If not, there will not be any extra trade and the exporting group Y would not find it worthwhile to lobby in favour of integration. But assume that t does indeed shift to the left and a new post-integration equilibrium emerges indicated by t^{*2}.

Here we have to abstract from another complication. The post-integration equilibrium is partly determined by the internal bargaining in the partner

the literature. See, e.g., R. Feenstra, G. Grossman, and D. Irwin (eds), *The Political Economy of Trade Policy* (1996); J. Bhagwati and A. Panagariya (eds), *Trading Blocs: Alternative Approaches to Analysing Preferential Trade Agreements* (1999).

country and by the bargaining between the two countries. How much the X curve shifts upwards depends on the gains that group X expects to make in the partner country, which in turn depends on the outcome of the internal lobbying contest between the corresponding groups in that country.

This admittedly very simplistic construction highlights, however, three interesting features of integration. First, the process of integration begins to roll when policy outcomes are packaged in the right way so as to give the right incentives. The policy outcomes which are packaged in this case are the linkage of the value of t in one country with the gains that exporters of that country hope to make in another, and vice versa.

Secondly, the ideal partner country is, among other things, also the one that offers the most attractive market to the potential supporters of trade liberalization. Perhaps arguments such as 'we will not surrender our national sovereignty' actually mean that 'it is not worth while for domestic lobbies to push for further integration'.

Thirdly, external commitments between partner countries are adhered to when internal commitments are adhered to. Or, to put it differently, integration works when there are domestic groups to counterbalance the actions of opponents and when the domestic political bargains can also be adhered to. This statement is neither unusual nor new. It has long been observed that among other things sovereign countries also wilfully 'tie their policy hands' by acceding to GATT and other international agreements. They do that in order to enhance the credibility of their commitment to liberal trade policies in the eyes of various domestic political groups.

We can now explore in more detail the significance of domestic commitments for the success of external commitments. Figure 3.2 shows the post-integration equilibrium. Let us say that the partner countries engage in discussions on some kind of regulation. Call that, again, 't'. As in actual life

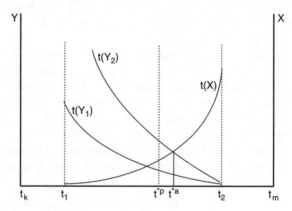

Figure 3.2. *Policy Implementation After Integration*

in the EU, partner countries agree principles which they incorporate in directives that have to be transposed and further elaborated by national authorities. Assume that the agreed principle t^{*p} may take values ranging from t^1 to t^2. The partner countries as a whole would prefer outcomes as close as possible to the agreed value or, if there is a deviation from that value, their next best option would be to have laxer forms of regulation tending towards t^1 rather than t^2 (because their exporters will have easier access to multiple partner-country markets which presumably far outweighs any losses suffered by their import-competing industries).

The actual result, however, that is shaped by domestic lobbies following the same process as that explained above is given by t^{*a}. That is a third-best outcome for the partner countries as a whole. We get this result because there is an asymmetric shift in $t(X)$ and $t(Y)$. This is for two reasons. First, the values of the implemented regulations are determined domestically by the lobbying action of national groups. If groups could be involved in the domestic policy processes of other partner countries, the results would be different. In real life, of course, this kind of involvement does occur. But it is not unreasonable to suppose that domestic groups are more effective in influencing the policy outcomes in their own market.

Secondly, while the curves $t(X)$ and $t(Y)$ are determined by the gains and losses in the domestic market, any shifts are caused by extra gains from greater exports (for X) or extra losses from greater imports (for Y). But since relaxation of t in the domestic market would not help exports of X but would harm instead the interests of Y, only $t(Y)$ shifts from $t(Y_1)$ to $t(Y_2)$. The lower the value of t, the greater the volume of imports and the bigger the shift of $t(Y)$. In fact, the curves in Figure 3.2 are drawn in such a way that the domestic equilibrium value of t without the possibility of imports is even to the left of the commonly agreed value of t^{*p}. The prospect of imports that harm the interests of group Y galvanizes them into action to lobby for regulation t to be framed as much as possible in their favour.

The heart of the problem related to the implementation of common policies is not just lax enforcement or interpretation of principles in a way that, although it is within the letter of the policy in question, deviates from the intention or the spirit of that policy. It is also due to the fact that domestic policy-making in essence 'decomposes' the processes that provided the 'package' that made integration possible in the first place.

Any solution to this problem must be twofold. It must restrict the discretion of the implementing authorities for creative interpretation of the common rules and build bridges for other groups and authorities in the partner countries to have their interests taken into account by domestic policy processes. Perhaps it is necessary to elaborate here the first part of the statement in the previous sentence because it may be construed as being contradictory to other statements in the main body of the text. Here it is advocated that discretion should be restricted, while in the rest of the Chapter it is argued that implementing authorities need to have decision-making discretion. Both statements are correct. Authorities need to have as much discretion as necessary to reach their targets. At the same time they need to be accountable so that they will not deviate from the spirit of the rules without good reason.

We can also see now that remedies such as independent arbitration, institutional dispute-settlement procedures, and courts are actually second-best solutions to the problems caused by mis-implementation of common rules in other countries. They may offset the effects of non-compliance without however addressing directly the root of the problem, which is too wide an interpretation of the agreed principles combined with vulnerability to domestic political pressure and lobbying activities.

The EU has tried several solutions to this problem ranging from more detailed legislation (restricting implementing discretion) to comparisons of national performance, to the establishment of independent national authorities with narrow mandates and specific obligations to pursue certain policy objectives. In this way the political expenditures of lobbies could become ineffectual because they may not be able to obtain outcomes that stretch the scope of discretion of the implementing authorities.

In conclusion, the credibility of national commitments is enhanced not by preventing domestic lobbies from attempting to influence policy (that would be unacceptable in democracies) but by narrowing the extent of creative interpretation of the rules by domestic policy-implementing authorities (e.g. through more detailed rules and narrower mandates), by providing incentives to them to resist political pressure (e.g. through explicit performance requirements and standards that make them more accountable) and by giving a 'voice' to the interests of the partner countries.

The problem is complex and therefore in real life no single remedy is likely to suffice. It would require a mixture of different remedies. Also one has to maintain some scepticism about the efficacy of recent trends towards benchmarking and cross-country comparisons as a means of inducing the Member States of the EU to improve their implementation record. Such measures are not useless, but the question is whether they can address the real issue, which is the structure of domestic policy implementation.

4

The 'Eastern Enlargements' of the European Union

ANDRÁS INOTAI

More than a decade after the fall of the Berlin wall, unfortunately rather too late, Europe has to be revisited and reinterpreted. There are a number of reasons why this task is urgent. The times are gone when (Western) Europe could consider itself as a closed entity and focus on its own narrow-minded stability, economic welfare, and social market economy. Both internal developments and external challenges require a reconsideration and redefinition of Europe's basic goals and its position and prospects in world politics and in the global market place. Globalization, repeatedly postponed EU reforms (e.g. on agriculture, institutional questions, budgetary issues), the substantial need for restructuring within member countries, and the coming waves of 'Eastern' enlargement—all of these factors point to the urgent need for a new approach.

Evidently, these challenges have a number of components and none of them can be ignored. However, enlargement to the 'East' touches upon all of them. First, the European Union can hardly become a more relevant player in global politics and the global economy without having the additional resources of the candidate countries and, today perhaps more importantly still, without stability in East Central and South Eastern Europe (EC+SEE). In this context, short-term or prospective membership of the EU provides undeniable stability and a modernization anchor. Secondly, all major EU reforms have to face the pressure of enlargement, which will substantially shape the character and instruments of indispensable reforms. It is increasingly understood in policy-making circles that the candidate countries have to play a more active role in creating the future of the continent, both in those areas which belong to the traditional *acquis* (e.g. agriculture) and in those which have become part of Community policies more recently (e.g. justice and internal affairs, common foreign and security policy). Thirdly, autonomous developments in the candidate countries will have an impact on the future of the continent. Their impact, both direct and indirect, will to a large extent depend on the timing and pattern of integration into present and unfolding EU structures.

This Chapter is divided into two main parts. First, some common characteristics of the candidate countries will be summarized in order better to understand the driving force, expectations, and dilemmas connected with their accession to the EU. Secondly, selected strategic issues in preparing for the implementation of Europe's 'project of the century' will be addressed from the viewpoint of both the EU and, more particularly, the candidate countries.

1. SOME COMMON FEATURES OF THE CANDIDATE COUNTRIES

Although developments in EC+SEE are just some of the factors influencing the future of the continent, their relevance has been increasing and will continue to do so. Accordingly, it may be helpful to point out some of the basic characteristics of the region which are rooted in its history, geographic location, economic potential, and social texture. This approach is needed despite, or rather because of, the recognition that the region is extremely heterogeneous in its history, security needs, politics, economic performance, maturity as regards EU membership, and also in cultural terms. However, all of these countries form part of a larger Europe, and not only in the context of security.

A. A Buffer Zone Over Centuries

During the last 1,000 years, EC+SEE has always been a buffer zone, between West and East, and sometimes between North and South. Colonization accompanied by modernization stemming from the West (initiated by the 'Drang nach Osten') and domination without modernization from the East either followed each other or overlapped. The first case is illustrated by German *v* Russian/Soviet endeavours, while the second can best be indicated by the tri-partition of Poland. The struggle between Western and Eastern Europe, with rather different values and instruments but obviously pursuing the same basic interests in expanding their respective security zones towards the East or the West, has sometimes been interrupted by other influences. While the Nordic factor played only a limited role in shaping the basic characteristics of this part of Europe (the Swedish invasion during the Thirty Years' War and partly in the early eighteenth century), the consequences of the Southern factor, namely the Ottoman Empire, have been much more lasting. Today, the recent expansion of NATO towards East Central Europe, and membership of the Czech Republic, Hungary, and Poland, have shifted this security buffer zone, at least in military terms, towards the East. However, the existence of the historically established buffer zone, still *within* the continent, has not been abolished. Urgent steps are needed to (re)define the future borders of Europe in terms of security. This approach has to take into account the interests of the new neighbours on the other side of the 'buffer zone', but not at the expense of those who are expected to become part of the new security umbrella.

B. Economic Periphery and Peripheralization

In economic terms, EC+SEE has historically belonged to the semi-periphery of European development.[1] Of course, there has always been a big difference between the semi-peripheral situation of Bohemia or Austria, under German/ Habsburg rule and geographically part of Central Europe, and that of South Eastern Europe under Ottoman domination and geographically distant from Western European centres of modernization. The historically generated development gaps, manifested not only in differences in income, but, and more significantly, in differences in mentality and behaviour, can be identi- fied not only across countries but also within a single country. The best example would be the very diversified development level and cultural land- scape in the Habsburg Empire. The fact that most countries of the region acquired new frontiers after 1918 and, not less importantly, that new coun- tries have been emerging since 1989 did not eliminate this diversity, but put it into a different geographic framework. As a result, development gaps between their western and eastern parts can be observed in almost all countries, (e.g. in Austria between Tyrol/Salzburg and Burgenland, between Western, Central, and Eastern Poland, in Slovakia between the Bratislava region and the eastern part of the country, between Western and Eastern Hungary, between Ljubljana and Eastern Slovenia, and between Western and Eastern Romania). Nevertheless, the economic modernization of East Cen- tral and South Eastern Europe cannot be considered in narrow sub-regional terms. European stability and economic development both require a com- prehensive approach for the whole region, even if, as a result of catching up, currently existing differences will not be narrowed spectacularly (or even at all) in the short term.[2]

---

[1] In its historical development, Europe has always had various economic peripheries. Some of them (Scandinavia with the exception of Finland at the turn of the 20th century), were able to catch up by their own efforts while others, several decades later, needed the European Community as a modernization anchor (Greece, with very doubtful results; Ireland, Spain, and Portugal with better results).

[2] Catching up in Scandinavia or in the Iberian peninsula did not happen through institution- ally determined regional separation, but through a comprehensive effort to offer better prospects for the whole region. This, of course, could not avoid the temporary widening of the develop- ment gap between regions differently developed or, rather, differently prepared for absorption of modernization resources (see the contrast between Catalunya and Andalucia).

In the first years of transformation, one of the biggest mistakes of the international economic and financial community was that it failed to differentiate between the characteristics of the semi-peripheral situation of EC+SEE and the 'classic' periphery in global terms. Since textbook economics and widespread economic experience after World War II provided both theories on economic peripheries and lessons on how to overcome economic underdevelopment in the traditionally underdeveloped countries of Latin America and parts of South-East Asia, they did not deal with the specific factors of the semi-peripheral development of European countries in general, nor with their very specific (mis-)development under Soviet domination in particular.[3]

Thus, at the moment of the dramatic changes in EC+SEE after 1989, international organizations and experts attempted to implement the same policies which had been applied successfully (or unsuccessfully) by Eastern and South-Eastern Asian countries or by some Latin American countries. They did not comprehend that the respective European region was not underdeveloped in the same way as other parts of the world were underdeveloped. It was mis-developed, mis-structured, and mis-functioning. The countries of East Central and South Eastern Europe have had a very high concentration of industrial production. The problem was not how to convert a mainly backward agricultural economy into a more industry-oriented economy (as was the case with Thailand, Indonesia, Peru, or Morocco). The problem was the opposite: all of these countries concentrated too heavily on industry. Generally, it is easier to change an agrarian economy into an industrial one (where an industrial economy did not previously exist) than to destroy already (mis-)developed structures. In the latter case, one has to create a new structure, not from scratch, but by carefully considering what can be kept of the old structure and how the significant opposition of vested interests can be broken.

The second difference, long overlooked, was that, unlike classic underdeveloped countries, EC+SEE countries have developed a welfare system based on the mixed effort to overcome underdevelopment, to implement socialist ideology, and to improve on capitalism. The system was based on highly subsidized basic needs, covering food, services, education, health care,

---

[3] Soviet-dominated East Central and South Eastern Europe was not a topic for research in the United States and in Western Europe, in economic terms. While much energy was devoted to analysing the military, ideological, and political capacities and influence of the so-called Soviet bloc, its economic, social, and cultural features were widely ignored. As a result, at the outset of transformation, almost nobody in the 'Western world' was prepared to understand the non-security and non-ideological factors of the change. Two, partly fatal, consequences derived from this ignorance. First, the transformation was considered as an ideological and political exercise, deprived of its fundamentals. Secondly, the basic elements of the *sustainability* of transformation were largely absent in 'high-level' surveys.

and housing. These policies were carried out in countries which had a relatively low level of economic development. To compare their situation to that of other parts of the world, the figures around 1990 show the following. The highly industrialized countries had a *per capita* income of 25,000 dollars per year. Of these 25,000 dollars they spent 20 per cent on social welfare. The East Central and South Eastern European countries had a *per capita* income of about 5,000 dollars, and spent more than 25 per cent of it on social welfare. With the same level of economic development, although with a dramatically different distribution of income, Latin America was able to give 12 per cent of the same 5,000 dollar *per capita* figure to social expenditure. Long before the systemic change, it became clear that the social welfare system could not be sustained in the medium term, even by prolonging the old system. On the other hand—and this is the basic challenge for the future—it is easier to introduce some sort of social welfare system in societies that did not have one previously (Latin America and South-East Asia) than to 'streamline' one in those societies which not only have been accustomed to a social welfare system (a special form of 'social subsidy mentality') but desperately need one as part of indirect (non-cash) income. The difficulty of the situation is aggravated if the reforming of the social welfare umbrella has to be brought about during a meaningful fall in real wages.

The third and partly promising difference has been the high level of education in all East Central and South Eastern European countries.[4] This is the major asset or, more precisely, ten years ago it was the major asset of the region. In the era of the information society this is an important element in making use of the 'latecomer's advantage'. One of the fundamental dilemmas of the future development of the whole of Europe is whether this potential can be used adequately (before it is destroyed in EC+SEE).

The final point is that in several parts of the world high-income countries and low-income countries are geographically separated. Western Europe is separated from Africa. The USA is separated from Latin America. Japan is separated by sea from China and the other Asian countries. So if there is geographical (physical) separation, differences in income may persist without creating political tension. However, if two countries have a common border and the two countries are at a very different level of overall economic development in general, and, moreover, on a diverging level as expressed in income per head in particular, the conflict is pre-programmed. In this case something has to be done. In the case of the USA and Mexico, there is the Rio Grande and there is a physical barrier on the Mexican–US border to prevent

---

[4] Education includes much more than institutionalized teaching and learning. It comprises flexibility, innovative/creative/problem-solving capacity, cooperative behaviour, tolerance, social cohesion, etc. All of these factors have already been appreciated in worldwide competition.

Mexicans from entering the USA illegally. But what about Europe? To the satisfaction of all Europeans, the Iron Curtain was lifted and the physical barriers between the two parts of Europe with highly differing income levels eliminated. This was an absolutely necessary step in order to reunite Europe. The next step is clearly not to return to separation between high-and low-income neighbouring countries but, on the contrary, to create conditions for relatively quick and sustainable catching-up. This has in the last decade been one of the basic challenges to a European strategy, and will remain so for many years.

C. Cultural and Ethnic Diversity

The regions of East Central and, in particular, South Eastern Europe are multicultural regions, with all of the corresponding problems and potential advantages. The region is divided by different religions, including Roman Catholic, Protestant, Orthodox, Jewish, Muslim, to mention only the most prominent ones. Even more importantly, ethnic diversity is a characteristic of some parts of the region, mainly in South Eastern Europe. It can be said that ethnic diversity has always been a feature of the region, both within the Austro-Hungarian monarchy but also previously in Poland, and in the Balkans. After the collapse of the Austro-Hungarian monarchy the situation did not change, except that countries which had been multi-ethnic became more homogenous and others which had been more homogenous became multi-ethnic. Hungary was a multi-ethnic country in the Austro-Hungarian monarchy and became a homogeneous country after 1918, while large minorities remained within the new boundaries of its neighbouring countries. Religion, ethnicity, and social values are increasingly intertwined. This part of Europe can only overcome its historical burdens if the advantages of multicultural cooperation prevail against justified or perceived complaints of the past. At the same time, the rest of Europe, by no means free from similar problems (Northern Ireland, the Basque Country, Corsica, etc.), also has to understand the character of East Central and South Eastern Europe in order to create a new and more unified (harmonious) Europe. One can only hope that everything that has happened, and is unfortunately still happening, in former Yugoslavia will be not only a necessary but also a sufficient lesson— for all of us.

D. Top-down versus Bottom-up Development Patterns

In order to understand the behaviour of East Central and South Eastern Europe, with regard in particular to the integration process, one must realize that, for historical reasons, most countries of the region are the historical product of top-down development. They had a centralized state, a state that

was in charge of organizing the economic and social life and the administrative structure of a given country. In contrast, in most Western European
countries the main approach to development was from the bottom up, driven
by self-organizing units at local and regional levels, which always tried to
limit the role of the state. Why was the state practically organizing the
economic and social life in Central and Eastern Europe? This fact has
historical roots: since the region was a buffer zone, it always needed a strong
state to protect national identity and physical integrity. It needed a strong
state to withstand different pressures from different directions. Moreover, for
most countries of the region, the collapse of the Roman Empire and several
centuries of disorder in Western Europe meant the growing influence of a
strong Byzantium. Byzantine rule was based on a very high concentration of
state influence. It deprived small communities of the possibility of endogen-
ous development. Everything depended on the central power, on top-down
measures. Nobody was interested in starting a grass-roots effort—everyone
expected the central power to do a lot for them, and, at the same time, the
central power throttled any effort that could threaten it. The results were
both positive and negative: individual survival techniques, high levels of
flexibility, and innovative behaviour on the one hand, and a subsidy mentality, corruption, tax evasion, and overriding of centrally-set rules on the other.
This behaviour did not start after World War II, although some of its
elements were strengthened during Soviet domination and, unfortunately,
and even more so, in the first years of transformation. I do not know whether
this is a return to the past in order to go back to historical roots, or a return to
the past in order to overcome them.

E. Failure at the Threshold?

Throughout their history, the countries of Central and Eastern Europe
considered it a major political priority to catch up with Western Europe,
not only in levels of income but, in various periods, and more particularly, in
culture, social values, and institutions. And some of these countries, in several
periods of their history, seemed to be ready and able to catch up. According
to several economic and social indicators, some of them had reached the
threshold of integration into the mainstream of Western European development when suddenly, overnight, all their hopes were broken. This happened
sometimes because of wars, sometimes because of mistaken policies, and
sometimes because of foreign pressure or intervention, which could always
easily be blamed for the failure. However, the problem of having stopped
several times at the threshold has deeper roots as well. It has to be understood
that while the catching-up process was evident in macroeconomic terms (high
growth, more trade, even more investment), the absorption capacity for
sustainable modernization either remained insufficient or had a time delay

in comparison with evident economic performance. Statistically, a country may already have been capable of overcoming the modernization threshold but internally, in its institutional and, more importantly, psychological development, it was still lagging behind. The last decade of transformation has provided a number of extremely important lessons in this context. At the beginning of the transformation, each country shared two common objectives: political democracy and (some kind of) a market economy. Nobody has ever doubted the sincerity of these objectives. However, more than ten years after the transformation began, differences among (and not only between!) East Central and South Eastern European countries are larger than they were at the end of Soviet domination. The emergence of structural differences is rooted not only in economic policies but in many other areas. This also has to be reckoned with when all the countries are striving for (quick) membership of the European Union.

F. Modernization Anchor Outside the Region

This point is very much related to the previous issue. Over the last 500 years, as a result of the discovery of the Americas, Europe turned to the Atlantic and EC+SEE became a European 'hinterland', unable to participate in decisive global political and economic processes. Nevertheless, its only opportunity to break out of underdevelopment was provided by an Atlantic-oriented and prosperous Western Europe. East Central and South Eastern Europe was not in a position to develop a special pattern of sustainable development, while all countries of the region developed a highly successful pattern of sustainable tolerance and survival.[5] Thus, successful modernization and escape from the trap of underdevelopment and the (semi-)periphery has always required external support. International experts advising the countries of the region to reinforce regional trade and economic relations after the collapse of the CMEA have completely ignored or misunderstood this historical context. There have been very few countries in the world that have been able to develop their own modernization anchor in the last few centuries. Those who did have a mixed record: the dramatically failed socialist experience of the ex-Soviet Union as compared with the (still) working Chinese model. However, most successful modernizing countries were small and, from the very beginning of modernization, had to rely on an external anchor. Of course, such reliance does not make genuine national policies unnecessary. On the contrary, only rational and sound policies are in a position to link the country to the selected modernization anchor (in this context, the rather different

---

[5] Sometimes, the survival experience left some space and hope for future modernization. In other cases, it developed structures which have impeded any modernization. Here one can find one of the basic development dilemmas of this part of Europe.

experience with the modernization anchor of the United States for East and South-East Asia, as compared with Latin America, is obvious).

East Central and South Eastern Europe has no other choice than the European Union as its economic modernization anchor.[6] The experience with enlargement of the European Union shows that less developed countries, once they join the EU, have been able to enter an unprecedented modernization path provided two conditions are met. The first is that the new member country was well prepared for participation in integration (Ireland, Portugal, Spain *v* Greece). The second is that enough time was left to create the critical mass of the 'modernization jump' (Ireland needed 15 years to start the engine of the 'Celtic tiger'). Since geography does play a major role in successful or failed modernization, East Central and South Eastern Europe, as part of the geographic core of Europe, has a better chance, costing less time and less money, to modernize successfully than the geographically peripheral regions of the continent fortunate enough to become part of European integration at an earlier stage.

During the centuries of repeated (and mostly failed) modernization efforts, EC+SEE had three different external anchors. One was (intensive) foreign trade. This meant growth based on favourable external conditions and, in the last few centuries, driven mainly by exports of agricultural commodities. Domestic economic progress depended on the growth of these commodity markets (the Italian market, the German market, or more recently the market of the Austro-Hungarian monarchy). If these markets grew rapidly, foreign trade did so too. Overall growth was also quicker. However, we know that business cycles question the sustainability of such processes. Once foreign markets entered into recession, the crisis immediately hit the exporting countries and, lacking adequate internal factors, stopped (or even reversed) the modernization process. The second anchor was an 'imposed anchor' by a foreign country which also politically dominated an EC+SEE country. Here, however, we have to draw a clear distinction between two very different 'imposed anchors'. One imposed anchor transmitted a more developed pattern than the development level of the given country (Italy in the Middle Ages, later Germany or the Austro-Hungarian monarchy). The other pattern was forcefully imported from a less (and, more importantly, differently) developed country in comparison to the development level and pattern of the EC+SEE region. For centuries and for a large part of this region the Ottoman Empire and, in a rather contradictory form, the Soviet Union after 1945 followed this pattern. Despite their different roots and development levels, both 'imposed modernization patterns' had one common denominator. If something is imposed, the question is to what extent the society is ready to absorb these patterns, to what extent the society and the institutions

---

[6] The security anchor of the region, however, remains NATO, as for Western Europe.

are ready to cooperate and to assimilate them, and how, on the basis of imposed elements, a new, genuine, and particular pattern can be created. Finally, the third model is a modernization path based on the benign pressure of the external anchor. The growing integration into EU structures through trade, investment, adoption of the *acquis communautaire*, and participation in some Community policy areas, with the clear prospect of full membership, can be considered as the best example of this model.

The fact that the region's modernization anchor is located outside its geographic frontiers explains the limits to regional cooperation. Although more intensive cooperation is badly needed in many areas (e.g. in politics, security, and environmental protection), intra-regional economic relations (trade, capital, technology flows) cannot question the dominant position of the European Union. However, once these countries become members of the EU, the prospects for regional cooperation are expected to improve spectacularly, in trade, investment, and joint regional infra-structural and environmental projects.

G. Economic Modernization versus National Sovereignty

Throughout its history, East Central and South Eastern Europe has been characterized by a permanent struggle between economic modernization, on the one hand, and political independence, on the other. National independence was the utmost priority of the noble middle class in all countries of the region. This middle class, however, was never financially strong enough, or economically independent enough, to become the (exclusive or core) driving force of genuine economic modernization. Quite the opposite: economic modernization was anchored outside the country. This middle class always feared that if modernization could be imposed on the country, it might lose its position and feudal privileges. Accordingly, it continually opposed modernization steps in order to protect the country against any kind of foreign influence.

This notion has extremely important implications in the enlargement process. Today, we can see that there is a certain split in the society of many countries. On the one hand, they know that their economic modernization anchor is the EU. On the other hand, they would like to keep their full political sovereignty. This is mainly the case in those countries which have a very difficult historical past, where national sovereignty has been questioned several times or even abolished. In addition, some countries were not nation states at all before 1989. The question is what is the future of a nation state in a globalizing world, a world in which even the strongest nation states of Europe find it increasingly difficult to protect the so-called national interest in the way they have done for centuries? Shared sovereignty, interdependence, practical strategic alliances, flexibility, are the most important requirements in order to protect and implement so-called national interests in the twenty-first century. This is no longer the old nineteenth-century nation state pattern. And in some Central and Eastern European countries some kind of a return to the old pattern can be observed. This approach, however, would result in a historical catastrophe. Thus a well-prepared accession process could prevent substantial negative developments for the CE+SEE region, for the EU, and for the whole of Europe.

2. REFLECTIONS ON THE 'EASTERN' ENLARGEMENT OF THE EUROPEAN UNION

More than a decade after the fall of the Berlin wall and the unprecedented changes in Central and Eastern Europe, the enlargement of the European Union towards the transforming and partly transformed countries seems to have become an integral part of the EU's integration strategy. A long time was required by Spain and Portugal to progress from the birth of democratic institutions to membership of the EU. Certainly, both countries were labelled market economies. However, if we look at their development level, economic structure, degree of private ownership, and international competitiveness in the late 1970s and early 1980s, at least some of the present candidate countries appear much stronger. Obviously, one can argue that the EU of the early 1980s and of today are substantially different. The *acquis communautaire* is qualitatively superior to that of 20 years ago. However, the association agreements and the consequent preparation for membership have made some of the candidate countries much more integrated into the EU structures than the Mediterranean countries were immediately before accession. Moreover, the problems, challenges, and tasks of today's Europe can hardly be compared with those of two decades ago.

A. Strategic Goal without Strategic Plan

Following a decade of gradual progress with more or less dynamic development, the transforming countries of Central and Eastern Europe first signed association agreements with Brussels (between 1991 and 1996), and then were invited to start official negotiations on accession (from 1998 and 2000, in two groups). At present, the negotiation process is well under way. The Commission's Strategy Paper on Enlargement of November 2000, containing a road map for negotiations, and the ambitious plans and actions of the Swedish Presidency (in the first half of 2001) have obviously been supporting the process, which has resulted in an 'upgrading' of the enlargement issue within the general agenda of the EU. However, there have been many other factors which have played or are playing an important role in raising enlargement into the priority strategic areas of Community activity. Not all of them, though, necessarily lead to identical assessments of what to do, and when and how to do it.

First, the record of political, economic, and institutional relations between the candidate countries and Brussels as well as the EU Member States has fundamentally shaped progress in the last decade and created a special intrinsic (authentic) dynamism for the enlargement process. The candidate countries' share of the total trade of the EU increased from less than 3 per cent a decade ago to 12.3 per cent of total EU exports and 9.6 per cent of total EU imports.[7] The ten candidate countries (CCs) have proved to be the most dynamic trade partner of the EU on a global comparison. While the EU's total exports grew by 63 per cent between 1995 and 2000, its exports to the CCs increased by 112 per cent. Similar development can also be registered on the import side (84 and 118 per cent, respectively). The driving factors were the creation of bilateral free trade in manufactured goods, privatization in the CCs, the often decisive role of foreign direct investment, and institutional development towards a functioning and increasingly competitive market economy.

Secondly, the negotiation process itself provided a special dynamism. As more and more chapters have been closed, including some of the most delicate ones (e.g. the four freedoms of the single market, and the environment), enlargement has had to be considered not as a remote objective but as a strategic issue on the EU's current agenda.

Thirdly, the agreement on reform of the institutional structure of the EU signed in Nice has practically removed the last self-made barrier on the way to enlargement. As a result, the road seems to be cleared, and accession is now dependent on two factors, namely the level of preparation of the CCs and the finalization of the negotiations.

Fourthly, global challenges have also contributed to the increasing importance of 'Eastern' enlargement. For most businesses involved in Central and Eastern Europe, either as an important market for goods and services or as an equally important location for internationally competitive production, it became clear that the sustainability of predictable and rapidly growing business opportunities also required the legal and institutional(ized) integration of the CCs into EU structures. Although, in current GDP terms, the new entrants do not offer huge economic potential, the growth potential of the region, the rapid increase in productivity, the emergence of new and competitive structures, and a large number of promising investment opportunities leading to economies-of-scale savings (e.g. in infrastructural devel-

---

[7] All data, if not otherwise indicated, is taken from or calculated on the basis of Eurostat. *External and Intra-European Union Trade*, No. 6 (2000) and No. 4 (2001).

opment or environment protection) all mean that the importance of these countries must not be underestimated. More importantly, there are a number of hidden resources in the region at the threshold of the knowledge society (e.g. the general level of education, high-quality manpower, outstanding achievements in selected areas of research and development, the high level of flexibility of the citizens, good adjustment capacity to the changing environment).[8] Some of these factors will obviously be increasingly important as a result of the coming global challenges and the answers to be given to them. Finally, the CCs represent a major contribution to the EU's global external trade balance. Between 1995 and 2000, the EU's cumulative global trade surplus amounted to 45 billion euros, while its surplus from trade with the CCs reached almost 100 billion euros, or more than twice the former figure. Both in 1999 and in 2000, the EU's global trade deficit (14 and 86 billion euros, respectively) sharply contrasted with its trade surplus with the CCs (16 and 17 billion euros, respectively).

The strategic importance of enlargement can be argued for in another way too. Should enlargement not take place or be delayed, stability in Europe will be seriously at risk. Controlling an unstable situation or ensuring apparent, superficial stability would require damage limitation with very high financial costs. Even if the EU grew more rapidly than in recent years, most of the increase in growth would have to be spent on preserving stability. In consequence, practically no resources would remain to improve the EU's (and Europe's) position in global politics and in the world economy.

Fifthly, civil/ethnic wars and the remaining high level of uncertainty in most of the former Yugoslav republics and in some other parts of Southern and Eastern Europe are forcing the EU to take a clear position concerning its role and objectives in a region which, for the moment, does not belong to the countries negotiating accession. In any event, the EU's growing commitment to stabilizing this part of the continent has also contributed to upgrading the enlargement process and seeing it in a broader context.

Sixthly, politicians in Brussels, the Member States, and the candidate countries have noticed that public support for the enlargement project may (further) decrease if no action is taken. Otherwise, as has until recently been

---

[8] According to a recent study prepared by the European Commission, the candidate countries (except Estonia) have a lower share of population with high-school education; however, they are clearly better educated at secondary school level. While in Portugal 78 % of the population between 25 and 59 has basic education only (Spain 62, Italy 54, Greece 49, Ireland 49, Belgium 40 %), this share is substantially lower in the candidate countries (less than 25 % in all 'first-wave' candidate countries and in the Baltic states). See Institut der deutschen Wirtschaft, *iwd*, Cologne, 25 Oct. 2001, 8. Even more interestingly, according to a study by the OECD, Hungary ranks sixth in the group of countries 'most likely to succeed in knowledge industries'. See Marsh, 'New Millennium's Winners and Losers', *Financial Times*, 29 Oct. 2001.

the case, enlargement will be considered as one of many tasks for the future but not as *the* strategic goal for the present. In this context, the credibility of the EU is at stake. On the one hand it is a major stability factor, and on the other it cannot be divided according to different geographic areas. Any loss of credibility in parts of Europe would necessarily affect the EU's credibility in other parts of the world too.

Finally, the ongoing debate on the future of Europe, which will be launched as a key area of activity during the Belgian Presidency, also needs the active participation of the CCs, both in their present position and, of course, even more, as new members of an enlarging Community.

Today, most experts agree that enlargement belongs to a package of the most urgent strategic issues to be solved or answered by the EU. However, agreement on its strategic nature has not yet been accompanied by agreement on a transparent 'travel plan' (rather than road map) for how, when, under which conditions, with what kind of sequencing, and with the participation of which countries the enlargement process should be set going. There is one general guideline only. It states that countries can join once they are ready to join, which generally means that they have finished negotiations on accession and the accession documents have been ratified. This principle should, however, be strengthened by an additional condition: no candidate country has the right to take any other country hostage. In other words: no country that is not yet ready to join has the right to stop others who are ready from joining.

At present, nobody knows to what extent the above-mentioned principle will be applied in the clearly difficult decisions on enlargement, nor to what extent further considerations—political, strategic, or other—will gain momentum in the future.

Even the speed of the negotiation process may be hampered by intra-EU disputes (consider the latest example of Spain temporarily blocking the presentation of the common EU position on the free movement of persons). It is not difficult to predict that further stumbling blocks still lie on the road to accession. In addition, short-term election considerations may interfere with the enlargement process (labour issues in Germany or, more importantly, the EU's agricultural position and elections in France). If we add that some extremely complicated technical issues have to be settled by negotiating various chapters, both public opinion and the attention of politicians could easily be diverted from the strategic importance of enlargement. This means that enlargement as a strategic question for the whole of Europe needs to be constantly emphasized.

B. Shared Objectives—Growing Differences in the Candidate Countries

All CCs have clearly recognized the strategic relevance of their accession to the EU. Thus, all of them have made substantial efforts to accommodate their domestic economic and institutional structures to EU requirements. Also, they have started a communication campaign and, not less importantly, have been equipped for negotiation. Nevertheless, the situation is rather similar to the starting of the transformation process more than a decade ago. At that time too, all countries wanted to go in the same direction (political democracy and market economy). However, their capacity to implement reforms and create a functioning and competitive economy proved to be rather different. Also, due to different historical legacies, different levels of preparation for transformation, different social contexts, and different geographic locations, Central and Eastern European countries opted for different instruments, followed different ways, and tried different sequencing for the implementation of specific policy measures.

It is obvious that the absorption and adjustment capacities of the individual CCs in relation to the economic, legal, and institutional requirements of the *acquis communautaire* are also quite different. Moreover, these differences are partly rooted in their present situation based on the diverging development of the last ten years. Differences can be identified on at least four levels.

First, there are manifest differences among the individual candidate countries. These can be registered in macroeconomic features (growth, inflation, unemployment, budget deficit, current account) and, perhaps more importantly, in microeconomic performance (the degree of privatization, the role of foreign direct investment, productivity growth, structural change, competitiveness, but also legal stability and transparency).

Secondly, economic relations with the EU also reveal clear differences. 70 per cent of the EU's exports to CCs and 68 per cent of its imports from CCs are with only three Central European countries (Poland, Czech Republic, Hungary). More than 60 per cent of the Ell's trade surplus is due to one bilateral relationship, namely trade with Poland. The export structure of the CCs to the EU shows similar large differences. While more than 63 per cent of Hungary's exports to the EU consist of machinery, computers, electronics, and transport equipment (generally considered to be 'technology-intensive' goods), the same product group represents a proportion of EU-related exports of 49 per cent for the Czech Republic, 45 per cent for Slovakia, 41 per cent for Slovenia, 35 per cent for Poland, and less than 20 per cent for all the other CCs (data for 2000). Obviously, different specialization patterns have already developed across Central and Eastern Europe, due to the level of economic development, the method of privatization, and the role of foreign capital, mainly of transnational companies, in the given economy. In addition, different export patterns result in different unit prices of exports. One ton of manufactured goods exported by Hungary to Germany equals DM 16,163 (8,100 euros) (very similar to the German total of DM 16,635 (8,400 euros)). By contrast, one ton of similar exports to Germany by the

Czech Republic is priced at DM 6,427 (3,250 euros), with Poland at DM 4,489, (2,250 euros) and Latvia at DM 2,749 (1,400 euros).[9]

Thirdly, differences can be identified within each candidate country by comparing various central areas of EU maturity. For example, some countries are well prepared in economic terms. One can state that, in everyday practice, they have already become members of the EU. The legal adjustment process is a trickier issue. Of course, despite some delay almost everywhere, the transposition of EU laws and regulations has been ongoing, and in some countries is expected to be finished by the end of 2002. A different issue is, however, the enforcement of EU-compatible rules. This has to be a two-way process, consisting of a top-down approach directed by the national legislation and a bottom-up process driven by the activities and absorption capacity of citizens, business, and other organizations. In this context, foreign capital originating in an EU country has generally transferred to a candidate country not only financial resources, technology, marketing knowledge, but also part of the *acquis communautaire.* This aspect must not be ignored in the process of legal accommodation. No candidate country can state that it is fully prepared for membership in the institutional context. Several institutions have still to be created or strengthened, and some of them can start effective work only at the moment of entering the EU (e.g. those linked to the common agricultural policy). Finally, the level of public support in the individual CCs is also rather uneven. In some countries, support is expected to remain sufficiently high in case of a referendum, while in others it may decrease as painful compromises have to be accepted in the process of negotiation. In any event, dialogue with the public and the preparation of society for accession is an outstanding task, since it is not only politicians, business leaders, experts, or members of the negotiating teams who will join the EU, but also societies. Their maturity will largely determine whether the new country will become a successful member or not.

Fourthly, and most recently, growing differences have also been emerging in the speed (and quality) of the negotiations. It has been repeatedly and rightly stressed that differences in the number of provisionally closed chapters do not matter very much, since even one unfinished chapter would block the closure of negotiations. It has also been emphasized that, as long as the negotiation process lasts, all previously and provisionally closed chapters may be reopened.

However, differences in the number and/or quality of closed chapters ('core' chapters *v* 'soft' ones) are great, and this is indicative. If some countries have closed 20 to 23 chapters by the end of the Swedish Presidency (the end of June 2001), while others have closed only 15 or 16, the difference can

[9] Figures calculated from: Statistisches Bundesamt. Fachserie 7. Reihe 3, *Aussenhandel nach Ländern und Warengruppen. Zweites Halbjahr und Jahr 2000* (2001).

hardly be ignored. And this emerging 'gap' could be strengthened by a 'qualitative breakthrough', meaning that the most advanced negotiating countries may have finished work on the four chapters on 'freedom' (goods, services, labour, and capital), as well as on such issues as environment or taxation.

The evident acceleration of the negotiation process during the Swedish Presidency does not result exclusively from the Commission's road map. It is also the outcome of more flexibility on both sides. The EU has been ready to offer the CCs transitional periods in various areas, while the latter have withdrawn a number of previously formulated requests for derogations from EU rules at the moment of accession. In some cases, one had the impression of cross-country 'competitive withdrawal' (similar to competitive devaluation). No doubt, these steps can be assessed in a positive way, if the gains expected from the accelerated process and the earlier finalization of negotiations resulting in earlier membership are significantly higher than the additional costs of adjustment *before* accession. It is not known whether the decisions on the withdrawal of some requests were based on carefully prepared impact studies or were part of longer-term negotiation tactics to be implemented at a given stage of the talks, or else were simply dictated by a fear of lagging behind the others. It is, however, clear that all changes should be communicated to and discussed with the interested parties in the given candidate country (business sector, interest groups, or wider public).

C. The Agenda Ahead

According to the Commission's road map, the best prepared countries may finish negotiations on all chapters by mid-2002, or the end of the Spanish Presidency. To stick to this ambitious plan, several conditions have to be fulfilled. First, the EU has to present its common position papers in the remaining chapters on schedule (e.g. the agricultural chapter cannot await the French elections). Secondly, the Nice Treaty on institutional reforms has to be ratified by the national parliaments and the Irish 'no' has to be 'ironed out', since the chapter on institutions cannot be addressed before ratification by the Fifteen. Thirdly, both Belgium and Spain have to work as hard as Sweden did and does, and be driven by a strategic approach instead of entering narrow-minded disputes on some issues. Unfortunately, due to the relevant financial implications of the chapters which are pre-eminent on the agenda of the Spanish Presidency (regional policy, budget, agriculture), delays cannot be ruled out. Still, the enlargement process is unlikely to be stopped, since the consequences would be very detrimental for the whole of Europe.

At the present stage of negotiations, three important developments deserve special attention. First, the low level of solidarity among the candidates. The point has been reached where everybody is following his or her own interests, and a space for individual interest implementation has been opened. This does not signify a fundamental lack of cooperation, dialogue, or mutual information. However, no country should complain of being betrayed by others that have been making more progress in selected chapters. Secondly, differences in the room to manœuvre and in domestic limitations (constraints) of the negotiation teams are becoming manifest. Each country's capacity for compromise and agreeing new (less favourable) commitments is linked to the level of acceptance by its own politics and society. Certainly, pre-election periods do not favour more flexible negotiating behaviour. But the real problem is in society's flexibility. Governments and chief negotiators can always be replaced, but societies cannot. And social attitudes seem to be rather different even on a Central European comparison. New positions, partial or total giving up of some objectives, and restructured compromises can generally be absorbed better in Hungary or the Czech Republic than, for instance, in Poland. Thirdly, negotiations on accession are by no means about accession only. This is a good opportunity for all EU member countries to try to rearrange their previous positions within the Community and create better ones for themselves, or to insist on already-achieved benefits. Until now, officially, the EU has repeatedly refused to name any date or any composition of the 'first' group to join the Union. Nevertheless, 2004 has been mentioned in various EU documents, and a few CCs have envisaged in their preparations the year 2003. The latter is possible only if a few countries are able to complete negotiations by mid-2002 and, for whatever reason, a quick ratification process can be carried out.

What is much more important is the designing of a comprehensive and clear 'travel plan' for enlargement. If the final goal of the EU (and of the CCs) is to create stability in Europe, the process of enlargement has to remain open to all countries with which Brussels has started negotiations, and, most likely, to some new candidates from former Yugoslavia. Evidently, such a huge project needs time, transparency from the outset, and public support. In order not to threaten the project, and, consequently, in order to sustain and strengthen continental stability, the following approach seems viable.

First, a small group of well-prepared countries should join the EU as quickly as possible (not later than 2004). This group will not burden the EU's decision-making structure, institutions, or budget. Their easy adjustment to EU structures will mitigate or even break the growing opposition to 'Eastern' enlargement among Western European politicians and the broader public. This is the way to generate support for further (and more difficult) enlargements and keep the EU door open to other candidates. The other approach ('big bang') would threaten to destroy the enlargement process, because it would bring into the EU differently prepared countries, with substantial financial needs and slower adjustment capacities, with negative impacts on the decision-making process and the everyday work of institutions. An eventual delay of enlargement in order to wait for less prepared countries would be extremely detrimental both for the advanced candidates and for the credibility of the EU. A 'big bang' enlargement that involved differential treatment of differently prepared countries, on the other hand, would make the adjustment process non-transparent, unmanageable, chaotic, and even more bureaucratic. However, the main argument against the 'big bang' approach is that it would enhance political and public opposition or even hostility to any further enlargement. As a result, some countries which, for obvious stability reasons, should join in the future but are not yet adequately prepared, would not be accepted, and would remain outside the new Europe, with disastrous consequences.

Secondly, parallel to the small-group enlargement, a ten-year enlargement schedule of the EU should be presented, with at least two further dates for potential enlargement, but without identifying any candidate country as destined to join on a specific date. In this context, the Copenhagen criteria will need to be applied in the future as well. Those countries which remain outside the first wave of enlargement should be involved in a number of Community programmes. Some of these have already been opened up to the present candidate countries (e.g. research and development framework programmes and educational projects). There is no doubt that new areas should be opened, since European integration progresses differently in different sectors. For instance, the security requirements of the continent, accompanied by financial considerations, may dictate a reassessment of where the new external (Schengen) borders of the Union should be drawn. Large infrastructural projects must be planned and realized by including future member countries. Also, cross-border cooperation at the new borders of the EU must be strengthened. Finally, all countries which are expected to belong to the not-too-distant 'future Europe' should be invited actively to participate in the discussion about the architecture of the new Europe and be offered the chance to help shape it from their present positions.

Thirdly, and finally, accession provides the first-wave countries not only with new opportunities but also with a new quality of responsibility. They will have to start work in order to join the Union at the highest level of preparation and to strengthen public support for quick further enlargements. In addition, as new members, they will have to work very intensively for more regional economic cooperation based on enhanced regional stability and on the shifting of the European growth centre towards the territory of the new entrants. Finally, they must remain, or become, advocates of a Union with an open-ended enlargement policy.

Table 4.1. *Share of the Ten Central and Eastern European Candidate Countries in Total Extra-regional Trade of the European Union (in per cent of total EU extra-regional trade)*

	1995	1998	1999	2000
EU exports	9.3	12.3	12.1	12.3
EU imports	8.1	9.5	9.8	9.6

Source: Eurostat, External and Intra-European Union Trade, No. 4. 2001, and own calculations

Table 4.2. *Trade between the European Union and the CEECs* (2000, Euro mn)*

	EU exports	EU imports	EU balance
total extra-regional	933,895	1,019,881	−85,986
CEECs-10	114,634	97,460	+17,174
Poland	33,726	23,108	+10,618
Czech Republic	23,713	21,417	+2,296
Hungary	22,955	21,842	+1,113
Romania	8,658	7,604	+1,054
Slovenia	8,067	6,259	+1,808
Slovakia	6,528	6,966	−438
Estonia	3,225	3,149	+76
Bulgaria	3,205	3,062	+143
Lithuania	2,557	2,162	+395
Latvia	2,000	1,891	+109

*Bulgaria, Czech Republic, Estonia, Hungary, Latvia, Lithuania, Poland, Romania, Slovakia, Slovenia

Source: Eurostat. External and Intra-European Union Trade. Monthly Statistics. No. 4. 2001.

Table 4.3. *Selected Indicators of Trade Relations Between the European Union and the CEECs-10* Year 2000*

	Country exports	Share of EU imports	Coverage exp/imp. (for CEECs)	growth 2000/1999 (1999 = 100) EU exp.	EU imp.
EU total extra-regional	100.0	100.0	91.6	122.9	130.0
CEECs-10	12.3	9.6	117.6	122.6	127.8
Poland	3.61	2.27	68.5	116.4	131.4
Czech Republic	2.54	2.10	90.3	128.7	127.2
Hungary	2.46	2.14	95.2	124.5	123.9
Romania	0.93	0.75	87.8	136.8	131.7

(continues)

Table 4.3. *(continued)*

	Country Share of EU exports	Coverage imports (for CEECs)	growth exp/imp. EU exp.	2000/1999 (1999 = 100) EU imp.	
EU total extra-regional	*100.0*	*100.0*	*91.6*	*122.9*	*130.0*
CEECs-10	*12.3*	*9.6*	*117.6*	*122.6*	*127.8*
Slovenia	0.86	0.61	77.6	116.6	118.2
Slovakia	0.70	0.68	106.7	118.3	116.9
Estonia	0.35	0.31	97.6	133.6	166.5
Bulgaria	0.34	0.30	95.5	118.6	136.2
Lithuania	0.27	0.21	84.6	121.9	133.5
Latvia	0.21	0.19	94.6	120.2	134.3

* Bulgaria, Czech Republic, Estonia, Hungary, Latvia, Lithuania, Poland, Romania, Slovakia, Slovenia

Source: Eurostat. External and Intra-European Union Trade Monthly Statistics. No. 4. 2001, and own calculations.

Table 4.4. *Increment and Dynamics of Trade Between the European Union and the Ten Central and Eastern European Candidate Countries (1995–1999)*

	EU exports increment Euro bn (1995	1999/1995 = 100)	EU imports increment Euro bn (1995	1999/1995 = 100)
total extra-EU	184.9	132.3	226.7	141.6
CEEC-10	38.6	172.9	31.2	170.3
—Estonia	1.0	176.0	1.0	210.2
—Latvia	0.7	171.6	0.3	124.4
—Lithuania	1.0	199.8	0.6	164.6
—Poland	13.1	185.7	5.2	142.2
—Czech Republic	6.3	154.6	7.7	185.8
—Slovakia	2.2	170.0	2.9	193.0
—Hungary	9.6	211.1	9.7	227.7
—Romania	2.4	164.7	2.4	169.9
—Bulgaria	0.6	128.9	0.4	121.9
—Slovenia	1.6	131.0	1.0	124.5

Source: Eurostat, External and Intra-European Union Trade, No. 6.2000, and own calculations

Table 4.5. *Trade Balance of the European Union with the Ten Central and Eastern European Candidate Countries, 1995–1999 Cumulative*

	Euro bn	
total extra-EU	+ 131.1	− 13,771
CEEC-10	+ 82.4	+ 16,073
—Estonia	+ 3.4	+ 504
—Latvia	+ 0.6	+ 214
—Lithuania	+ 2.6	+ 433
—Poland	+ 43.3	+ 10,890
—Czech Republic	+ 14.1	+ 1,230
—Slovakia	+ 1.2	− 560
—Hungary	+ 6.9	+ 1,028
—Romania	+ 3.3	+ 468
—Bulgaria	+ 0.4	+ 394
—Slovenia	+ 6.5	+ 1,472

Source: Eurostat. External and Intra-European Union Trade, No. 6. 2000, and own calculations.

Table 4.6. *Commodity Structure of Exports by CEECs into the European Union (in per cent of total exports to the EU) Year: 2000*

Country	0+1	2+4	3	5	7	6+8
EU total extra-regional imports	5.3	4.9	14.3	6.9	38.0	27.2
Poland	5.4	3.1	4.9	4.7	34.9	45.6
Czech Republic	1.6	4.3	2.1	4.7	49.2	36.8
Slovakia	1.0	3.5	3.4	5.0	45.7	38.1
Hungary	4.5	2.3	1.4	4.8	63.4	22.2
Romania	2.1	4.7	0.4	3.1	18.9	70.4
Bulgaria	5.8	5.6	2.1	6.8	9.9	68.9
Slovenia	1.0	2.6	0.0	4.7	41.0	48.3

Notes: 0+1 food, beverage and tobacco
2+4 raw materials
3 energy
5 chemical products
7 machinery and transport equipment
6+8 miscellaneous manufactured goods

Source: Eurostat. External and Intra-European Union Trade. Monthly Statistics. No. 4. 2001, and own calculations.

Table 4.7. *Unit Prices of German Imports from Selected Countries 2000*

Imports from	DM/ton all commodities final manufactured goods*		German price level = 100 all commod. final manuf. goods*	
total German imports	2,103	16,635	100.0	100.0
Hungary	7,075	16,163	336.4	97.2
Bulgaria	3,624	11,472	172.3	71.0
Romania	5,912	10,271	281.1	63.5
Slovenia	6,807	9,936	323.7	61.5
Slovakia	2,647	8,986	125.9	55.6
Czech Republic	1,682	6,427	80.0	39.8
Estonia	988	5,499	47.0	34.0
Poland	971	4,489	46.2	27.8
Lithuania	1,296	4,427	61.6	27.4
Latvia	766	2,749	36.4	17.0
Ireland	21,946	147,607	1043.6	913.2
Portugal	10,005	22,078	475.7	136.6
Austria	3,895	12,877	185.2	80.0
Spain	4,654	12,470	221.3	77.2
Greece	3,636	5,011	172.9	31.0

* Final manufactured goods account for 70 to 90 per cent of total German imports from Central and Eastern Europe. Thus, they adequately indicate the structural development level of the selected economies.

Source: own calculations based on: Statistisches Bundesamt. Fachserie 7. Reihe 3. Aussenhandel nach Ländern und Warengruppen (Spezialhandel) Zweites Halbjahr und Jahr 2000. Wiesbaden, 2001.

Table 4.8. State of the Accession Negotiations at the End of the Swedish Presidency (end of June, 2001)

Chapters	Hungary	Czech Rep.	Poland	Estonia	Slovenia	Cyprus	Malta	Lithuania	Slovakia	Latvia	Bulgaria	Romania
1. Free movement of goods	provisionally closed	provisionally closed	provisionally closed	provisionally closed	provisionally closed	provisionally closed	provisionally closed	provisionally closed	provisionally closed	provisionally closed	chapter opened	to be opened
2. Free movement of persons	provisionally closed	chapter opened	chapter opened	chapter opened	chapter opened	provisionally closed	chapter opened	chapter opened	chapter opened	chapter opened	to be opened	to be opened
3. Free movement of services	provisionally closed	provisionally closed	provisionally closed	provisionally closed	provisionally closed	provisionally closed	provisionally closed	provisionally closed	provisionally closed	provisionally closed	chapter opened	to be opened
4. Free movement of capital	provisionally closed	provisionally closed	chapter opened	provisionally closed	provisionally closed	provisionally closed	chapter opened	provisionally closed	chapter opened	provisionally closed	chapter opened	chapter opened
5. Company law	provisionally closed	provisionally closed	chapter opened	provisionally closed	provisionally closed	provisionally closed	provisionally closed	provisionally closed	provisionally closed	provisionally closed	provisionally closed	chapter opened
6. Competition & state aid	chapter opened	chapter opened	chapter opened	chapter opened	chapter opened	chapter opened	chapter opened	chapter opened	chapter opened	chapter opened	chapter opened	chapter opened
7. Agriculture	chapter opened	chapter opened	chapter opened	chapter opened	chapter opened	chapter opened	to be opened	chapter opened	chapter opened	chapter opened	to be opened	to be opened
8. Fisheries	provisionally closed	provisionally closed	chapter opened	provisionally closed	provisionally closed	provisionally closed	chapter opened	provisionally closed	provisionally closed	chapter opened	provisionally closed	chapter opened
9. Transport	chapter opened	provisionally closed	chapter opened	chapter opened	chapter opened	provisionally closed	chapter opened	chapter opened	chapter opened	chapter opened	chapter opened	chapter opened
10. Taxation	provisionally closed	chapter opened	chapter opened	chapter opened	chapter opened	chapter opened	chapter opened	chapter opened	chapter opened	chapter opened	to be opened	to be opened
11. EMU	provisionally closed	provisionally closed	provisionally closed	provisionally closed	provisionally closed	provisionally closed	provisionally closed	provisionally closed	provisionally closed	provisionally closed	to be opened	to be opened
12. Statistics	provisionally closed	provisionally closed	provisionally closed	provisionally closed	provisionally closed	provisionally closed	provisionally closed	provisionally closed	provisionally closed	provisionally closed	provisionally closed	provisionally closed
13. Social policy & employment	provisionally closed	provisionally closed	provisionally closed	provisionally closed	provisionally closed	provisionally closed	chapter opened	provisionally closed	provisionally closed	provisionally closed	to be opened	to be opened
14. Energy	provisionally closed	chapter opened	provisionally closed	chapter opened	provisionally closed	provisionally closed	provisionally closed	chapter opened	provisionally closed	chapter opened	to be opened	to be opened
15. Industrial policy	provisionally closed	provisionally closed	provisionally closed	provisionally closed	provisionally closed	provisionally closed	provisionally closed	provisionally closed	provisionally closed	provisionally closed	to be opened	to be opened
16. SMEs	provisionally closed	provisionally closed	provisionally closed	provisionally closed	provisionally closed	provisionally closed	provisionally closed	provisionally closed	provisionally closed	provisionally closed	provisionally closed	provisionally closed

Chapter												
17. Science & research	provisionally closed	provisionally closed	provisionally closed	provisionally closed	provisionally closed	provisionally closed	provisionally closed	provisionally closed	provisionally closed	provisionally closed	provisionally closed	provisionally closed
18. Education & training	provisionally closed	provisionally closed	provisionally closed	provisionally closed	provisionally closed	provisionally closed	provisionally closed	provisionally closed	provisionally closed	provisionally closed	provisionally closed	provisionally closed
19. Telecommnications	provisionally closed	provisionally closed	provisionally closed	provisionally closed	provisionally closed	provisionally closed	provisionally closed	provisionally closed	chapter opened	chapter opened	chapter opened	chapter opened
20. Culture & audiovisual	provisionally closed	provisionally closed	provisionally closed	provisionally closed	provisionally closed	provisionally closed	provisionally closed	provisionally closed	provisionally closed	provisionally closed	provisionally closed	chapter opened
21. Regional policy	chapter opened	chapter opened	chapter opened	chapter opened	chapter opened	chapter opened	chapter opened	chapter opened	chapter opened	chapter opened	to be opened	to be opened
22. Enviro-nment	provisionally closed	provisionally closed	chapter opened	provisionally closed	provisionally closed	provisionally closed	chapter opened	chapter opened	chapter opened	chapter opened	to be opened	to be opened
23. Consumers & health protection	provisionally closed	provisionally closed	provisionally closed	provisionally closed	provisionally closed	provisionally closed	provisionally closed	provisionally closed	provisionally closed	provisionally closed	provisionally closed	provisionally closed
24. Justice & home affairs	chapter opened	chapter opened	chapter opened	chapter opened	chapter opened	chapter opened	to be opened	to be opened	to be opened	to be opened	to be opened	to be opened
25. Customs union	provisionally closed	provisionally closed	provisionally closed	chapter opened	provisionally closed	provisionally closed	chapter opened	chapter opened	chapter opened	chapter opened	chapter opened	chapter opened
26. External relations	provisionally closed	provisionally closed	provisionally closed	provisionally closed	provisionally closed	provisionally closed	provisionally closed	provisionally closed	provisionally closed	provisionally closed	provisionally closed	provisionally closed
27. Common foreign & security policy	provisionally closed	provisionally closed	provisionally closed	provisionally closed	provisionally closed	provisionally closed	provisionally closed	provisionally closed	provisionally closed	provisionally closed	provisionally closed	provisionally closed
28. Financial control	provisionally closed	chapter opened	provisionally closed	provisionally closed	provisionally closed	provisionally closed	provisionally closed	chapter opened	chapter opened	chapter opened	chapter opened	to be opened
29. Financial & budgetary	chapter opened	chapter opened	chapter opened	chapter opened	chapter opened	chapter opened	chapter opened	chapter opened	chapter opened	chapter opened	to be opened	to be opened
Number of provisionally closed chapters	22	19	17	19	21	23	18	17	17	15	10	7

Note: Chapter 30 on institutions has not yet been opened up with any candidate country. The content of Chapter 31 (others) is not yet known.

Source: European Union Council of Ministers, as quoted by *Világgazdaság*, 30 July 2001. p.16.

5

The Evolution and Application of EU Membership Conditionality

KAREN E. SMITH

This Chapter analyses the evolution of EU membership conditionality and its application *vis-à-vis* the applicant countries, that is: Bulgaria, Cyprus, Czech Republic, Estonia, Hungary, Latvia, Lithuania, Malta, Poland, Romania, Slovakia, Slovenia, and Turkey. It examines why these countries have been subjected to tougher membership conditions than previous applicants, and how the EU has used membership conditionality to try to influence their domestic and foreign policies. The Chapter also argues that the consistent application of its membership conditions could provide the EU with a more justifiable way to judge present, and future, applicant countries than other criteria such as cultural affinity, geographical proximity, or geo-strategic calculations. The problem is that membership conditionality has not been applied consistently, and other considerations will continue to play a role in enlargement decisions. This will diminish the force of the EU's membership conditions as a means for both protecting and promoting the integration process, and influencing applicant countries.

The first section of the Chapter examines the broad reasons why the EU sets conditions for membership in the first place. The second section describes the evolution of the EU's membership conditions. The third section analyses how the EU has applied membership conditionality, and the challenges it has consequently faced, in its relations with the applicant countries from Central and Eastern Europe, while the fourth does the same with respect to Cyprus and Turkey. The future of EU membership conditionality is considered in section five. The Chapter concludes with a consideration of the advantages of membership conditionality compared to other factors affecting decisions to enlarge the EU.

1. WHY SET CONDITIONS FOR MEMBERSHIP?

Most clubs set explicit conditions for joining, if only that new members agree to obey the club's rules; many also have unspoken, implicit expectations of the suitability or not of prospective members. The conditions reflect the values and interests of the club and its membership. Expanding a club to include new members inevitably means some change in the way the club operates and the functions it performs; membership conditions are a way to protect the club's basic values and interests from radical change brought on by membership expansion. This should coincide with the expectations of membership applicants: they are seeking to join the club in its current state and presumably wish to keep it that way.[1]

The European Union (a kind of club, after all) sets conditions for new members, and has rules that all members must obey. These reflect the very special, and evolving, nature of the EU. As Paul Taylor has argued:

the institutions of the European Union are a unique achievement. They emerged as an effective way of governing a set of states which retained their sovereignty, but which nevertheless agreed to form a system possessing a very high degree of common management. The combination of interests and values which could sustain this system had taken a good many years to evolve, and it represented an achievement which should not be abandoned easily. It involved a long process of learning and adjusting, of socialization in the ways of the Community.[2]

The European Communities started as a customs union; the Union's remit now extends to policy-making in areas as diverse as the environment, education, foreign and defence policy, asylum and immigration policy, and combating crime. A single currency circulates in 12 of the 15 Member States. Community law is supreme over national law, and decisions can often be made by the Member States voting by qualified majority.

There are thus considerable achievements to be protected. It should not be surprising that as the Union has evolved, the conditions for becoming a member have become more demanding. When new members enter the EU, they must accept the changes that have already been made. The hurdle of membership conditions moves higher as the obligations of membership increase.

But membership conditions are also to help protect the future integration process. Deeper integration becomes ever more difficult with a larger EU, although admittedly widening has thus far not impeded the integration process. But as the number of Member States grows even further, it is feared that size will matter: it will be much more difficult to agree to extend either

---

[1] Although joining a club with the aim of transforming it from within is not an unusual occurrence.

[2] P. Taylor, *The European Union in the 1990s* (1996), at 99.

the scope of integration (adding new policy areas to the process) or the level of integration (such as increasing the use of qualified-majority voting). In fact, some proponents of enlargement support it precisely because it will slow down—or render impossible—further integration. This has spurred many Member States to push for reforms that are to enable the EU to continue to deepen even after it widens.

Deepening integration has arguably been the EU's priority: since the end of the Cold War, there have been three new treaties (Maastricht, Amsterdam, and Nice), yet only one enlargement (to Austria, Finland, and Sweden). But while some of the reforms agreed in the treaties have their own logic (the single currency, for example), others have been designed explicitly to enable widening to occur without unduly jeopardizing the functioning of the EU, although they have been widely criticized as inadequate in this respect. The experience of the difficult negotiations leading up to the treaties (especially Amsterdam and Nice) only sharpens the dilemma: if the current Member States find it difficult to agree on reforms, how will an even larger group be able to do so? The applicant countries have been left out of negotiations on the EU's future, although many of them will have joined before the end of the 2004 intergovernmental conference, which is to decide on a 'constitution' for the EU. It appears that the current Member States are trying to change the rules of the game to protect their club, in accordance with their wishes, before it becomes more difficult after enlargement.

Yet the arguments for enlargement are strong. By enlarging, the EU would incorporate more states, thus spreading its model of ensuring peace and security via economic and political integration ('projecting political stability'[3]). As Christopher Hill has noted, enlargement decisions 'can be seen as a commitment to a major new foreign policy on the part of the EU, that of changing the map of Europe to the East and to the South .... [T]he aim is to extend the zone of economic prosperity and "democratic peace" as a prophylactic against war, nationalism and autocracy.'[4]

Setting strict membership conditions provides a partial solution to this 'widening *v* deepening' dilemma, but by no means resolves it. The EU declares its openness to further enlargement, but the conditions provide some protection of its achievements and ambitions. Yet meeting the conditions is no easy task for states engaged in a transition to the market economy and democracy (and, in some cases, to statehood itself), and strict application of membership conditionality could even prevent—or excessively delay—the pursuit of an inclusive EU, and thus the vision of a more stable and secure Europe. This dilemma has haunted the EU since the end of the Cold War.

---

[3] European Commission, 'Enlargement Strategy Paper 2000', Brussels, 8 Nov. 2000, 3.
[4] Hill, 'The Geo-Political Implications of Enlargement', in J. Zielonka (ed.), *Europe Unbound: Enlarging and Reshaping the Boundaries of the European Union* (2002).

Another solution to the widening *v* deepening dilemma is 'flexibility': allowing Member States to delay applying certain laws for a given period of time (transition periods), or to opt out of policy-making in certain areas (opt-outs), or to opt in to policy-making in certain areas ('enhanced integration', among a smaller group of Member States). Flexible solutions have been used throughout the Union's history, and are enshrined in Treaty law. They may help ensure that integration, at least among some Member States, continues even in the wake of enlargement. But flexibility also risks unravelling the Union: by destroying the principle that all must play by the same rules, it could undermine mutual solidarity and weaken the commitment of existing Member States.[5] While the current Member States devised flexible solutions for themselves, they have, since 1992, effectively ruled out flexibility for newcomers, at least in terms of the laws and practices already agreed. Flexible solutions applied in the past are not available to newcomers, although it is highly likely that they would continue to be used in future negotiations in an enlarged EU, particularly if new Member States have trouble fully implementing the existing *acquis*. But for the moment at least, the refusal to reopen flexible arrangements for the applicant states may help limit the confusion of 'variable geometry' within the EU, even if it makes it more difficult for applicant states to meet the conditions—and thus heightens the inclusion-exclusion dilemma.

In addition to protecting the club, 'membership conditionality' is used by the EU as a foreign-policy instrument, to influence applicant (and future applicant) countries' domestic and foreign policies. Setting membership conditions for joining international organizations is a form of conditionality. Conditionality entails the linking, by a state or international organization, of benefits desired by another state to the fulfilment of certain conditions.[6] It is essentially an exercise of power by the actor that is using conditionality; the *demandeur* is in a position of relative weakness, particularly if the benefit on offer is especially desired. Conditionality can be thought of as a type of foreign-policy instrument, a means used by policy-makers in their attempts to get other international actors to do what they would not otherwise do.[7]

As the queue of applicant countries has grown, membership conditionality has become a very powerful, if not the most powerful, foreign-policy instrument of the EU. It is exploiting its power of attraction. For several states (such as the Central and East European states), the EU is a bastion of democracy, prosperity, and security; for others (such as European Free Trade Association members), staying out of the world's largest economic

[5] Taylor, *supra* note 2, at 105.
[6] Stokke, 'Aid and Political Conditionality: Core Issues and State of the Art', in O. Stokke (ed.), *Aid and Political Conditionality* (1995), at 11–13.
[7] D. Baldwin, *Economic Statecraft* (1985), at 8–9.

bloc is too costly. This power of attraction has been translated by the EU into great leverage over the *demandeurs*, through insistence on their meeting all of the membership conditions. The use of membership conditionality is both an indication of, and a contributing factor to, a more cohesive and assertive international role for the EU.

Of course, membership conditionality is an odd foreign-policy instrument. It is limited geographically, because EU membership is open only to 'European states'. And it is limited temporally, because applicant countries will eventually become part of the EU and will obviously no longer be the subjects of EU foreign policy. But within the framework of these limitations, the EU has wielded this instrument, at times quite assertively and to great effect. The influence of external pressure on indigenous dynamics within countries is not and can never be overwhelming: third countries may be unwilling or unable to meet externally-imposed demands, for a wide variety of reasons. Yet the Central and East European countries (CEECs) are particularly susceptible to external pressure because they so desire to 'return to Europe', meaning membership of the EU (and NATO). This does not mean that the CEECs always and fully comply with EU demands, as discussed in section three. But they are still trying to meet the conditions, rather than dismissing their validity and withdrawing from the accession process.

2. WHAT ARE THE EU'S MEMBERSHIP CONDITIONS?

The conditions for EU membership have been set out in Treaty Articles, European Council statements, and legal agreements between the EU and candidates. The basic condition, European identity, was the only condition set out in the Rome Treaty. Article 237 proclaimed, 'Any European state may apply to become a member of the Community'. During the Cold War, membership eligibility was not such a troublesome issue, because membership for states outside the Western part of the continent was unthinkable. Other West European countries were either not interested or undemocratic (and hence implicitly unsuitable). The first enlargement of the European Communities, to Britain, Ireland, and Denmark, did not take place on the basis of any other explicit membership criteria, although Britain's suitability for EC membership came under considerable scrutiny prior to its accession on 1 January 1973.

In the mid-1970s, however, membership conditions became an explicit matter of concern, because of the unfolding events in southern Europe: Greece, Portugal, and Spain were making a transition from authoritarian rule to democracy. In April 1978, the European Council declared that 'respect for and maintenance of representative democracy and human rights in each Member State are essential elements of membership in the European Communities'.[8] This was a clear signal to Greece, Portugal, and Spain that they could join the Community if they proceeded with democratization, and was intended to support and encourage democratic forces within those countries.[9] However, the Commission's opinions on the three applications only briefly note that democracy has been restored or established, without elaborating on specific criteria used to reach such a conclusion.[10] Much more importance was given to consideration of the applicant's economic and administrative capacities, which became an implicit membership condition. The three southern European countries were by and large poorer than the other Member States,[11] so their capacity to function within the Community was a concern. In the case of Greece, an early version of the 'good-neighbourliness' condition appeared (see below), although it was less a condition and more an assertion of good intent. The Commission and Council declared that Greece's accession should not adversely affect the Community's relations with Turkey; Greece announced that it would not impede the strengthening of ties with Turkey.[12] The implications of enlargement for the functioning of the Community's policies and the efficiency of its decision-making procedures and institutions were also an issue. In its opinion on the Greek application, for example, the Commission declared that further enlargement called for an acceleration of the integration process.[13]

The Community did not, however, apply membership conditionality consistently. In the Commission's opinion, Greece was not ready for membership on economic grounds, and it recommended a transitional period first. The Council disagreed, as the view prevailed that Greece's democratic transition must be supported by opening full membership negotiations. Political considerations won out over the strict imposition of membership conditionality, an early illustration of the difficulties of applying condition-

---

[8] Copenhagen European Council, 7–8 Apr. 1978, 'Declaration on Democracy', *EC Bulletin*, no. 3 (1978), at 6.

[9] See Pridham, 'The Politics of the European Community, Transnational Networks and Democratic Transition in Southern Europe', in G. Pridham (ed.), *Encouraging Democracy: The International Context of Regime Transition in Southern Europe* (1991).

[10] European Commission, 'Opinion on a Greek Application for Membership', *EC Bulletin Supplement* no. 2/76, 9; European Commission, 'Opinion on Portugal's Application for Membership', *EC Bulletin Supplement* 5/78, 7; and European Commission, 'Opinion on Spain's Application for Membership', *EC Bulletin Supplement* 9/78, at 9.

[11] Spain's GDP *per capita* was, however, higher than Ireland's. See Kennedy, 'Ireland and European Integration: An Economic Perspective', in D. Keogh (ed.), *Ireland and the Challenge of European Integration* (1989) 33.

[12] Siotis, 'Greece: Characteristics and Motives for Entry', in J.L. Sampedro and J.A. Payno (eds), *The Enlargement of the European Community: Case-Studies of Greece, Portugal and Spain* (1983) 68.

[13] Commission, 'Opinion on a Greek Application for Membership', *supra* note 10, at 9.

ality. Such considerations did not, however, work in Turkey's favour. Turkey applied for EC membership in 1987; in 1989, the Commission's opinion stated that it would not be appropriate or useful to open accession negotiations with Turkey, as Turkey was not ready for membership based on economic and political grounds. The Turkish application has since remained on the table.

The end of the Cold War had the effect of dramatically increasing the number of states wanting to join the Community. The queue of membership applicants grew to include members of the European Free Trade Association (EFTA), and all of the Central and East European countries expressed a desire to join them (see Table 5.1.). It became imperative for the Community to set out more explicit requirements of membership, to impose order on a clamour of membership demands that threatened to engulf the Community, and, more significantly, to endanger the process of deepening begun with the 1987 Single European Act and 1989 Delors report on Economic and Monetary Union, and continued with the 1992 Maastricht Treaty.

In a report to the June 1992 Lisbon European Council, the Commission restated that there were three basic conditions for membership: European identity, democratic status, and respect of human rights. These conditions were not further elaborated upon by the Commission. Instead, attention was

Table 5.1. *Applications for EU Membership*

Turkey	14 April 1987
Austria	17 July 1989
Cyprus	3 July 1990
Malta	16 July 1990
Sweden	1 July 1991
Finland	18 March 1992
Switzerland[14]	26 May 1992
Norway[15]	25 November 1992
Hungary	31 March 1994
Poland	5 April 1994
Romania	22 June 1995
Slovakia	27 June 1995
Latvia	13 October 1995
Estonia	24 November 1995
Lithuania	8 December 1995
Bulgaria	14 December 1995
Czech Republic	17 January 1996
Slovenia	10 June 1996

[14] Switzerland's membership application was 'frozen' after Swiss voters rejected participation in the European Economic Area, in Dec. 1992.

[15] Norway completed accession negotiations in 1994, but Norwegian voters then rejected EU membership (again).

given to ensuring that enlargement would not endanger the Community's achievements. The Commission thus insisted that applicant countries had to accept the Community system, the *acquis communautaire*, and be able to implement it. The *acquis* was considerably larger than it ever had been. As the Commission noted, the 'accession of new members will be to a Community with new characteristics', including a single market with no internal frontiers, an economic and monetary union, and a common foreign and security policy.[16] Hence, an applicant state had to have a functioning and competitive market economy, and administrative and legal institutions capable of implementing Community law.

Particularly important was the Commission's insistence that applicant states agree to accept the *entire acquis*. During the Maastricht Treaty negotiations, there were pressures for exceptions, derogations, and opt-outs, some of which were accepted.[17] These pressures all derived 'from the claims of states which had acceded after the European Community had been set up'.[18] Newcomers had already proved to be awkward partners for the original six Member States, when it came to agreeing the future direction of the Union. The Commission wanted to prevent the extension of these flexible solutions to the long queue of membership *demandeurs*—thus limiting potential confusion, as well as the possibility that past deals, often difficult to reach, would be reopened.

The insistence on accepting the entire *acquis*, with no opt-outs, applied even to the neutral EFTAns: Austria, Finland, and Sweden. These countries would have little difficulty implementing the *acquis* in most areas, except for the Maastricht provisions on the common foreign and security policy (CFSP). The Commission, though, was clear. Applicants had to accept the common foreign and security policy, including the development of a common defence policy: '[a]n applicant country whose constitutional status, or stance in international affairs, renders it unable to pursue the project on which the other members are embarked could not be satisfactorily integrated into the Union'.[19]

In setting out these conditions, the Commission was trying to protect the Union: '[t]he impact of future enlargement on the capacity of the community

---

[16] European Commission, 'Europe and the Challenge of Enlargement', *EC Bulletin Supplement* 3/92, at 9.

[17] Two examples: Britain and Denmark opted out of the third stage of Economic and Monetary Union, and Britain would not agree to the Social Chapter.

[18] Taylor, *supra* note 2, at 104.

[19] European Commission, 'Europe and the Challenge of Enlargement', *supra* note 16, at 11. This even though (non-neutral) Denmark was granted an opt-out from the common defence policy in the Maastricht Treaty. The neutral applicant states could take comfort in the Maastricht Treaty's wording that the Union's common defence policy 'shall not prejudice the specific character of the security and defence policy of certain Member States' (Art. J.4(4)).

to take decisions merits the most careful reflection and evaluation. Non-members apply to join because the Community is attractive; the Community is attractive because it is seen to be effective; to proceed to enlargement in a way which reduces its effectiveness would be an error'.[20] The Commission argued forcefully that 'widening must not be at the expense of deepening. Enlargement must not be a dilution of the Community's achievements'.[21]

The decision to open negotiations with the EFTAn applicants was a relatively easy one to take: they had few difficulties complying with the conditions, and the EFTAn enlargement would pose relatively few problems for EU policies and institutions. Three EFTAns thus joined the EU on 1 January 1995. Enlarging further, however, was another matter.

In June 1993, the Copenhagen European Council opened the way for enlargement to Central and Eastern Europe and endorsed the Commission's stance on membership conditions. The decision to enlarge was a controversial one, as the Member States were divided over whether to prioritize widening or deepening. The spread of violence and instability in Eastern Europe (especially in the former Yugoslavia and the former Soviet Union) strengthened the arguments for widening. But imposing membership conditions reassured Member States that deepening would not be endangered. The Copenhagen European Council declared that the associated countries from Central and Eastern Europe could join the EU, but that candidate countries must meet the famous Copenhagen conditions. Candidate countries must have achieved:

- a functioning market economy with the capacity to cope with competitive pressures and market forces within the EU;
- stability of institutions guaranteeing democracy, the rule of law, human rights, and respect for and protection of minorities; and
- the ability to take on the obligations of EU membership including adherence to the aims of economic and political union.

Crucially, the European Council also declared: 'The Union's capacity to absorb new members, while maintaining the momentum of European integration, is also an important consideration in the general interest of both the Union and the candidate countries'.[22] In other words, the EU must be able to absorb new members and maintain the momentum of integration. Hence the 1996–1997 intergovernmental conference was to revise the treaties to this end. The resulting Amsterdam Treaty was a disappointment, as the December 1997 Luxembourg European Council in fact recognized: 'as a

---

[20] Ibid., at 14.

[21] Ibid., at 10.

[22] Conclusions of the Presidency, European Council in Copenhagen, 21–22 June 1993, SN 180/93, 13.

prerequisite for enlargement of the Union, the operation of the institutions must be strengthened and improved in keeping with the institutional provisions of the Amsterdam Treaty'.[23] The Amsterdam 'leftovers' had to be addressed at yet another intergovernmental conference, resulting in the still disappointing Nice Treaty. The Member States are to embark on yet another round of intergovernmental negotiations in 2004. Thus, the EU's ability to absorb new Member States has been continuously debated, but not satisfactorily achieved, since the Copenhagen European Council.

In the meantime, the emphasis has rested on the applicant states meeting the conditions, which are rather vague. The Copenhagen European Council did not prioritize the conditions, although the EU's priorities have since become somewhat clearer. Of the three conditions, democracy is the most fundamental. The political conditions of EU membership were reiterated in the 1999 Amsterdam Treaty, which was the first Treaty update of Article 237 of the Rome Treaty. Article 6 of the Amsterdam Treaty stated: 'the Union is founded on the principles of liberty, democracy, respect for human rights and fundamental freedoms, and the rule of law, principles which are common to the Member States'. Under Article 49, any European state that respects these principles may apply to become a member of the Union. By explicitly giving this condition a Treaty basis, the EU Member States have signalled its fundamental importance. In addition, the Helsinki European Council in December 1999 made it clear that democracy is *the* prerequisite for beginning negotiations on EU membership (see section three below).

Once the democracy prerequisite has been met, the demand that applicant countries actually implement the *acquis* seems to come a close second in importance. The market economic condition is given less attention. This may be because it is so vague (see below), and because a certain amount of 'slippage' can be absorbed; after all, eastern Germany was incorporated within the EC when market economic conditions (capable of sustaining competition within the single market) arguably did not exist there. This is especially the case because the EU is not promising aid to the new Member States on anything like the scale of transfers from western to eastern Germany. In any event, implementing the *acquis* in practice also requires undertaking market economic reforms: for example, implementing EC competition laws cannot be divorced from the transition to a market economy.

Implementing the *acquis* is crucial for the smooth operation of the Union. And the extent of the *acquis* is one of the most distinguishing features of the Union, which clearly sets it apart from other international organizations. The Member States must trust that each will play by the rules and implement collectively-agreed laws. This is why so much importance has been given to

---

[23] Conclusions of the Presidency, European Council in Luxembourg, 12–13 Dec. 1997, DOC/97/24, 2.

this condition. In May 1995, the Commission published a White Paper on preparing the applicants for integration into the single European market, and argued that the operation of the single market could not be disrupted by enlargement. The White Paper set out the main measures that the applicants should take in each sector, along with a sequence for the approximation of legislation on the single market.[24] The Madrid European Council, in December 1995, also declared that the 'gradual, harmonious integration' of an applicant state requires that it has adjusted its administrative structures.[25] For the Commission, this means that the *acquis* must not only be transposed into national legislation, but, more importantly, that legislation must be implemented effectively through appropriate administrative and judicial structures (*before* accession).[26]

Not only did the Copenhagen European Council resist prioritizing the membership conditions, it also left the content of the conditions quite vague. Elaborating upon them was the European Commission's job. The Commission's first detailed explanation of what the conditions actually meant is provided in 'Agenda 2000' (July 1997), which contained the Commission's opinions on the membership applications of the ten CEECs.[27] The clearest explanation of the conditions thus came at the same time as the justifications for proposing that membership negotiations should or should not be opened with particular candidates.

In assessing the extent to which the candidate countries met the political condition, the Commission examined the formal institutions of democracy (the constitution, political institutions, and so on), and how democracy is practised.[28] Agenda 2000 does not provide a list of detailed criteria, but

[24] European Commission, 'White Paper: Preparation of the Associated Countries of Central and Eastern Europe for Integration into the Internal Market of the Union', COM(95)163 final, Brussels, 3 May 1995.

[25] Presidency Conclusions, European Council in Madrid, 15–16 Dec. 1995, in *EU Bulletin*, no. 12 (1995), 18.

[26] See, e.g., European Commission, 'Enlargement Strategy Paper 2000: Report on progress towards accession by each of the candidate countries', Brussels, 8 Nov. 2000, 21.

[27] European Commission, 'Agenda 2000: For a Stronger and Wider Union', *EU Bulletin Supplement* 5/97.

[28] The Commission did not refer to the membership criteria of the Council of Europe, possibly because all the applicants had already joined it. Membership of the Council of Europe has been considered the basic prerequisite for EU entry, because the Council of Europe also sets democratic conditions for membership. In 1993, the Council of Europe formally set membership conditions (until then implicit): the people's representatives must have been chosen by means of free and fair elections based on universal suffrage; freedom of expression and notably of the media must be guaranteed; rights of national minorities must be protected; and the state must sign the European Convention on Human Rights within a short period: Winkler, 'Democracy and Human Rights in Europe: A Survey of the Admission Practice of the Council of Europe', 47 *Austrian Journal of Public and International Law* 2–3, (1995), at 155.

instead lists a variety of areas where the candidates perform either well or badly, which gives some indication of what the Commission considers a fully functioning democracy to entail.[29] These can be summarized as:

- the constitution must guarantee democratic freedoms, such as political pluralism, the freedom of expression, and the freedom of religion;
- independent judicial and constitutional authorities;
- stability of democratic institutions permitting public authorities (including police forces, local government, and judges) to function properly;
- the holding of free and fair elections, and the recognition of the role of opposition;
- respect for fundamental rights as expressed in the Council of Europe's Convention for the Protection of Human Rights and Fundamental Freedoms (including acceptance of the protocol allowing citizens to take cases to the European Court of Human Rights); and
- respect for minorities, which includes adoption of the Council of Europe's Framework Convention for the Protection of National Minorities, and Recommendation 1201 of the Council of Europe's Parliamentary Assembly.

The Commission made few references to international standards, other than Council of Europe conventions on human rights. Democracy has not been defined in international conventions, but work has been done on this in the European context.[30] The Copenhagen document on the human dimension, agreed by the Conference on Security and Cooperation in Europe in June 1990, contains a list of democratic principles.[31] Agenda 2000, however, does not refer to it, even though it was agreed by all of the applicant (and EU member) states. The EU's judgements on democracy in the applicant countries could be better justified if it relied more widely on such European precedents. This may not be an issue with respect to the CEECs, but could become one with respect to Turkey and other future applicant states.

The Commission's definition of the economic criteria is even vaguer. Agenda 2000 lists several detailed conditions which determine the existence of a functioning market economy, and the capacity to withstand competitive pressure and market forces within the Union.[32] The requirements for a functioning market economy include:

[29] 'Agenda 2000', *supra* note 27, at 40–41.
[30] Theorists also differ over definitions of democracy. See Fox and Roth, 'Democracy and International Law', 27 *Review of International Studies*, 3 (2001), at 341.
[31] Supplementary Document to the Charter of Paris for a New Europe, Conference on Security and Cooperation in Europe, reprinted in *EC Bulletin*, no. 11 (1990), 137.
[32] 'Agenda 2000', *supra* note 27, at 42–43.

- liberalized prices and trade;
- the absence of significant barriers to market entry and exit;
- a legal system which regulates property rights and allows laws and contracts to be enforced;
- macroeconomic stability, including sustainable public finances and external accounts; and
- a well-developed financial sector, allowing savings to be channelled towards productive investment.

The capacity to withstand competitive pressure within the Union requires:

- a functioning market economy;
- a sufficient amount, at an appropriate cost, of human and physical capital (including infrastructure and education);
- government policy which enhances competition;
- trade integration with the Union; and
- a good proportion of small firms, since a dominance of large firms could indicate a reluctance to adjust to the market.

As the Commission noted, it is more difficult to judge the 'competitive' condition than to identify the existence of a functioning market economy. This, it can be added, leaves considerable room for leeway in determining whether countries meet it.

As for the adoption and implementation of the *acquis*, the Commission can simply note the extent to which the some 85,000 (and growing) pages of Community legislation have been transposed into national laws. Determining whether the *acquis* is being implemented and enforced, however, is even more difficult: the key criterion is having the administrative and judicial capacity to apply it. For the Commission, this means applicants' administrations have to be 'modernized', administrators have to be 'properly trained and remunerated', and judges must be trained in Community law.[33] Given how important the *acquis* condition is, the vagueness of the EU's detailed definition of it causes concern, not least among the applicant countries.

One part of the *acquis* condition that is not discussed in Agenda 2000, or elsewhere for that matter, is adherence to the aims of economic and political union. This is undoubtedly because the current Member States would not agree on what an economic and political union entails, so that it is easy enough for the applicant states to declare their compliance. The inclusion of such a condition in the first place reflected concern that enlargement will impede further integration, but the silence about it probably indicates how difficult it has become to agree on a future direction for the EU.

[33] Ibid., at 46.

Furthermore, neither the Copenhagen European Council conclusions nor Agenda 2000 address the most basic condition for membership, 'European identity'. Yet this has become increasingly controversial. 'European' has not been explicitly defined by the Commission or the Council. Morocco's application could be dismissed in 1987 because it did not meet that condition, but 'where Europe ends' is now considerably more difficult to determine. While much discussion has focused on whether Turkey is a European state, it seems to pass unnoticed that the Republic of Cyprus is even further away, and is closer to the Middle East and north Africa than to most of the EU. Geography has become virtually meaningless in determining eligibility. This will be discussed further in section five.

In addition to the three basic Copenhagen conditions, another condition has since been set: 'good neighbourliness'. Good-neighbourliness implies a willingness to cooperate with neighbours, but also—more concretely—to resolve disputes peacefully, if necessary by referring them to the International Court of Justice (ICJ). Compliance with this condition would guard against the 'importation' of foreign policy problems into the EU with enlargement.

Good neighbourliness has been stressed on a number of occasions. In 1992, the Czech Republic and Slovakia were carefully watched to ensure that their breakup was peaceful: '[i]t was decisive to both parties to ensure that the divorce was carried out in a way which was deemed civilized by the West and which allowed both of the new states to carry over all of the arrangements with the EU'.[34] In 1993, Hungary and Slovakia were successfully pressed to refer a dispute over the Gabcikovo dam to the ICJ.[35] A key objective of the 1994–1995 Pact for Stability was to encourage the Central and East European applicant countries to reach bilateral good-neighbour agreements on borders and the treatment of minorities. In Agenda 2000, the Commission stated that 'before accession, applicants should make every effort to resolve any outstanding border dispute among themselves or involving third countries. Failing this they should agree that the dispute be referred to the International Court of Justice'.[36] The Helsinki European Council reiterated this condition: applicants had to resolve outstanding border disputes before accession or refer them to the ICJ.[37]

---

[34] Waever, 'The EU as a Security Actor: Reflections from a Pessimistic Constructivist on Post-sovereign Security Orders', in M. Kelstrup and M. C. Williams (eds), *International Relations Theory and the Politics of European Integration: Power, Security and Community* (2000), at 261.

[35] See G. Munuera, *Preventing Armed Conflict in Europe: Lessons from Recent Experience*, Chaillot Paper no. 15/16 (1994), at 8–11.

[36] 'Agenda 2000', *supra* note 27, at 51.

[37] Presidency Conclusions, Helsinki European Council, 10–11 Dec. 1999, para. 4. This condition was aimed at Turkey in the first instance, but builds on previous declarations *vis-à-vis* the other applicants.

The four formal membership conditions—democracy and protection of human and minority rights; a functioning market economy; implementation of the *acquis*; and good neighbourliness—add up to a considerable list of membership requirements, which are far more exacting than those of other European organizations such as the Council of Europe and NATO, and certainly reflects the unique nature of the EU.

One question to consider is whether the candidate countries consider the EU's membership conditions to be acceptable in and of themselves. Several observers have noted that the CEECs have been virtually unable to voice objections to the conditions, and that 'applicant state preferences have been consistently marginalized'.[38] This is a case of the EU *imposing* its preferences on the applicant states, which means that non-compliance in practice becomes one way for the CEECs to indicate their objections, and that public opinion in the CEECs may not be easily persuaded of the v   of compliance with the conditions. This is also a problem of owne   uropean laws are largely "imposed" from outside with little regard   habits, tradition, preferences and resources, both human and materia   ean laws and standards are formally adopted, but in practice they are   er ignored or implemented in an opaque manner'.[39] Of course, the   have chosen to apply for EU membership: they are the *demanu* naturally the EU is imposing its preferences. But the application of me   ship conditionality illustrates in itself a preference for deepening over the imperatives of a wider, more inclusive EU, and criticism of this basic choice is implicit in the comments above.

Empirical research has, however, shown that candidate countries accept the validity of the EU's membership conditions. Ania Krok-Paszkowska and Jan Zielonka interviewed the heads of delegations to the EU from the current applicant countries and 'aspirant' applicants (such as Albania, Croatia, and Ukraine) about their perceptions of EU enlargement, including membership conditionality.[40] Krok-Paszkowska and Zielonka found that, '[w]ith only a few qualifications, they [the elites] basically agreed with the principle and logic of the EU's policy of conditionality vis-à-vis the candidate states'.[41] What they are worried about is the subjective nature of the economic (especially the capacity to withstand competitive pressure) and *acquis* conditions, which cannot be measured objectively.[42] Furthermore, the elites noted

[38] Checkel, 'Compliance and Conditionality', ARENA Working Paper WP 00/19 (2000), at 7.

[39] Zielonka, 'How New Enlarged Borders Will Reshape the European Union', 39 *Journal of Common Market Studies* (2001) 513.

[40] A. Krok-Paszkowska and J. Zielonka, *The EU's Next Big Enlargement: Empirical Data on the Candidates' Perceptions*, RSC Working Paper no. 2000/54 (2000).

[41] Ibid., at 2.

[42] Ibid., at 5.

that the EU Member States themselves are not perfect when it comes to implementing fully the *acquis*.[43] The Commission has to take Member States to the European Court of Justice to enforce Community law, even in the crucial area of the single market, and 'name and shame' those that have not transposed EC law into national law on time.

Another area of double standards can be identified: the Amsterdam Treaty provisions on EU membership do not include respect for the rights of minorities; the Copenhagen membership conditions, however, do.[44] Minority rights are controversial within the EU, as the Member States are divided over the concept. France, for example, is more inclined to emphasize individual rights and has not ratified the Council of Europe's Framework Convention on National Minorities (nor have Belgium, Greece, Luxembourg, the Netherlands or Portugal).[45] The EU is thus insisting that applicant states, but not current Member States, protect minority rights, although admittedly the minority-protection regime within the EU is gradually strengthening.[46] The Copenhagen conditions reflect the view that protection of minority rights will help prevent ethnic conflict; and the EU certainly wants to avoid 'importing' ethnic conflict when it enlarges. But imposing different standards on applicant countries from current Member States does not provide the EU with a great deal of legitimacy, and could store up problems for the enlarged EU. Double standards could fuel resentment on the part of applicant states, which is not the best way to ensure that the collectivity functions well after enlargement. Reciprocity and mutual trust between the new and old Member States—the grease of the integration process—could be that much more difficult to build, if the applicant states feel the conditions were unfair.

Beyond the perceptions of the basic fairness of the EU's membership conditions, it is also important that the EU is perceived to be applying membership conditionality fairly. If conditionality is applied inconsistently, it can lose force: applicant countries will question why they have been targeted as non-compliant, while others have not, and will suspect that there are more important considerations behind EU decisions on enlargement, such as geopolitical stability or friendships between applicant states

[43] Ibid., at 6.

[44] See G. Amato and J. Batt, *Minority Rights and EU Enlargement*, Report of the First Meeting of the Reflection Group on the Long-Term Implications of EU Enlargement: The Nature of the New Border, RSC Policy Paper no. 98/5 (1998).

[45] Council of Europe, Signatures and ratifications of the Framework Convention for the Protection of National Minorities, Status as at 3 Sept. 2001, http://conventions.coe.int/Treaty/EN.

[46] e.g., under the Amsterdam Treaty, the EU can combat discrimination based on racial or ethnic origin (Art. 13). See de Witte, 'Politics versus Law in the EU's Approach to Ethnic Minorities', in J. Zielonta (ed.), *supra.* note 4.

and EU Member States. Again, there are worrying implications for the EU post-enlargement: treating future Member States differently could create resentment, which is then carried into an enlarged EU.

3. THE APPLICATION OF MEMBERSHIP CONDITIONALITY *VIS-À-VIS* THE CEECS

The membership conditions are not the EU's first use of conditionality with respect to the Central and East European countries. From 1988, the Community hoped to encourage its eastern neighbours to carry out political and economic reforms by making trade and cooperation agreements, aid, and association ('Europe') agreements, conditional on satisfying certain criteria, including democracy, the rule of law, human rights, and respect for and protection of minorities. The Community considered reforms to be necessary to ensure stability and security in Europe, a traditional liberal internationalist view (and one that reflects the West European experience), and it was willing to use both carrots and sticks to achieve these goals. Hence the conclusion of agreements and provision of PHARE aid to Bulgaria and Romania were delayed, whereas the Community moved rapidly to conclude agreements and provide aid to the fastest reformers, such as Poland and Hungary.

The use of conditionality was largely a security strategy, and certainly an indication of the Community's assertiveness in trying to shape post-Cold War Europe. The use of conditionality to influence domestic and foreign policies of the CEECs continued after Copenhagen, and arguably the promise of membership increased the EU's influence: the tastiest 'carrot' was finally on offer.

The Copenhagen conditions were specified for those countries that had concluded (or were in the process of concluding) Europe (association) agreements with the Community, which at the time meant six countries: Hungary, Poland, Bulgaria, Romania, the Czech Republic, and Slovakia. In December 1994, the Essen European Council affirmed that Europe agreements would be concluded with the three Baltic republics and Slovenia, because they met the requisite conditions.[47] Thus, four new countries joined the potential membership queue. The decision is surprising because it follows so closely the difficult decision to enlarge at Copenhagen, and entailed little discussion of the implications of expanding the list of potential applicants. How many other European countries could also join the membership queue?

[47] Conclusions of the Presidency, European Council in Essen, 9–10 Dec. 1994, in *EU Bulletin*, no. 12 (1994), point I.13. This is further compounded by the June 1994 decision of the Corfu European Council to include Malta and Cyprus in the next round of enlargement.

Expanding the queue means that the EU can exercise influence over a greater number of countries, but, as discussed in section five, this is becoming an increasingly difficult strategy to pursue.

In the run-up to the publication of the Commission's opinions on the membership applications, the EU used membership conditionality to influence the domestic and foreign policies of the applicant countries. This went beyond merely encouraging them to implement the *acquis* or to pursue market economic reforms: the EU criticized domestic political processes and outcomes, and foreign policy choices, and expressed strong preferences for particular changes. The EU's demands were not, though, always met with full compliance.

The prospect (though never explicitly articulated by the EU) of being excluded from EU membership negotiations helped convince the CEECs to overcome their reluctance and participate in the EU's Pact for Stability.[48] The Pact for Stability was one of the first CFSP joint actions.[49] The EU coordinated a multilateral framework, between May 1994 and March 1995, within which the CEECs were encouraged to conclude agreements with each other on borders and the treatment of minorities, as well as to use regional round tables to agree cross-border cooperation projects. Considerable pressure was put on Hungary and Slovakia, and on Hungary and Romania, to conclude good-neighbourly agreements: the EU presidency, and sometimes the troika, made several visits to promote negotiations. While Hungary and Slovakia did reach an agreement just before the final Pact conference, Hungary and Romania did not do so until a year later. There was domestic opposition in all three countries to these agreements, but the governments still concluded them.[50]

The EU also intervened to criticize domestic politics in the CEECs, and call for reforms, with varying degrees of success. For example, the EU contributed greatly—alongside others such as the OSCE's High Commissioner for National Minorities—to the protection of human and minority (ethnic Russian) rights in the Baltic states, through its use of membership conditionality.[51] During the period of the Meciar government in Slovakia, the EU delivered *démarches* and issued numerous warnings that Slovakia

---

[48] The Pact for Stability was initially an initiative of the French prime minister, Edouard Balladur. The French proposal, put forward in June 1993, did suggest that EU membership would be offered only to those states that had settled problems liable to threaten European stability. 'French Proposal for a Pact on Stability in Europe (Copenhagen, 22 June 1993)', statement translated by the Press Department of the French Embassy in London. EU Council decisions, however, do not make the same explicit link.

[49] Council Decision 93/728/CFSP, 20 Dec. 1993 in OJ 1993 L 339/1.

[50] *Agence Europe*, 22 Mar. 1995; 'Hungary Calls on Romania to Compromise in Talks', *Reuter*, 20 June 1995.

[51] See N. Gelazis, *The Effects of EU Conditionality on Citizenship Policies and Protection of National Minorities in the Baltic States*, RSC Working Paper no. 2000/68 (2000).

must meet democratic norms before it could join the EU.[52] Yet the Meciar government did not alter its behaviour in response and remained in power until 1998, when Slovaks elected a pro-western coalition government. When, in 1994 and 1995, Romania appeared to be heading towards more nationalist and racist politics, the EU indicated bluntly and repeatedly that these would not help Romania's application for membership.[53] From mid-1995, the Romanian government changed course, and broke with extremist parties; a reformist government was elected in November 1996.

Obviously, then, the pressure on the CEECs before the Commission issued its opinions on the membership applications in July 1997 was quite high. But it was also increasingly apparent that other considerations would play a role in enlargement decisions. There was debate within the EU over how many countries should join initially: should the EU go for a more easily manageable first enlargement, and only let in a few (two or three) CEECs? Or should it go for the big-bang approach, and let in as many as feasible, thus prioritizing enlargement (and the vision of a peaceful and stable Europe) over the deepening of integration among only some of Europe's states?[54]

One of the concerns that lay behind these debates was the impact of leaving countries out of the first round of enlargement. The Commission had to decide the merits of each application, judging each candidate separately, and the Council would then decide to open negotiations accordingly. Here the application of membership conditionality—part of, after all, a strategy to spread peace and security—could actually end up destabilizing applicant countries. If there were no membership conditions, enlargement would be wholly an inclusive process, but this was obviously not feasible. With membership conditions, inevitably some applicants will meet them before others. Differentiating between applicant countries means excluding some, at least initially. In principle, this should spur progress with reforms, if applicants are confident of the objective application of membership conditionality.

But differentiation has potentially large implications for relations between the CEECs before enlargement, and for those countries left out of the first round(s) of enlargement. Those countries first admitted will enjoy the economic and political advantages associated with EU membership, notably participation in the common agricultural policy (CAP) and structural funds.

---

[52] Public *démarches* were presented to the Slovak government on 23 Nov. 1994 and 25 Oct. 1995. Fisher, 'Turning Back?', *Transition*, 30 Jan. 1995, at 62; P. Javurek, 'US, EU Formally Express Disquiet on Slovak Turmoil', *Reuter*, 25 Oct. 1995.

[53] 'Getting Nastier', *The Economist*, 4 Feb. 1995; 'Paris, Bonn Remind Romania of EU Entry Conditions', *Reuter*, 18 July 1995.

[54] See the discussion on the options available in Danish Institute of International Affairs, *European Stability: EU's Enlargement with the Central and East European Countries*, report for the Danish Parliament (1997).

Even though these policies will be reformed prior to the first round of enlargement, and even though additional aid has been granted to the CEECs in
the run-up to their accession to the EU, the new Member States will receive
more aid than the states left outside. The new Member States will also benefit
from inclusion in the single European market (and consequent increased
attractiveness as a destination for foreign direct investment), while the outsiders will still be subject to the possible use of contingent protection (anti-
dumping and safeguard measures) and rules of origin regarding trade with
the Union. Economic disparities could widen between the two groups of
states.[55]

Political relations between the newly enlarged EU and those states left out
could become more difficult. For example, controls at the borders between
the new Member States and non-Member States must be strengthened,
because the new Member States will need to adhere to EU immigration
standards. Relations between Central and Eastern European countries have
been strained over issues such as the treatment of minorities (as in Hungary
and Slovakia, or Hungary and Romania); differentiation could contribute to
those tensions. Furthermore, the effects of exclusion from the EU could be
exacerbated by exclusion from NATO, a problem particularly for those
countries not (yet) in the EU's official membership queue (such as the
South-East European states, or Ukraine).

Thus applying membership conditionality could be destabilizing, as it isolates
and excludes (for a time) some states. This is especially risky because some
applicants are located in dangerous areas of Europe (the Balkans), or along the
Russian border (the Baltic republics). Alienation from the EU could consequently reduce the EU's leverage on these countries, in terms of pressure to
proceed quickly with painful or controversial reforms. We have seen, in the case of
Turkey, how difficult it is for the EU to exercise influence when membership
prospects appear distant or, more worryingly, slight or non-existent.

The EU has tried to lessen the negative implications of differentiation in
three successive ways: by taking a multilateral approach to relations with the
CEECs and their neighbours; by establishing an inclusive 'accession process';
and by opening negotiations with all of them.

First, the EU tried to balance its largely bilateral approach to relations with
the CEECs with a multilateral one.[56] After the Copenhagen European
Council, the EU set up a 'structured relationship', which was to help
integrate the CEECs into the EU. This included regular meetings between
the Council and all of the associates on EU matters, within all three pillars,

---

[55] See S. Senior Nello and K. E. Smith, *The European Union and Central and Eastern
Europe: The Implications of Enlargement in Stages* (1998), at 33–55.
[56] Several observers had criticized the bilateral approach. Richard Baldwin argued that the
Europe agreements had set up a 'hub-and-spoke' bilateralism, which hindered East-East trade:
R.E. Baldwin, *Towards an Integrated Europe* (1994), especially at 129–136.

the Community, the CFSP, and Justice and Home Affairs. The CEECs have objected to the multilateral approach; it seemed to signal that they were all being treated similarly, and that the Union was not differentiating between slower and faster reformers. Those countries that considered themselves to be at the head of the membership queue were particularly unhappy that their membership prospects could be held back because they were being grouped with slow-pokes. One observer, Péter Balázs, charged that the Union was 'homogenizing' its relations with the Central and East European countries.[57] But the multilateral approach gave way to bilateral relations with the replacement of the structured relationship by the accession process (see below).

The EU also tried to encourage regional cooperation, among the applicants and further afield. Aid has been given to regional cooperation initiatives such as the Central European Initiative, the Council of Baltic Sea States, and Black Sea Economic Cooperation. The Pact for Stability also created regional round-tables, which were to agree on projects furthering regional cooperation. Differentiation would be balanced by greater cooperation across Europe, including between an enlarged EU and outsiders. This has the best potential of reducing the inclusion–exclusion problem, but the strategy has not been terribly successful in reducing the centrality of the EU and bilateral relations between it and Central and East European countries.

The other two ways of lessening the impact of differentiation are in practice just ways of postponing it, because they merely deal with the impact of exclusion from membership *negotiations*, not from membership itself. The second way the EU has tried to lessen the effects of differentiation is by designing an inclusive 'accession process'. This was launched at the same time as the decisions were made in 1997 to differentiate between two groups of applicant countries, and begin membership negotiations with only one of them.

In July 1997, the European Commission published its opinions on the applications (in Agenda 2000). The Commission evaluated each application on the basis of reports from the applicants, information from the Member States, European Parliament reports, and the work of other international organizations (such as the Council of Europe) and non-governmental organizations (NGOs). The Commission recommended that membership negotiations be opened with five countries (the so-called 'ins'): the Czech Republic, Estonia, Hungary, Poland, and Slovenia (in addition to Cyprus). Although no candidate country met all of the membership conditions, these five states came closest to doing so. The other five countries (so-called 'pre-ins') did not, and of these Slovakia was singled out as the only country which did not meet the political condition.

[57] P. Balázs, *The EU's Collective Regional Approach to its Eastern Enlargement: Consequences and Risks*, CORE Working Paper 1/1997 (1997), at 11–21.

The Commission's recommendation was not universally welcomed within the EU—several Member States, including Italy, Denmark, and Sweden, and some MEPs argued that talks should be opened with all ten applicant countries, to avoid the destabilizing effects of excluding some of them.[58] These sorts of arguments—for an alternative model of lessening the effects of differentiation—swept aside much earlier arguments for limiting the first intake even further, to fewer than five states. The decision to include Estonia and Slovenia, in addition to the three countries traditionally considered the frontrunners (the Czech Republic, Hungary, and Poland) was undoubtedly influenced by NATO's June 1997 decision to expand to only three countries in the first instance, the Czech Republic, Hungary, and Poland. In the interests of geopolitical stability, the first round of EU enlargement would have to be more inclusive.

In December 1997, the Luxembourg European Council agreed with the Commission's recommendation, and in March 1998 membership negotiations formally began with the Czech Republic, Estonia, Hungary, Poland, and Slovenia (as well as Cyprus).[59] Several pre-ins, most notably Romania but also Lithuania and Latvia, expressed considerable dismay at the decision to exclude them from the first round of talks.

To lessen the negative implications of differentiation, the Luxembourg European Council also approved an 'accession process' for all applicant countries. This was to ensure above all that the excluded applicant states still perceived EU membership as a real possibility. 'Accession Partnerships' were concluded with all the candidate countries; these are detailed agreements setting out a multi-annual programme for adopting EU legislation and meeting the Copenhagen conditions. They are updated annually. Additional EU aid is promised, but is conditional on meeting the objectives set out in the Accession Partnership. In response, the candidate countries have adopted national programmes for meeting the conditions and adopting the *acquis*.

The priorities and objectives in the Accession Partnerships are sometimes quite vague, and sometimes astonishingly detailed. A sample of the short-term and medium-term objectives in Romania's 2000 Accession Partnership is given here.[60] In the short term (2000), Romania is to:

- guarantee adequate budgetary provisions for the support of children in care, and undertake a full reform of the child-care system;
- restore macroeconomic stability, particularly by implementing structural reform;

[58] J. McEvoy, 'Differences Burst into Open on EU Enlargement', *Reuter*, 22 July 1997; S. Helm, 'EC Holds Hand Out as States Make Grade', *The Independent*, 17 July 1997.

[59] Presidency Conclusions, Luxembourg European Council, 12–13 Dec. 1997, at 2.

[60] European Commission, 'Accession Partnership 1999: Romania', http://www.europa.eu.int/comm/enlargement/dwn/ap_02_00/en/ap_ro_99.pdf.

- ensure the functioning of a land market;
- implement single-market legislation in areas such as public procurement, intellectual and industrial property rights, chemicals and foodstuffs, and VAT;
- prepare a national employment strategy;
- enforce the Environmental Impact Assessment directive;
- strengthen border controls; and
- adopt a new penal code.

In the medium term, Romania is to:

- improve the social and economic conditions of the Roma;
- complete the privatization process;
- adopt new legislation on pharmaceuticals;
- develop the capacity to implement and enforce the common fisheries policy;
- strengthen regulatory structures for nuclear safety;
- develop a national policy on social and economic cohesion;
- align visa legislation and practice with that of the EU; and
- ensure training of prosecutors, judges, and lawyers in EU law.

Overall, the Accession Partnerships illustrate the extent to which the EU is seeking to influence the domestic and foreign affairs of membership candidates. It should be noted that the Commission has found reason to criticize all of the applicant countries for not fully implementing the obligations in the Accession Partnerships.[61] Given how vague some of the Accession Partnership objectives are, this is hardly surprising. It illustrates how difficult it is, or will be, to prove that membership conditionality is being applied fairly and objectively.

In addition to the Accession Partnerships, the EU made it clear that the decision on starting membership negotiations could be amended prior to the first stage of enlargement, if other countries are considered ready for membership. In other words, the pre-ins can join the ins if they make adequate progress towards meeting the conditions, as listed in the Accession Partnerships in particular.

This second way of lessening the effects of differentiation—an inclusive accession process—started to unravel because, paradoxically, it actually worked faster than the EU anticipated. The carrot of inclusion in the first round motivated several pre-ins—Latvia, Lithuania, and Slovakia (the Slovaks having elected a democratic government)—to make fast progress in fulfilling the terms of the Accession Partnerships. Already at the start of 1999,

---

[61] See, e.g., a progress report on Hungary, one of the 'frontrunners': European Commission, 'Regular Report from the Commission on Hungary's Progress towards Accession', COM(1998)700 final, 17 Dec. 1998, at 48–51.

it was generally anticipated that Latvia, Lithuania, and Slovakia would be invited to commence membership negotiations. Including them, however, would have left Bulgaria and Romania as the only pre-ins.

While the accession process might otherwise have been expected to lessen the negative implications of leaving only two countries out, geopolitical considerations soon made this an unpalatable option. The Kosovo crisis in the first half of 1999 and the ensuing instability throughout the Balkans led to a consensus within the EU that Bulgaria and Romania should not be further isolated. In addition, both had steadfastly supported the NATO action against Serbia; some 'reward' seemed justified, and certainly the blow of exclusion from EU membership negotiations had to be muffled. Isolating and potentially antagonizing them could further destabilize an already unstable region, and would certainly not help to stabilize it.

In October 1999, the Commission recommended that negotiations be opened with all five CEEC pre-ins (in addition to Malta). The primary justification for the Commission's recommendation was that these five countries by and large met the *political* criteria for membership, although Bulgaria and Romania did not meet the other conditions.[62] This further established the principle that the political criteria are the most important: membership negotiations can take place only with democracies. It was also a convenient way of handling the Turkish application: Turkey was excluded from negotiations because it did not yet meet the political conditions (see below).

The Helsinki European Council, of 10–11 December 1999, approved the Commission's recommendations, and in February 2000, membership negotiations started with the five remaining CEEC applicants. This was the third way of coping with the problems of differentiation: postpone it further by taking an all-encompassing approach to the opening of negotiations. All applicants could be included, with the exception of Turkey (a separate 'problem').

In June 2001, the Göteberg European Council stated that the frontrunners could join the EU in time for the 2004 European Parliament elections. The issue was then one of how many frontrunners there might be.

By choosing to open negotiations with all of the CEECs, the EU has only deferred the problem of differentiation. The negotiations were supposed to

---

[62] Bulgaria and Romania were given additional specific conditions to be met before the Helsinki European Council. Bulgaria had to decide on acceptable closure dates for a nuclear power plant and show evidence of making progress on economic reforms. Romania had to reform its child-care institutions and show evidence of making progress on economic reforms. Both countries were judged to have met these conditions sufficiently by December 1999. But, as the Accession Partnership shows, child care is still a problem in Romania, indicating how willing the EU was to ignore lapses in favour of an inclusive negotiation process.

be differentiated—so that as soon as a country has met all of the conditions, the negotiations will be concluded. This still means differentiation—but exclusion from membership, not membership negotiations—and all this implies for outsiders. What is instead obvious is that the process of concluding negotiations will not, and cannot, be so clear-cut as to guarantee that only those applicant countries that fully meet the conditions will join. Numerous other considerations jostle with the strict application of membership conditionality.

For a start, it was virtually inconceivable that the first round of enlargement would exclude Poland, regardless of how far Poland was behind the other frontrunners. Reconciliation between Germany and Poland is so symbolic, so central to the entire rationale for the enlargement process, that leaving Poland out is almost as unimaginable as trying to halt German unification back in 1990. But there were concerns about its readiness. Would the application of conditionality be 'fudged' in its case? Or would the others have to wait for Poland to catch up? Both were rather unpalatable alternatives, though both have their advantages as well, as they signal the priority of reconciliation. Considerable pressure was placed on Poland to meet the conditions.

Furthermore, differentiation implied that countries will accede one by one, as each concluded negotiations. This is extremely impractical. For example, the threshold for a qualified majority would have to be constantly recalculated, and the distribution and redistribution of seats within the European Parliament would become quite complex once the limit of 732 MEPs had been exceeded. Accession of groups of countries seems more practical, but how large should the groups be? If they are too large, then the implications for the EU's budget, policies, decision-making procedures, and institutions are that much greater. Yet one way of eliminating (or severely reducing) the problem of differentiation would be to enlarge to a very large group of applicants. Enlargement Commissioner Günter Verheugen stated in September 2001 that ten countries could join in the next round of enlargement: all of the applicants except for Bulgaria, Romania, and Turkey.[63] This option soon gathered considerable momentum, such that by 2002 it was widely perceived to be a certainty. This made it all the more difficult for the EU to take any other decision and dash the expectations raised. The Seville European Council in June 2002, for example, declared its determination to conclude accession negotiations with ten candidate countries (all but Bulgaria, Romania, and Turkey).[64] The December 2002 Copenhagen European Council then did so. This naturally raised serious concerns about how the EU would cope

---

[63] *European Voice*, 6–12 Sept. 2001.
[64] Conclusions of the European Council, Seville, 21–22 June 2002: 6.

with such a large enlargement, but it also signalled that the imperatives of widening outweighed those of deepening.

What this all means, in the end, is that decisions to conclude accession negotiations with particular countries are not based solely on fulfilment of the conditions. Politics will intervene, which will undoubtedly make the decisions even more controversial. There is thus plenty of leeway to fudge the application of conditionality. But doubts about the objective application of conditionality could end up undermining the potential effectiveness of it—particularly in those (few) countries left out of the first round of enlargement, and in countries that have not yet applied. Furthermore, if the conditions are supposed to protect the EU's achievements and the integration process in general, then fudging them in practice presumably has serious implications for the way the EU will operate in the future.

4. THE APPLICATION OF MEMBERSHIP CONDITIONALITY *VIS-À-VIS* MEDITERRANEAN STATES

The Copenhagen conditions were stipulated for the CEECs, although they have since become the standard conditions for all applicants, including those from the Mediterranean. The case of Malta will not be dealt with here, as there are relatively few problems with its membership bid (except domestically, within Malta); it by and large meets the political and economic conditions, and it is making progress in implementing the *acquis*.[65] The use of membership conditionality with respect to the other two Mediterranean applicant countries, however, is far from uncontroversial.

The Republic of Cyprus applied for membership in 1990. The island of Cyprus is divided: most Greek Cypriots live in the south, and most Turkish Cypriots in the north. The Republic of Cyprus is the only internationally recognized government on the island, but it effectively controls only the southern part of the island. Turkish troops are present in the north, in the 'Turkish Republic of Northern Cyprus' (an entity recognized only by Turkey). Since the 1970s, the UN and others have tried to resolve the situation, to no avail.

In June 1993, the Commission's opinion on the application was largely positive: not only did the Republic of Cyprus meet the necessary political and economic criteria, but the Commission was also convinced that Cyprus's accession would 'increase security and prosperity' and help 'bring the two communities closer together'. It stated that 'Cyprus' integration with the Community implies a peaceful, balanced and lasting settlement of the

---

[65] See European Commission, 'Enlargement Strategy Paper 2000: Report on Progress Towards Accession by Each of the Candidate Countries', Brussels, 8 Nov. 2000, at 48–50.

Cyprus question'. The Commission felt that a positive signal should be sent that Cyprus is eligible 'and that as soon as the prospect of a settlement is surer, the Community is ready to start the process with Cyprus that should eventually lead to its accession'.[66] In June 1994, the Corfu European Council agreed that Cyprus should be involved in the next enlargement. A year later, the Cannes European Council declared that negotiations with Cyprus should be opened six months after the conclusion of the 1996 intergovernmental conference. Formal membership talks with Cyprus opened in March 1998. The prospect of a settlement, however, seemed no surer than it had been in 1993.

The Union has repeatedly stated that it supports a just and lasting settlement of the Cyprus question, and that the prospect of accession will provide an incentive for this. But it has not stated that accession will be blocked should no settlement be reached, and it has continued to negotiate with the Republic of Cyprus although no representatives of the Turkish Cypriot community are included in the delegation (the Republic of Cyprus is effectively negotiating the entry of the entire island). The Helsinki European Council stated that 'a political settlement will facilitate the accession of Cyprus to the European Union'. But 'if no settlement has been reached by the completion of accession negotiations, the Council's decision on accession will be made without [this] being a precondition'.[67] And so it was: the December 2002 European Council concluded the negotiations in the absence of a settlement.

Conditionality has not been applied consistently with respect to the Republic of Cyprus, as good neighbourliness has been ignored. The EU seems to be hoping that the carrot will be enough to spark a solution. The EU has declined to use its leverage openly and explicitly, never threatening to use the stick with respect to the Republic of Cyprus. The Greek position has by and large prevented the Union from doing so, although the other Member States also appear to be reluctant. Instead, the EU has put pressure on Turkey: the Helsinki European Council's declaration on good neighbourliness certainly places pressure on Turkey to contribute to a resolution of the issue, and the EU has pressed (unsuccessfully) the Turkish Cypriots to agree to join the negotiating delegation.[68] How successful this approach will be depends also on the state of the EU's relations with Turkey.

There are also reasons to doubt that the other membership conditions are being applied consistently in the case of Cyprus. As Jolanda van Westering has argued, the division of Cyprus is the source of numerous violations of

[66] Cited in G. Avery and F. Cameron, *The Enlargement of the European Union* (1998), at 95–96.

[67] Presidency Conclusions, n. 37 above, para. 9(b).

[68] For an overview of the EU's approach to the Cyprus problem, and a discussion of four possible scenarios for the future, see Nugent, 'EU Enlargement and the "Cyprus Problem" ', 38 *Journal of Common Market Studies* (2000).

fundamental freedoms, relating to the lack of freedom of movement within the country, foreign travel, and emigration: 'there are no stable institutions guaranteeing respect of democratic order and fundamental freedoms in Cyprus'.[69] The Republic of Cyprus is negotiating the accession of the entire island; yet the northern part probably does not meet the economic conditions of EU membership.[70] And a former president of the Republic of Cyprus maintains that if Cyprus joins under conditions as they currently stand, then 'the territory of Cyprus as a whole will belong to the Union but the *acquis* will be applied only in the areas controlled by the Cyprus Government'.[71] This sets up quite a dangerous precedent for the EU. The main point here is that Cyprus was apparently put on a fast track to membership, even though there are serious doubts that it meets all the conditions. Politics have so far prevailed over the objective application of membership conditionality.

This makes the treatment of Turkey appear so glaringly inconsistent. Since the Commission's 1989 negative opinion on Turkey's membership application, the Commission, Council, and European Parliament have persistently raised problems regarding Turkey's human rights and democracy situation, and the European Parliament has used these issues to block (temporarily) aid and the customs union. Yet the Union would not credibly hold out the prospect of membership, thus diminishing the potential of conditionality. Turkey watched the EFTAns and the CEECs jump the membership queue, while various European politicians cited cultural and religious factors for its exclusion, and Greece placed obstacles in the way of closer relations (thus reneging on the verbal promises made before its accession to the Community). Turkey had every reason to suspect that it would never become a member of the club even if it had a fully functioning democracy and exemplary human rights record. This doubt seemed to be confirmed when the December 1997 Luxembourg European Council placed Turkey in its own separate category of applicant state, although it confirmed its eligibility for membership. This prompted it to suspend its relations with the EU. The EU's leverage over Turkey diminished.[72]

Since then, relations have improved somewhat. The Helsinki European Council classified Turkey as an official candidate (entailing inclusion in the pre-accession strategy and conclusion of an Accession Partnership), although it made it clear that membership negotiations would be opened only once the Copenhagen political conditions have been met. Consequently, the EU's influence seems to have increased. It is still not clear how willing Turkey is to

[69] Van Westering, 'Conditionality and EU Membership: The Cases of Turkey and Cyprus', 5 *European Foreign Affairs Review* (2000), at 113.
[70] Ibid., at 111.
[71] Vassiliou, 'Why Enlargement Will Be a "Win-Win" Situation for Cyprus, Greece and Turkey', *European Voice*, 13–19 Sept. 2001.
[72] See D. Barchard, *Turkey and the European Union* (1998).

undertake the necessary reforms (such as outlawing the death penalty). Turkish elites, as Lauren McLaren notes, do not put as much emphasis on key political and foreign policy reforms as the EU does.[73] The extent to which Turkey must undertake political, economic, and even constitutional reform—as well as contribute to a resolution of the Cypriot issue—to meet the EU's membership conditions could spark a backlash and rejection of the EU. But for now, it appears that the EU has gained some influence, by indicating that membership is actually a possibility and suggesting that membership talks could begin as early as 2005, if the political condition is met. This may not persist in the event of Cyprus's accession to the EU, and renewed doubts about the EU's objectivity. The exclusion of Turkey from the allocation of EP seats and Council votes in the Nice Treaty, unlike all of the other applicant states, does not help generate faith in the EU's intentions.

The cases of Turkey and Cyprus illustrate the problems inherent in using conditionality inconsistently, but they also set a worrying precedent for the future use—and effectiveness—of membership conditionality.

5. THE FUTURE OF MEMBERSHIP CONDITIONALITY

Two issues arise with respect to the future use of membership conditionality. First, what leverage does the EU have over states once they accede to the EU? Secondly, can membership conditionality be effective beyond the current applicant states?

Conditional membership is a 'consumable power resource'—once it has been used up, once the applicants have joined the EU, it could be difficult to exercise leverage over them. The carrot has been offered and consumed. Of course, failure to comply with Community law can be sanctioned in the European Court of Justice, but this is a lengthy process—and, crucially, it still relies on Member States' willingness, and ability, to abide by ECJ rulings. As Jan Zielonka notes, 'It took current EU members many decades to arrive at common laws and similar legal practices, and there is no reason to believe that applicant countries with their complex historical backgrounds can achieve a process of genuine legal and administrative approximation within a few short years.'[74] The uniform application of Community law will certainly be difficult to achieve, and enforce, in an enlarged EU, though possibly only in the short or medium term.

How to deal with a country that backtracks on the political conditions is also a concern, given that most of the current applicants are new democracies. This prompted the inclusion of a membership suspension clause in the

---

[73] McLaren, 'Turkey's Eventual Membership of the EU: Turkish Elite Perspectives on the Issue', 38 *Journal of Common Market Studies* (2000), 124–9.

[74] Zielonka, *supra* note 39, at 513.

Amsterdam Treaty. Some of a Member State's membership rights can be suspended if it has seriously and persistently breached principles of liberty, democracy, respect for human rights and fundamental freedoms, and the rule of law. The Nice Treaty provides for a consultation process with a state suspected of violating these principles, before any decision to suspend membership rights is taken.

A rather mixed precedent was set in the case of Austria. In February 2000, 14 Member States imposed diplomatic sanctions against Austria, after the far-right Freedom Party was included in a coalition government. The Amsterdam Treaty provisions were not invoked in the Austria case, but the 14 Member States did signal that domestic political processes are a matter of collective concern, the basic message of those Amsterdam Treaty provisions. While the sanctions were problematic (they were pre-emptive, as no violations of principles had actually taken place, and there were no criteria for lifting them), at least internal EU behaviour came close to matching the demands made on third countries by the EU. The Austria experience, however, also illustrated the difficulties of sanctioning states that are already inside the club: Austria threatened to disrupt EU business including the 2000 intergovernmental conference, and to hold a referendum on relations with the EU, as public opinion massively opposed the sanctions.[75] In June 2000, a compromise was reached. Three 'wise men' were to report on whether Austria was violating human rights; in September, they found that the Austrian government was committed to European values and respected human rights better than some EU Member States, and that the Freedom Party exploited xenophobia, but was working according to the government's commitments. The Fourteen then dropped the sanctions on 12 September.[76] The Austrian affair illustrates how much of a challenge it will be to discipline a current Member State.

This much is also obvious from the experience of the European organization which has more practice sanctioning Member States than any other: the Council of Europe.[77] Article 3 of the Council of Europe statute states that 'every member of the Council of Europe must accept the principles of the rule of law and of the enjoyment of all persons within its jurisdiction of human rights and fundamental freedoms'. Article 8 states that any member which has seriously violated Article 3 may be suspended from its

[75] MacAskill, 'Austria expects end to isolation', *The Guardian*, 26 June 2000.
[76] 'The EU 14 give way to Austria', *The Economist*, 16 Sept. 2000.
[77] Art. 1 of the agreement establishing the European Bank for Reconstruction and Development (EBRD) states that only countries complying with political criteria such as respect for democracy and freedom of speech can receive loans. Yet no country has had its loans suspended because of political concerns, although the EBRD's Board of Directors has found that compliance with Art. 1 was inadequate in a few countries. Activities have been curtailed in Belarus and Tajikistan. See the EBRD *Annual Report* (various years).

rights of representation and requested by the Committee of Ministers to withdraw.

Compliance with membership standards was already a problem during the Cold War in respect of two member states, Greece and Turkey. Both were ruled by military regimes for a period: Greece between 1967 and 1974 and Turkey in the early 1980s. This raised the issue of whether sanctions should be imposed on them, even though they remained important NATO allies. Greece was suspended from the Parliamentary Assembly in 1967; in December 1969, the Committee of Ministers was prepared to request Greece to withdraw from the Council of Europe. But before it could take the decision, Greece decided to withdraw on its own. It did not rejoin until 1974. Turkey was suspended from the Parliamentary Assembly between 1981 and 1984, but not from the Committee of Ministers; Turkey was simply too important an ally to kick out of the Council of Europe.

Since the end of the Cold War, the Council of Europe's membership has expanded rapidly and controversially to countries such as Russia and Croatia.[78] When they were admitted in 1996, neither country fully fulfilled the membership conditions. The Council of Europe member states, however, considered that Russia had to be 'at the table', so that it could be socialized into Western democratic practices. It was also considered foolhardy to exclude Russia at a time when Russia was feeling isolated and alienated over NATO enlargement.[79] Yet Russian compliance with the conditions did not improve after its accession. In May 1998, a parliamentary committee noted that Russia had still not fulfilled several key obligations. In April 2000, the Parliamentary Assembly even suspended the voting rights of the Russian delegation over the violation of human rights in Chechnya. But the Committee of Ministers did not follow suit.[80] Rather than press Russia, the member states chose not to alienate it, at a time when Russia's relations with the West were tense (as a result of the Kosovo war in particular). This experience shows how difficult it can be for the member states of an organization to agree to suspend the membership of a fellow member state. Higher political imperatives tend to get in the way.

[78] See Gelin, 'L'Adhésion de la Russie au Conseil de l'Europe à la Lumière de la Crise Tchétchène', 99 *Revue Générale de Droit International Public* (1995). A similar argument arose in the case of Croatia (membership could allow Croatia's socialization), and once Russia has been allowed in, the case for excluding a country like Croatia became much weaker.

[79] Doyle, 'Council of Europe Accepts Russia, Boosts Yeltsin', *Reuters*, 26 Jan. 1996; 'France Backs Russia to Join Council of Europe', *Reuters*, 25 Jan. 1996.

[80] 'Assembly Suspends Voting Rights of Russian Deputies and Calls on Committee of Ministers to Report Back in June on Possible Suspension', *Agence Europe*, 8 Apr. 2000; 'Assembly Keeps Pressure Up on Russia for Political Settlement to Chechen Conflict', *Agence Europe*, 30 June 2000.

Jeffrey Checkel has argued that compliance with membership conditions cannot be expected with the sole use of conditionality: an approach based on dialogue and interaction is also needed, better to persuade and teach the applicant country or new member state and involve it in the process of accepting and internalizing the new standards of behaviour. He uses the example of the Council of Europe and Ukraine, a new member state, to illustrate the benefits of combining conditionality with an approach based on dialogue: after both pressure and persuasion from the Council of Europe, Ukraine declared the death penalty to be unconstitutional.[81] Such an approach can clearly yield desirable results, but it should be noted that it requires a long-term effort. The socialization of (so many) new Member States may take too long for the EU to continue to function as it does, which is why meeting the conditions assumes so much importance in the EU's case.

The second issue regarding the future of EU membership conditionality is its utility in relations with states not yet even in the membership queue. The EU developed its membership conditionality primarily with respect to the current applicant states. Very little serious consideration has been given to whether the EU should extend beyond the applicants. If Slovenia and Bulgaria can join, then why cannot the remaining Balkan countries also join? And why should the EU not embrace Ukraine, Belarus, and Moldova one day? or even Russia? All of these countries (and more besides) have expressed an interest in joining the EU. The EU's power of attraction provides it with potentially enormous leverage, to demand that countries not yet in the membership queue undertake the necessary reforms in order to meet the conditions. The EU can use this policy instrument to try to effect change, to shape the surrounding environment. And in areas where there is great need for this—South-Eeastern Europe, the Caucasus—the temptation to use the promise of membership to exercise influence is great. An outright refusal to offer eventual membership could even diminish the EU's influence.

In the midst of the Kosovo crisis, in April 1999, the German presidency proposed a Stability Pact for South-Eastern Europe. As an incentive to participate, Germany proposed that the EU hold out the prospect of association *and* make a clear commitment that the countries in the region could eventually accede to the EU. This would be a key incentive to encourage the countries to undertake political and economic reforms and to work on cooperating with each other.[82] The CFSP common position on the Stability Pact, of 17 May 1999, promised that 'the EU will draw the region closer to the perspective of full integration of these countries into its structures . . . with

---

[81] Checkel, *supra* note 38, at 12–16.
[82] German Presidency, 'A Stability Pact for South-Eastern Europe', para. IV.1, 12 Apr. 1999; http://www.bunesregierung.de/english/01/0103/3810/index.html.

a perspective of EU membership on the basis of the Amsterdam Treaty and once the Copenhagen criteria have been met'.[83]

The problem is that the offer of membership to so many more countries begins to appear quite unrealistic. First of all, the prospect of membership for most South-East European countries is so distant—even 20 years—that there is little reward for the politicians of today to try to meet the conditions. Secondly, the offer of additional rounds of enlargement assumes that after the EU has enlarged to the 12 current applicant states (and presumably Turkey at some point), the EU would be capable of enlarging further. But it may never be able to deliver on its promise, either because the EU simply collapses under the weight of so many members and turns into something more akin to the Organization of Security and Cooperation in Europe (if it continues to exist at all), or because a unanimity of Member States in favour of enlargement cannot be reached. The EU may not even be such a desirable organization to join when it has 28 Member States. How long can the EU exploit its power of attraction before it becomes a farce?

But even in the short run, the promise of eventual membership could backfire. If EU membership conditionality is to have some effect on potential applicant states, it will need to be applied consistently now. Which countries join the EU first will be closely watched, not just by the other applicant countries, but by potential applicants as well. If the EU appears to loosen the conditions, then potential applicants will have less incentive to try to meet them. If some countries appear to be excluded for reasons other than the fair application of membership conditionality, then potential applicants will have reason to question the validity of the conditions. Those countries with large Muslim populations, for example Albania and Bosnia-Herzegovina, will watch closely to see how the EU treats Turkey: if the EU is perceived to have an anti-Muslim bias—regardless of whether the country meets the conditions—then the EU will find it difficult to convince them to comply with the conditions.

6. CONCLUSION

The application of membership conditionality can be problematic. There is a need to balance inclusion and exclusion, to counter the negative effects of differentiating among membership candidates on the basis of their fulfilment of the conditions. There is also a need to give consistent signals, to apply conditionality consistently with respect to all applicants, so that none have

---

[83] 'Common Position of 17 May 1999 concerning the launching of the Stability Pact of the EU on south-eastern Europe', Document no. 99/097, *European Foreign Policy Bulletin online*, http://www.ieu.it/EFPB/Welcome.html.

reason to believe that there are other routes to accession. This is particularly difficult when the membership conditions are so vague that they are open to various interpretations, which allows plenty of room for other considerations, such as geopolitical stability, to play a role in enlargement decisions.

But the Copenhagen conditions, however imperfect, are still probably the best way for the EU to handle the continuously growing number of membership *demandeurs*, and as a framework for public debate about it. If the EU is loathe to exclude other European countries forever, then standing by the membership conditions is the best way to determine which of them should join when. Some notion of cultural or (even worse) religious affinity with 'Western Europe' is simply out of place in a Union that prides itself on its diversity, and, indeed, *is* diverse. Indigenous cultural heritages of applicant countries are frequently reduced to providing evidence of some link with 'West European values',[84] which should be discouraged as a matter of principle, not least because of the risk that it fosters a 'clash of civilizations'. If 'culture' figures highly in enlargement decisions, then inclusion in the EU becomes in practice highly exclusionary, a process of leaving out the Other/ Others.

Geography, when examined closely, actually does not provide an objective way of justifying the exclusion of peripheral countries: once the boundaries of the EU are pushed ever outwards then the periphery moves as well. Once Cyprus and Malta are members, for example, then enlarging to Israel, Lebanon, Tunisia, or any other Middle Eastern and North African state is no longer beyond the realms of the imaginable, especially as imagined by those in the periphery. In comparison, judging whether states are democratic, have functioning market economies, get along with their neighbours, and can implement the *acquis* seems much more fair.

There is always the issue of how far the EU can expand and still function as it does, especially given the unique nature of the Union system. And one condition of enlargement is that the EU can continue to deepen as it enlarges. At some point, there must be a *n* of Member States above which the Union simply ceases to work, whether this is because decision-making becomes impossible or because richer Member States refuse to redistribute wealth to newcomers, or because reciprocal trust evaporates. But determining that *n* is not a cut-and-dried decision: the Union is more than double its original size, and yet is much more integrated than it was at its inception. It would be hard to rule out categorically *a priori* that another doubling of the membership— to countries that accept and implement the *aquis*—would prevent further

---

[84] References to the contributions of this or that applicant country to European history or philosophical traditions or religious heritage, etc., can be found throughout much of the information on their case for joining the EU that applicant countries make available to the public.

integration, at least in the long term. This is thus yet another shaky ground for solving the inclusion–exclusion dilemma.

The basic predicament here is that the EU appears to be launched on a process of continual expansion, beyond the borders of the current applicant states. The wisdom of this can be seriously doubted (after all, there is no reason why the EU must necessarily cover the entire continent; a number of overlapping regional organizations could have been envisaged to help ensure stability and prosperity). But it is going to be very difficult for the EU to back away from the promises already made; and it will find that those promises have far-reaching consequences. The EU does currently have a fair (in theory if not in practice) means of determining inclusion and exclusion: the membership conditions. Unfortunately, they have not been applied consistently or fairly. The dilemmas thus raised will continue to haunt the EU and make future enlargement decisions all the more challenging as a result.

6

Strategies for Democratization and European Integration in the Balkans

MILADA ANNA VACHUDOVA

1. INTRODUCTION

The European Union (EU) is widely recognized as the international actor with the most influence in promoting ethnic reconciliation, shoring up democracy, and supporting the economic revitalization of the Balkans. The EU's influence is immediate—providing humanitarian aid, economic assistance, market access, and political support. It is also long-term—shaping the tenor of domestic politics by offering the prospect of EU membership. This long-term influence may be more diffuse, but it is ultimately more powerful. The prospect of EU membership provides substantial and consistent incentives for moderation and reform on the part of regional elites. The World Bank's 2001 report noted that its strategy for the region is 'built upon the assumption that a credible commitment to integration with European and global structures, especially the European Union, is a critical ingredient of success, as it will serve as an external driver of reform and intra-regional integration'.[1]

The EU's policies toward the Balkans have become embedded in the much broader process of EU enlargement that has followed the collapse of communism in Europe's eastern half. By 1999 the EU had assembled an impressive list of 13 officially recognized candidates and five proto-candidates for membership. Negotiations began in 1998 with 'the Luxembourg group': Hungary, Estonia, Poland, Slovenia, the Czech Republic, and Cyprus. Negotiations began in 2000 with 'the Helsinki group': Slovakia, Latvia, Lithuania, Bulgaria, Romania, and Malta. Turkey also became an official candidate in 1999, although the start of the negotiations was postponed due to insufficient domestic reform. Meanwhile, the EU-led Stability Pact of 1999 promised candidate status to the States of the Western Balkans— Croatia, Macedonia, Albania, the Federal Republic of Yugoslavia (FRY),

[1] World Bank, 'The Road to Stability and Prosperity in South Eastern Europe: A Regional Strategy Paper', (2001), at 9.

and Bosnia-Herzegovina—as soon as democratic standards were upheld and economic requirements met.

This enlargement of the EU is unusual because of the great number of candidates, but also because of their institutional and economic backwardness. Earlier applicants for EU membership had less to do: East European applicants have to create democracy and completely rebuild the economy and the state administration, while attempting to adopt the whole of the EU's *acquis communautaire*, which is itself growing day by day.[2] They lack some of the apparent prerequisites of successful democratization—and nowhere is this more evident than in the Balkans. Alongside little economic wealth, feeble state institutions, and weak civil societies, some Balkan states have had to contend with troubled relations between ethnic minorities and majorities, and with the cycles of political extremism brought on by ethnic cleansing and war.

The states that are considered part of the Balkans or South Eastern Europe (SEE) are Bulgaria, Romania, Croatia, Macedonia, the Federal Republic of Yugoslavia (FRY), Bosnia-Herzegovina, and Albania—along with EU member Greece. At the Laeken summit in December 2001, the European Council expressed strong support for the so-called 'big bang' variant of EU enlargement that would bring eight post-communist states—Estonia, Hungary, Latvia, Lithuania, Poland, the Czech Republic, the Slovak Republic, and Slovenia into the EU at once (along with Cyprus and Malta). It declared: 'the European Union is determined to bring the accession negotiations with the candidate countries that are ready to a successful conclusion by the end of 2002, so that those countries can take part in the European Parliament elections in 2004 as members'.[3]

If the big bang does take place, all of Eastern Europe's post-communist states outside the Balkans (and the former Soviet Union) will have become EU members by 2005. This means that after 2005 the overriding challenge of the ongoing accession process will be to keep the seven Balkan states anchored in the process of European integration. At the Feira summit in June 2000, the European Council confirmed that 'its objective remains the fullest possible integration of the countries of the region into the political and economic mainstream of Europe.... All the countries concerned are potential candidates for EU membership'.[4]

---

[2] Vachudova, 'EU Enlargement Overview', 9 *East European Constitutional Review* (2000) 4, at 64–69. See also K. Smith, *The Making of EU Foreign Policy* (1999); Sedelmeier and Wallace, 'Eastern Enlargement: Strategy or Second Thoughts?' in H. Wallace and W. Wallace (eds), *Policy Making in the European Union* (2000), at 427–461; and Sedelmeier, 'EU Eastern Enlargement in Comparative Perspective', 8 *Journal of European Public Policy* (2001) 4, at 662–670.

[3] European Council, Presidency Conclusions of 14 and 15 Dec. 2001, SN 300/01, at 3.

[4] European Council, Presidency Conclusions of 19 and 20 June 2000, SN 200/00, at 13.

This Chapter explores how the EU has worked to anchor the seven Balkan states into the process of European integration. Since 1999, the clear prospect of EU membership has provided a relatively constant set of incentives for elites to pursue strategies of regional peace-building, ethnic tolerance, and economic reform. Before 1999, this prospect was much less clear—and the logic of qualifying for membership certainly failed to overpower domestic forces with very different political agendas in Croatia or Serbia. The prospect of eventual EU membership failed to motivate leaders in many Balkan states to follow a path of reform compatible with joining the EU as rapidly as possible. But it did not fail to motivate all of them: Slovenia demonstrates that a post-Yugoslav state (if not necessarily a 'Balkan' one) could muscle its way into the first wave of EU enlargement by succeeding in its political and economic reforms. Poverty may have foreclosed this path to Albania or Macedonia, but not to Croatia or even the FRY. Here, the roadblock to EU membership was the nationalism and the opportunism of certain political elites in conditions of state creation, economic insecurity, and intermingled ethnic geography.

Given the fact that the EU was so unsuccessful in promoting democracy, protecting ethnic minority rights, and preventing war in the 1990s in the former Yugoslavia, can it be successful in the 2000s? Does the EU have better tools for influencing domestic politics in Balkan states than it did ten years ago? Or have domestic conditions changed such that the EU's tools are more effective? I show in this Chapter that both are true. The EU has developed better tools for promoting the integration of the Balkans into Europe—chiefly because its strategy toward the Balkans has become anchored in the process of EU enlargement. This new strategy has stemmed directly from the EU's frustration with its own failures and its determination to become an effective international actor by strengthening its Common Foreign and Security Policy (CFSP). Meanwhile, the domestic conditions in the Balkans have become more conducive to EU influence as governments of extreme nationalists have been replaced by those of politicians (more) committed to liberal democracy and marketizing reforms.

Even though the EU has greater traction than ever on the political and economic developments in the Balkans, in some states the problems are so daunting that the EU's determination to promote successful reform will have to be very great indeed. Most important, because economic and institutional problems are so great and consequently EU membership itself is so distant, intermediate rewards for governments and societies staying the course are an imperative. This Chapter is divided into three parts. First, I will explore the nature of political change in the Balkan states after 1989 and account for the EU's lack of influence. Secondly, I will explore what strategies the EU adopted to replace extreme nationalists with politicians committed to reform as the first step toward stabilizing the region. Thirdly, I will examine how the

EU's evolving Common Foreign and Security Policy (CFSP) may combine with the EU's ongoing accession process to underpin a successful EU strategy for promoting the stabilization and economic revival of the Balkans.

2. DEMOCRATIZATION IN THE BALKANS AFTER 1989

In many Balkan states, what I call a 'nationalist pattern' of political change took hold in 1989 and caused the profound ethnicization of domestic politics.[5] For the first years after 1989, however, the EU and other international actors had only vague strategies for promoting democracy and ethnic tolerance in Eastern Europe. We can imagine post-communist states as falling along a spectrum: At one end were states such as Poland and the Czech Republic that needed little international pressure to implement democratizing and marketizing reforms in a political atmosphere of relative ethnic tolerance. At the other end of the spectrum were states emerging from the disintegration of Yugoslavia—states that apparently needed tremendous international intervention to prevent ethnic wars sparked by political leaders intent on securing and maintaining power through ethnic violence.[6]

A nationalist pattern of political change took hold in many states where no strong group of former oppositionists existed to take power from the communists in 1989. Nationalists, usually unreformed communists, won democratic elections by appealing to the fear of economic reform and the mistrust of ethnic minorities. Once in power, they harnessed domestic institutions to corrupt marketizing reforms and scapegoat ethnic minorities. In the fledgling states of the former Yugoslavia, they seized on the powerful project of emancipating and protecting the nation—an appealing alternative to overcoming the economic uncertainties and hardships of the transition. The concentration of power in the hands of these elites, unchecked by other political forces, allowed them to mislead electorates about the long-term costs of halting economic reform and of ethnic nationalism.[7]

In the nationalist-pattern states, governing elites promised the electorate slow economic reform, in order to prevent widespread unemployment. Rather than improving aggregate economic welfare, slow reform protected

---

[5] Vachudova and Snyder, 'Are Transitions Transitory? Two Models of Political Change in East Central Europe Since 1989', 11 *East European Politics and Societies* (1997) 1, at 1–35.

[6] S. L. Wooodward, *Balkan Tragedy: Chaos and Dissolution After the Cold War* (1995). See also Fearon and Laitin, 'Violence and the Social Construction of Ethnic Identity', 54 *International Organization* (2000) 4, at 845–877.

[7] For these costs in terms of exclusion from the EU's accession process, see Vachudova, 'The Leverage of International Institutions on Democratizing States: Eastern Europe and the European Union', European University Institute Working Papers (2001), RSC No. 2001/33, at 9–10.

and enriched communist-era managers, whose inefficient firms should have been restructured or forced into bankruptcy. Often, money poured from the state budget through these enterprises straight into the managers' pockets. Privatization also become remarkably corrupt, with governing elites handing out state property to economic cronies for a fraction of its actual worth.[8] For these intertwined circles of political and economic elites, comprehensive and transparent economic reforms, as demanded by the EU accession process, proved much too costly: why forego the ongoing benefits from partial reform? In the FRY and to a lesser extent in Croatia, the costs of economic rent-seeking combined with the costs of war to drive the population into poverty. Freedom House estimated that for FRY citizens economic misman-agement, war, and international sanctions reduced living standards by more than a third over the course of the 1990s.[9]

The nationalist pattern of political change did not automatically lead to ethnic violence. The governments in Zagreb and Belgrade fuelled ethnic conflicts to consolidate their political power, while the governments in Bucharest or Bratislava pursued political strategies that included ethnic scapegoating but that led to little or no ethnically motivated violence. In contrast to the peacefulness of East Central Europe, the Balkans suffered major wars in Croatia (1991–1992), Bosnia-Herzegovina (1992–1995), and Kosovo (1998–1999). In very broad terms, three interwoven factors account for the violence: (1) the break-up of a federal state, Yugoslavia, in conditions of complex ethnic geography; (2) the extreme nationalist project of Serbian president Slobodan Milosevic to create a Greater Serbia; and, more generally, (3) the opportunity for extreme nationalists to seize and maintain power in conditions of ethnic violence. The wars are outside the scope of this Chap-ter—but their brutal ethnic cleansing and destruction have left behind the ethnic polarization and economic devastation that must now be overcome to bring tolerance and prosperity to the Western Balkans.

A. The Development of EU Policy toward Post-communist Europe

While the EU developed some tools to dampen ethnic tensions in East Central Europe in the 1990s, it was unable to prevent, contain, or stop ethnic conflict in the disintegrating Yugoslavia. The most effective tools that the EU could use in promoting ethnic tolerance were based on the conditionality of EU mem-bership—but these took time to develop. In East Central Europe, the political

---

[8] Hellman, 'Winners Take All: The Politics of Partial Reform in Postcommunist Transi-tions', *World Politics* (1998) 50, at 233. See also Fish, 'The Determinants of Economic Reform in the Post-Communist World', 12 *East European Politics and Societies* (1998) 1, at 31–78.

[9] 'Yugoslavia (Serbia & Montenegro)', Freedom in the World Report, Freedom House, 15 June 2001, at 3.

changes were peaceful—and the EU had ample time to reconcile itself with the desire of these states to join the EU and to plot a strategy for their association to the EU. Scholars have argued that the *absence* of a coherent EU foreign policy toward the former Yugoslavia proved very costly: that the EU could have averted some or all of the violence and economic impoverishment of the Western Balkans by putting in place an ambitious, intrusive, and attractive EU enlargement project right away in 1990.[10]

Reluctantly, the EU committed itself to an eastern enlargement at the Edinburgh summit in December 1992.[11] It then began the process of developing the tools to interact purposefully with the eastern candidates. At the Copenhagen summit in June 1993, it set out the general political and economic conditions of membership in the 'Copenhagen Criteria'—but it did not evaluate the candidates in terms of these requirements. For the nationalist-pattern governments, the only ramification of manifestly failing to meet the Copenhagen requirements—even in the prominent area of ethnic minority rights—was the threat of exclusion from a first wave of EU expansion. Such exclusion seemed very distant in 1993—and indeed it would take the EU four more years to separate the 'ins' from the 'outs'. When the Opinions evaluating the candidates were published by the Commission in 1997, Romania and Bulgaria were among the states that were (diplomatically) called the 'pre-ins'. Since they had neither signed association agreements with the EU nor applied for membership, the other Balkan states were also outside the EU's emerging accession process.

After war broke out in Yugoslavia in 1991, EU governments were intent on changing the behaviour of post-communist governments elsewhere whose use of nationalism threatened the rights of ethnic minorities and peaceful relations with neighbouring states. The fist such attempt was the Balladur Plan of 1993 that was designed to use the carrot of future EU membership to encourage candidate states to settle national disputes: to pledge their acceptance of existing boundaries and their protection of the rights of national minorities. The prospect of a March 1995 conference did cause Hungary and

[10] Garton Ash, 'Europe's Endangered Liberal Order', 77 *Foreign Affairs* (March/April 1998) 2, at 51–65. On the EU's decision to expand see Schimmelfennig, 'The Community Trap: Liberal Norms, Rhetorical Action, and the Eastern Enlargement of the European Union', 55 *International Organization* 1, at 47–80. See also Kelley, 'Norms and Membership Conditionality', paper presented at the workshop 'International Institutions and Socialization in the New Europe', 18–19 May 2001, European University Institute; and Jacoby, 'Exemplars, Analogies and Menus: Eastern Europe in Cross-regional Comparisons', 12 *Governance* 4, at 455–78.

[11] During the negotiation of the Europe Agreements signed in 1991, the Polish, Czechoslovak, and Hungarian delegations had to struggle mightily to include a preamble stating that *they* understood the association agreements as a first step toward full EU membership—even though the EU refused to do so. See Brada, 'The Community and Czechoslovakia, Hungary and Poland', *Report on Eastern Europe*, 6 Dec. 1991, at 27–32.

Slovakia to sign a long-delayed treaty on good relations in which the Slovak government agreed to ambitious provisions for the protection of minority rights. It also caused Hungary and Romania to make advances in their troubled negotiation of a similar treaty. However, the nationalist governments of Slovakia and Romania, though they signed exemplary treaties with Hungary abroad, failed to abide by their provisions at home. The Balladur Plan exhibited the powerlessness of the EU to sway nationalist-pattern governments with the threat of exclusion from a distant first wave of EU expansion. A change of government was imperative: elections in Romania in 1996 and Slovakia in 1998 brought to power governments of moderate reformers that subsequently worked to satisfy the requirements of EU membership, including promoting ethnic tolerance.

The Dayton Peace Accords of 1995 drove this point home. It became clear that nationalist-pattern governments could neither be cajoled nor coerced into complying with Western standards of democracy and ethnic minority rights. The Dayton Accords backed by NATO troops did create a precarious peace in Bosnia-Herzegovina, Croatia, and the FRY. But however much or little they had backed down on the battlefield, the regimes of Slobodan Milosevic in FRY and Franco Tudjman in Croatia were clearly unwilling to pursue reforms at home. Meanwhile, the divided and weak government of Bosnia-Herzegovina was also marked by nationalism and corruption, for all that it was also becoming an international protectorate.

B. Applying Conditionality: The EU's Regional Approach

The Commission launched what it called the 'Regional Approach to the countries of South-Eastern Europe' in April 1997.[12] The Regional Approach created the structure for the Commission to apply conditionality very clearly to the states outside of the EU's accession process—Bosnia-Herzegovina, Croatia, the FRY, Macedonia, and Albania (the Western Balkans). In this way it mirrored the 'Pre-Accession Process' that in the meantime had been developed for the official candidates for EU membership, allowing the Commission to evaluate the progress of each candidate in an annual 'Regular Report'. The Regional Approach was similarly based on periodic assessments—but very general ones examining whether the governments of Bosnia-Herzegovina, Croatia, the FRY, Macedonia, and Albania were respecting basic Western standards of democracy and human rights. These assessments would determine whether each country would qualify for a cooperation agreement with the EU that would include trade concessions, and for direct aid that would come from the EU's PHARE programme.

[12] 'Council Conclusions on the Application of Conditionality with a view to developing a Coherent EU-Strategy for the Relations with the Countries of the Region', PRES/97/129, Annex 3, 29 Apr. 1997, at 3.

In all nationalist-pattern states, there was a gap between the 'formal commitment' to fulfilling the requirements of EU membership and their actual implementation by the government. This gap prevented them from reaching a standard of democratization that would make them credible candidates. In the case of the FRY, for example, the Commission decided to extend autonomous trade preferences for the year 1997 in response to a certain liberalization of the media and to calls by the opposition for an economic revival.[13] However, in 1998 the Commission concluded that the FRY failed to qualify for inclusion in the autonomous trade regime or for any EU aid 'notably due to the lack of respect for the fundamental principles of democracy and human rights'.[14] In the case of Croatia, the Commission in 1998 described the government's compliance with the conditions for closer association with the EU as 'selective'.[15]

For all three nationalist-pattern states—the FRY, Croatia, and Bosnia—the European Commission explained in a press release in 1998: 'compliance with conditionality . . . is not satisfactory. This concerns areas of democratic reforms, respect for human and minority rights, freedom of the media and the rule of law. In particular with regard to the countries that signed the Dayton/Paris Peace Agreement, improvements are also necessary concerning the return of refugees and displaced persons and cooperation with the International Criminal Tribunal.'[16] The ethnic cleansing of Kosovo by the regime of Slobodan Milosevic in the winter and spring of 1999 repeated his merciless use of ethnic conflict to hold on to power, and the bombing of the FRY that followed only underscored his complete intransigence in the face of foreign sanctions. NATO's bombs failed as surely as the EU's sanctions to bring about democratic reforms in the FRY by changing the policies of the Milosevic government. The bombs and the sanctions did, however, strengthen the hand of the rivals to Milosevic's rule, as discussed below.

For Macedonia and Albania, the situation was different. Both countries received trade preferences and aid through the EU's PHARE programme. However, state capacity was very weak, and elite commitment to democracy and ethnic coexistence was shaky. The weakness of the state and the backwardness of the economy, on the one hand, and the amount of attention

---

[13] Council Regulation 825/97/EC, OJ 1997 L 119/4. See also 'EU Declaration on the occasion of the Granting of autonomous trade preferences to the FRY', PRES/97/129, Annex 1, 29 Apr. 1997, at 2.

[14] European Commission, 'Compliance with the conditions in the Council Conclusions of 29 April 1997— Federal Republic of Yugoslavia', COM(98)237, 15 Apr. 1998, at 2.

[15] European Commission, 'Developments in the countries of the Regional Approach since 1996, The Stabilisation and Association Process for countries of South-Eastern Europe', Communication to the Council and European Parliament, COM(99)235, 26 May 1999, at 5.

[16] European Commission, 'The European Commission Maintains Trade Suspension for Croatia, FRY and Bosnia-Herzegovina', Press Release No. 31/98, 15 Apr. 1998, at 102.

and aid being provided by the EU and other external actors, on the other, did not add up to successful or substantial reform.

3. OUSTING NATIONALISTS AND SUPPORTING MODERATES

By 1998, the obvious core of the EU's strategy to stabilize the Balkans was the ouster of nationalist-pattern governments that had proved so intransigent in the face of Western pressure. What had been absent in these states at the moment of democratization was a united, Western-oriented political elite that was strong enough to defeat ethnic nationalists in national elections. The challenge then for the EU and other external actors was to create incentives for moderate elites to vie for power, and to cooperate with one another in order to win it.

In early 2000, the electorate in Croatia ousted Franco Tudjman's nationalist government and brought to power a broad coalition of Western-oriented parties who had run on a platform of earning EU membership as rapidly as possible—on the pattern of Romania in 1996 and Slovakia in 1998. Slobodan Milosevic's government similarly lost elections on 24 September 2000 to a broad, pro-reform coalition called the Democratic Opposition of Serbia (DOS). The existence and political strategies of the DOS were strongly conditioned by Western and especially EU support. In both Croatia and Serbia, the challenge was 'remaking' existing political elites into moderates, and convincing them to work together despite ideological and personal antipathies.

In the most deliberate attempt to influence domestic politics, the EU worked in 1999 and 2000 to remove Slobodan Milosevic's government from power in the FRY by spelling out for the electorate that ethnic nationalists in power preclude prosperity by way of eventual EU membership. Here the EU's strategy of creating a Western-oriented opposition to oust rent-seeking nationalists was even more obvious than in Croatia. Beginning in the summer of 1999, the EU and other Western actors pursued a strategy of openly supporting the political opposition to Milosevic in whatever form they could find them.

To this end, the EU sought to raise esteem for the discredited and disunited opposition parties of Serbia by providing them with tangible economic support and international recognition in a high-profile diplomatic relationship nicknamed 'Contract with Serbia'. The EU provided humanitarian and democratization assistance, including support for non-governmental organizations and the independent media. In addition, assistance was made available beginning in 1999 to democratically-run municipalities within Serbia under the EC's OBNOVA-CARDS programme. This included the 'Energy for Democracy' (EfD) programme that delivered great quantities of heating oil to municipalities controlled by the forces opposed to the Milosevic regime during the winter of 1999–2000.[17]

The EU also used economic instruments to undermine the power of the Milosevic regime. The EU imposed a total economic blockade on Serbia during the Kosovo crisis in an attempt to bankrupt the Milosevic regime.[18] It also drew up a blacklist of Serb businessmen close to the Milosevic regime whose foreign assets were frozen and who were blocked from travelling to the EU.[19] In June of 2000, the European Commission attempted to use sanctions in a more sophisticated manner to support opponents of the Milosevic regime. It published a list of Serbian companies who *would* be permitted to do business with Europe because they were not earning hard currency for Milosevic's regime.[20] The overall strategy was to empower the opposition while also tempting some of Milosevic's economic cronies to change sides and oppose the regime. One of the greatest successes of the Stability Pact and of the EU in the Balkans was certainly to send 'a powerful message to Serbia that democratic change would be supported by substantial aid'.[21]

Soon after the ouster of Milosevic in Serbia, the EU played an active and constructive role in the resolution of the crisis in Macedonia in 2001. The Ohrid peace agreement was signed between the Macedonian government and ethnic Albanian guerrillas on 13 August 2001, in order to end the armed conflict that began in February 2001. The agreement committed the Macedonian government to pass legislation giving official recognition to the Albanian language, and to reorganize the police force to include a proportion of ethnic Albanians such as is found in the general population. Since the Macedonian government was open to conditional Western assistance over the course of the 1990s—unlike the Croatian or Serb government—the question is why the EU and other international actors did not use conditionality to pressure Macedonian governments to improve the rights of Macedonia's ethnic Albanian population much earlier.

NATO took the lead in ensuring the success of the Ohrid peace agreement: Operation Essential Harvest collected approximately 3,800 weapons from the ethnic Albanian rebels. Operation Amber Fox protects the inter-

---

[17] European Commission, 'Federal Republic of Yugoslavia—the European Contribution,' *The EU & South Eastern Europe*, June 2001.

[18] Council Regulation (EC) 2488/2000, OJ 2000 L 287/19.

[19] Block and King, 'Milosevic's Cronies Struggle for Removal from Blacklist', *Wall Street Journal*, 1 Oct. 1999.

[20] Guzelova, 'Serbia sanctions seek to separate good from bad', *Financial Times*, 16 June 2000, at 3.

[21] 'Democracy, Security and the Future of the Stability Pact for South Eastern Europe', Report by the EastWest Institute and the European Stability Initiative, Apr. 2001.

national observers monitoring the implementation of the peace plan. But the EU also played a part in averting civil war between government forces and armed ethnic Albanian rebels. The special EU envoy François Leotard served as the chairman of a coordinating body that included the Atlantic Alliance, the OSCE, the UNHCR, and the Council of Europe. While NATO took charge of the security tasks stemming from the agreement, the EU coordinated the civilian tasks related to implementing the reforms stipulated by the Ohrid agreement.[22]

A. The Stability and Association Process (SAP)

Until the July 1999 launch of the Stability Pact for South-Eastern Europe, the EU's assistance to the Western Balkans focused on crisis management and reconstruction; the total EU assistance from all programmes totalled some 5.5 billion Euros until 1999.[23] In 1999, the EU developed the Stabilization and Association Process (SAP) that promised to harness the countries of the Western Balkans into the EU's enlargement process while organizing the immediate projects promoting democracy and economic reconstruction. The Commission described the SAP as a strategy designed to help the region secure political and economic stabilization while also developing a closer association with the EU.[24] The EU's 2001 budget for external actions was more than 8 billion euros, but almost 40 per cent of that sum was dedicated to pre-accession aid for the applicant countries to the EU. For the Western Balkans, the EU spent 839 million euros in 2001, about 10 per cent of its total budget for External Action in 2001. The EU spent 3,259 million euros on pre-accession aid to the candidates, including Romania and Bulgaria.[25] For 2002, the EU likewise spent about 40 per cent of its external action budget of 8 billion euros on Pre-accession Aid, and about 9.4 per cent on aid to the Western Balkans.[26]

The EU launched a new financial assistance programme in 2001 named CARDS—Community Assistance for Reconstruction, Democratization and Stabilization. CARDS supports the participation of Albania, Bosnia-Herzegovina, Croatia, the Federal Republic of Yugoslavia, and the Former

[22] 'Macedonia: Filling the Security Vacuum', *International Crisis Group Balkans Briefing*, 8 Sept. 2001, at 14.

[23] 'Federal Republic of Yugoslavia: Commission adopts new strategic framework for assistance', IP/02/08, 4 Jan. 2002, at 1.

[24] Council Regulation 2666/00, OJ 2000 L 306/1. See also European Commission, 'The Stabilisation and Association Process for countries of South-Eastern Europe', Communication to the Council and European Parliament, COM(99)235, 26 May 1999.

[25] European Commission, General Budget of the European Union for the Financial Year 2001, Jan. 2001, 1, at 7, 21.

[26] European Commission, General Budget of the European Union for the Financial Year 2002, Jan. 2002, 1, at 7, 21.

Yugoslav Republic of Macedonia in the EU's Stabilization and Association Process. For the period 2002 to 2006, the EU Member States have earmarked 4.65 billion Euros for the five states. Most of this assistance will be spent on projects drawn up jointly by the European Commission and the national governments, but about one fifth will be paid directly to the governments for national implementation.[27]

The CARDS programme offers support in four areas:

- integrated border management to help tackle cross-border crime, facilitate trade and stabilize the border regions;
- institutional capacity building to raise awareness of EU policy and laws;
- support to democratic stabilization and involvement of civil society in the region's development;
- support to help plan the integration of the region's transport, energy, and environmental infrastructure into the wider European networks.[28]

For each state, the Commission is writing a strategy paper that sets out the priorities for the CARDS assistance, akin to the Accession Partnerships that it has signed with the EU's existing candidate states. For example, the strategy paper published in January 2002 for the FRY identifies three priority areas: (1) good governance and institution building; (2) economic recovery, regeneration, and reform; and (3) social development and civil society.

Alongside the CARDS assistance, the Stabilization and Association Agreements (SAAs) promise to liberalize trade between the EU and the Western Balkan states. The EU already has a fairly liberal trade regime toward the Balkans, allowing more than 80 per cent of regional exports to enter the Union duty-free. Fully liberalized access to the EU markets is foreseen as part of the SAAs.[29] In the Stability and Association Agreements, the SEE countries (Croatia, Macedonia, Albania, the Federal Republic of Yugoslavia (FRY)) are asked to remove quantitative restrictions immediately and custom duties gradually over a period of ten years. For its part, the EU opens its markets to SEE goods—with a few exceptions. In the SAA agreement with Macedonia, for example, the EU retains some restriction on beef and fisheries products and wine.

The SAAs are considered the centrepiece of the EU's Stabilization and Association Process (SAP), and as such have substantially more significance than mere trade agreements. The five states of the Western Balkans that are eligible for SAAs must first each satisfy the EU's conditionality for opening

---

[27] Council Regulation 2666/00, OJ 2000 L 306/1, at 2.
[28] 'EU adopts new strategy for Balkans', *EurActiv*, 23 Oct. 2001.
[29] 'Stability Pact for the Balkans', *EurActiv*, 14 May 2001.

negotiations on signing these association agreements. The SAAs are thus at the forefront of the EU's increasingly focused strategy of using conditionality to promote political and economic reform. Once signed, the SAAs are the first formal step in the EU's accession process—to be followed eventually by opening negotiations for full membership. By the end of 2001, only Macedonia (in March) and Croatia (in July) had concluded SAAs with the EU. For the FRY, opening negotiations on a SAA was still conditional in 2002 on further democratic and economic reforms by the post-Milosevic regime. Progress in implementing reforms was (strictly) evaluated in periodic meetings of the EU–FRY Consultative Task Force.[30] For its part, Albania was described by the Commission in early 2002 as 'on the threshold' of negotiating an SAA thanks to its relative (but not absolute) progress on reform. For Bosnia-Herzegovina, however, an SAA was still far in the future as it could not yet even be considered a self-sustaining state.[31]

B. Intermediate Rewards for Moderate Governments

After the exit of nationalist governments in nationalist-pattern states, a significant challenge for the EU's accession process—and for expanding the liberal democratic core of Europe—is how to keep governments and societies committed to reform when the confluence of geography, conflict, economic backwardness, incompetence, and years of counterproductive government means that EU accession is still a long way off. Moderate, Westernizing governments are faced with the unenviable political task of implementing the difficult economic reform and ethnic reconciliation that were purposefully thwarted by the previous government. In Croatia and the FRY, the election of reformers resembled in some ways a new regime change: the elections were a watershed that surpassed the simple changing of the government. Political capital akin to that of the 1989 democratic revolutions, though weaker, was bestowed on the reformers to sweep out the corrupt unreconstructed communists and nationalists. But this political capital was not so great as to equip the new governments to solve all of the problems they faced upon taking office.

The economic decline of the last decade has yet to be reversed. According to the World Bank, none of the countries 'has yet established a firm foundation for sustainable growth and progress on improving living standards has also been disappointing'.[32] Some of the economic reforms necessary to move toward a functioning market economy may lead to further hardship for the

---

[30] See, e.g., European Commission, 'Fourth Meeting of the EU–FRY Consultative Task Force—Belgrade', 29 May 2002.

[31] For a useful overview of the SAP and of each country's progress, see 'The Stabilisation and Association process for South East Europe: First Annual Report, Report from the Commission', COM(2002)163, 4 Apr. 2002.

[32] World Bank, *supra* note 1, at 25–34.

population in the short term, and may therefore cause the governing parties to lose the next elections. A domestic backlash may even take place if difficult reforms are tied very closely to international demands.[33] The economic destruction of the last decade has been particularly acute in Serbia: the DOS government must make huge economic strides in order to mollify the population.[34] The DOS government must also deal with a huge refugee population, the largest in Europe, estimated at nearly 400,000 refugees from Croatia and Bosnia. The UNHCR estimated that during the winter of 2001–2002 some 40 per cent of these refugees still lived in very poor conditions. In response, the EU's Humanitarian Aid Office (ECHO) channelled food assistance through local NGOs.[35]

Revitalizing the economy must be accompanied by recovery from the ethnic conflicts that created deep divisions over the last decade. Ethnic reconciliation is a challenge in countries where the population has been conditioned to feel threatened by the minority, and where domestic political discourse has been heavily ethnicized. The moderate governments elected in Croatia and Serbia in 2000 were immediately pressured very heavily by the EU and other Western institutions to cooperate with the International Criminal Court by extraditing suspected war criminals to the Hague. They have also been required to step up efforts to encourage the repatriation of refugees from the wars in Croatia and Bosnia. To the extent that both governments are cooperating—and so far the level of cooperation seems notable if not impressive—then this is a great success for the EU's strategy of conditionality. However, it clearly undermines the popularity of the moderate governments.

The rewards short of EU membership which are the most effective in shoring up popular support for Westernizing governments in the Balkans are also the most difficult for the EU to deliver on account of the costs they will impose on the EU's Member States. These rewards include complete and unilateral access to the EU market for agricultural goods and visa-free travel to the EU for Balkan citizens.[36]

EU Member States are moving toward allowing unrestricted market access to South East European producers in all sectors in the new SAAs that are being signed with Macedonia, Bosnia-Herzegovina, Albania, Croatia, and

[33] In most East European states, popular support for EU membership decreases as domestic groups who may be disadvantaged by accession organize themselves and campaign against membership, and as governments substantiate difficult reforms with the task of qualifying for EU membership.

[34] Uvalic, 'Federal Republic of Yugoslavia', Working Paper 18/01 (2000), *One Europe or Several*, at 1–17. See also Pitic *et al.*, 'Yugoslav Economy after the War', Economics Institute, Belgrade (20 July 1999), at 1–13.

[35] 'Commission allocates a further EUR 2.5 million in humanitarian aid for Serbia', IP/01/1802, 12 Dec. 2001.

[36] Vachudova, 'The Trump Card of Domestic Politics: Bargaining Over EU Enlargement', 10 *East European Constitutional Review* (Spring/Summer 2001) 2, at 93–97.

the Federal Republic of Yugoslavia (FRY). The trade agreements signed with East Central European states in the early 1990s imposed restrictions and long transition periods on those sectors (steel, textiles, and agriculture) in which eastern producers were the most competitive. This catered to the interests of powerful producers within the EU, although studies showed that the impact of immediate and complete market access for East Central European goods on these producers would have been minimal. In the case of the SAAs, the EU is making a much greater effort to open its markets to the goods these poor and fragile states are most able to export. The barriers that remain for the export of some agricultural products to the EU market, however, are under-mining the EU's goal of helping the economic recovery of the region.

Meanwhile, visa requirements have fuelled anti-EU sentiment in the Western Balkans. Elites as well as ordinary citizens are frustrated, resentful, and feel like third-class Europeans because they have to obtain visas to travel to the EU. This resentment decreases the willingness of politicians and other public figures to portray themselves as pro-European, undermines the popu-larity of those who do, and feeds a sense of futility about ever being allowed into the European club. The sense of isolation will only mount as first-wave candidates to the EU implement Schengen visa policies in order to make good on their bids for membership. The removal of reforming countries from the EU's common visa list should be on the agenda as part of a strategy to strengthen the hand of pro-Western elites in the Balkans.[37]

The visa requirements for citizens of Balkan states travelling to the Schengen area stem from the fear and the reality of illegal immigration from the Balkans into the EU. The presence of Bulgaria and Romania on the EU's visa list for many years caused very considerable resentment. When Bulgaria was removed from the EU's visa list in 2000, it was a striking moment of national celebra-tion. Meanwhile, the greatest incentive for regional governments to spend a greater portion of their national budgets on better law enforcement and more effective border controls is to offer visa-free travel to the EU as a reward.

C. Can the EU Prevent the Return of Extreme Nationalist Governments?

Does the election of reformers mean that the commitment to EU-oriented reform will be an abiding one? In Croatia and Serbia, if the current oppos-itions win the next election, nationalist political parties will be returned to power. In what measure will they still rely on their previous political strategies

---

[37] Jileva, 'New Borders and Old Neighbors in Europe', *EES Newsletter*, Mar.–Apr. 2002, at 5–7. See also Vachudova, 'Eastern Europe as Gatekeeper: The Immigration and Asylum Policies of an Enlarging European Union', in P. Andreas and T. Snyder (eds), *The Wall Around the West: State Borders and Immigration Control in North America and Europe* (2000) 153.

of ethnic nationalism and economic corruption? If and when this return to power takes place, it will provide a test for whether the changes in preferences brought about by pro-Western economic policies and by participation in the EU's pre-accession process are enduring.

One of the most interesting ways in which the EU accession process locks in reform is by improving the credibility of policies designed to reform political institutions and the economy. As a report by the East-West Institute noted, 'International assistance is only effective where it supports credible domestic reform efforts emerging from the local political process. In all states of the region, there is a need for a constant effort to nurture and strengthen the policy consensus behind reforms, stressing the benefits, fostering realistic expectations and, wherever reforms involve short-term costs, explaining the rationale.'[38] A consensus behind reforms will help foreclose the political opportunities for anti-reform parties, including intolerant nationalists who use ethnic scapegoating to construct their domestic legitimacy.

To understand the challenges faced by the EU in integrating the seven Balkan states—Bulgaria, Romania, Croatia, FRY, Macedonia, Albania, and Bosnia-Herzegovina—we may imagine them as falling into three groups according to the capacity of an elected government to conduct meaningful reform. Bulgaria and Croatia are in the first group. The governments in both countries have been able to implement fairly successful reforms in conditions of relative political and social consensus. For Bulgaria, the EU played a significant role in keeping the pro-reform government of the Union of Democratic Forces (UDF) committed to reform during its term. The UDF lost the June 2001 parliamentary elections—but not to the Bulgarian Socialist Party that sought to slow reform and play on nationalist views.[39] For Croatia, the capacity of the state to govern along with relative economic prosperity could well allow it to overtake Romania.

Romania and the FRY are in the second group. Romania has been negotiating with the EU along with Bulgaria since 1999, but reforms have generally been unsuccessful because of a lack of consensus and state competence. The FRY meanwhile suffered a terrible decade at the hands of nationalist leaders, but it seems to have emerged with a state administration largely intact and with strong political leaders. In the third group we have Macedonia and Albania. Here, elected governments are weak and state administrations very feeble, so the project of overcoming tremendous economic

[38] 'Democracy, Security and the Future of the Stability Pact for South Eastern Europe', Report by the EastWest Institute and the European Stability Initiative, Apr. 2001.
[39] Koinova, 'Saxcoburggotsky and His Catch-All Attitude: Cooperation or Cooptation?', 2 *Southeast European Politics* (2001) 2, at 135–140; and Azmanova, 'The New Bulgarian Government: Awaiting an EU Response', *Challenge Europe*, European Policy Centre, 15 July 2001. See also 'Constitutional Watch: Bulgaria', 10 *East European Constitutional Review* 2/3 (2001), 9–11.

backwardness is daunting. Finally, in the fourth group we have Bosnia-Herzegovina along with Kosovo—entities that are run as international protectorates, so the question of promoting reform by creating the right incentives for local elites plays out at quite a different level.

4. THE EUROPEAN UNION AS AN EXTERNAL ACTOR

In 2001, the European Commission noted that 'through the process of enlargement, through the Common Foreign and Security Policy (CFSP), through its development cooperation and its external assistance programs the EU now seeks to project stability also beyond its own borders'.[40] The CFSP and the process of enlargement do seem to be coming together with the EU's external assistance programmes to project stability into the Western Balkans in the 2000s. But the EU's involvement in the Western Balkans for much of the 1990s was an embarrassing failure.[41] Indeed, the EU was unable to play a substantial role in stopping or even containing the successive wars in the former Yugoslavia—in Croatia, in Bosnia-Herzegovina, and in Kosovo. Arguably, the EU and its Member States made the war in Bosnia worse by their attempts to broker a diplomatic end to the conflict. Meanwhile, it was NATO intervention led by the United States that did put a stop to the conflicts in Bosnia, Kosovo, and Macedonia.

The EU's resolve to create a European Security and Defence Policy (ESDP) came at the close of a decade when the EU's foreign policy competence had been gravely put in question by the wars in the former Yugoslavia. The first step was taken in December 1988, when the British Prime Minister Tony Blair and the French President Jacques Chirac crafted the St. Malo declaration. 'The Union', they admonished, 'must have the capacity for autonomous action, backed by credible military forces, the means to decide to use them, and a readiness to do so, in order to respond to international crises'.[42] The St. Malo declaration, in particular its co-authorship by the British, was a response to the frustration and humiliation of the EU's inability to prevent, contain, or stop the wars in Bosnia. In the spring of 1999, the EU's inability to prevent ethnic cleansing in Kosovo or to intervene militarily to punish it only reinforced the EU's resolve to pursue a two-track strategy: taking charge of post-Kosovo reconstruction at the helm of the Stability Pact while committing to developing a stronger European security and defence policy.

[40] European Commission, 'Communication from the Commission on Conflict Prevention', 11 May 2001, COM(2001)211 final, at 5.

[41] Hoffmann, 'Yugoslavia: Implications for Europe and for European Institutions', in R. Ullman (ed.), *The World and Yugoslavia's Wars* (1996) 97.

[42] Joint Declaration on European Defence Issued at the British–French Summit, Saint-Malo, France, 3–4 Dec. 1998.

The EU has emphasized conflict prevention as the core of the CFSP. A report by the International Crisis Group notes the evolution of the EU's capabilities: 'The EU's . . . repertoire of conflict prevention tools, once limited by the exclusively "civilian" nature of a community of states operating largely in the economic sphere, is expanding as the EU acquires a greater capacity to use traditional levers of state power such as diplomatic pressure and even a degree of military force. For example, the "Rapid Reaction Force" . . . will put military options, such as the possibility of preventive deployment of troops, into the EU's toolbox of preventive measures for the first time.'[43]

A. Enhancing the EU's Role in the Stability Pact

The EU's foreign policy after the Kosovo crisis seemed for the first time to be based on the realization that EU enlargement itself may be the best way to promote peace, democracy, and economic growth in the whole of Europe.[44] The prospect of EU membership as a motor for political and economic change was explicitly set out in the EU-led Stability Pact for South Eastern Europe adopted at Sarajevo in July 1999. The Stability Pact brings all of the international institutions and government donors under one umbrella, including the United States and other non-EU countries such as Canada, Japan, and Russia. But the only actor with real political and economic leverage—with substantial rewards available to actors that comply consistently over time—is the EU. So while most commentators do not recommend disbanding the Stability Pact, they do recommend upgrading the role of the EU. In 2000 and 2001, the EU took up this challenge by devoting more attention to the Western Balkans, and by making different EU institutions—especially the Commission and the CFSP—work in closer tandem in the entire Stability Pact region.[45]

Whatever its reservations in relation to the EU's deepening security and defence identity, the United States is clearly eager to see the EU prove itself in the Balkans. For the USA, the goal of creating a self-sustaining peace in Bosnia and Kosovo that allows the withdrawal of NATO troops dovetails with the shift of responsibilities for the Balkans to the EU. This shift was described by a US official in early 2002 as follows: '[w]e no longer start

[43] International Crisis Group, 'EU Crisis Response Capability: Institutions and Processes for Conflict Prevention and Management', ICG Issues Report No. 2 (26 June 2001), at 8–9.

[44] Vachudova, 'The European Union Needs to Change Its Spots', *International Herald Tribune*, 12 Aug. 1999, at 8. See also M. Emerson and D. Gros, (eds), *The CEPS Plan for the Balkans* (1999).

[45] Cremona, 'Creating the New Europe: The Stability Pact for South-Eastern Europe in the Context of EU–SEE Relations', II *Cambridge Yearbook of European Legal Studies* (1999) 463. See also Emerson and Whyte, 'Options for the Stability Pact', CEPS Commentary, Nov. 2001, at 3.

meetings with Bosnia's leaders by pressing them to implement the 1995 Dayton Peace Accords; instead, we ask how they are doing in preparing for a Stabilization and Association Agreement with the EU. And during recent negotiations between Serbia and Montenegro, we politely told the leaders involved that the EU's Javier Solana was the international negotiator and had our support.[46]

The Centre for European Policy Studies has called for the EU to create the job of EU Special Representative for the entire region, ensuring coherence of EU policies toward the candidate states (Bulgaria and Romania) and the other states of the region.[47] This coherence is vital for the EU's 'traction' on the domestic politics of all candidate states, especially for those in the Balkans that will take many years yet to qualify for membership—and who may question, for reasons of geography or economic backwardness, whether the EU will ever let them in. As Emerson and Whyte note, 'The November 2000 summit conference in Zagreb of all of the EU and the Stability Pact states was an important event, establishing that the whole of the region sees its future in the EU, and that the EU accepts and welcomes this'.[48] The EU's SAA process has sought to balance a bilateral relationship with individual Balkan states that closely rewards each state's political and economic reforms with a regional approach that promotes cooperation among states. Indeed, the EU has tried to use conditionality to compel regional problem-solving and development projects—these being often against the preferences of the region's states.

The Commission has recently been given a new tool to increase its effectiveness: a Rapid Reaction Mechanism that is 'designed to enhance the EU's civilian capacity to intervene fast and effectively in crisis situations in third countries'. EU leaders have described conflict prevention and crisis management as forming the core of the EU's Common Foreign and Security Policy (CFSP). The Rapid Reaction Mechanism would essentially speed up the delivery of civilian experts from the Member States to crisis situations—experts, for example, in clearing mines, mediating between conflicting parties, or training the police and judges.[49]

The Community instruments include: 'human rights work, election monitoring, institution building, media support border management, humanitarian missions, police training and the provision of police equipment, civil emergency assistance, rehabilitation, reconstruction, pacification,

---

[46] Speech of Greg Schulte of the National Security Council, 'U.S. Strategy for the Balkans', Georgetown University, Washington, D.C., 20 Mar. 2002.

[47] Emerson, 'On the Forming and Reforming of Stability Pacts: From the Balkans to the Caucasus', CEPS Policy Brief 4, May 2001, at 3.

[48] Emerson and Whyte, 'Options for the Stability Pact', CEPS Commentary, Nov. 2001, at 3.

[49] Council Regulation 381/2001, creating a rapid-reaction mechanism, OJ 2001 L57/5, Art. 3, at 2.

resettlement and mediation'.[50] The main purpose of the Rapid Reaction Mechanism (RRM) is to deliver some of these instruments immediately, rapidly to stabilize a situation and pave the way for long-term assistance. In the past, Community instruments have been very slow in coming due to budgetary limitations and procedural delays. The RRM is a reaction in particular to criticism of the EU's very slow pace in delivering aid to the Balkans, particularly to Kosovo and Macedonia, after the creation of the EU-led Stability Pact in July 1999.

5. CONCLUSION: BRINGING THE CFSP AND ENLARGEMENT TO THE BALKANS

The EU's CFSP backed up by the ESDP may work in the Western Balkans because the EU has a range of effective tools that can be used for countries that are credible future members of the EU. In other words, the most powerful and successful aspect of EU foreign policy has turned out to be the incentive of EU enlargement—and the Western Balkans are the region where EU enlargement can be used to make the CFSP a success. The success of the CFSP will be measured by its ability to apply the instruments available to the EU—trade agreements, economic aid, investment, technical assistance, visa requirements, and the incentives of EU membership—to fulfilling its declared foreign-policy goals, even if this entails overruling the short-term interests of some Member States and incurring substantial economic costs. In order for the Balkans to become stable, democratic, and prosperous, the region's moderate elites must hold power and revitalize the economy. All the while, these elites must fend off extremist forces by convincing voters that difficult reforms of the economy and the state will lead to greater prosperity and to membership of the EU. For its part, the EU must help convince them by providing intermediate rewards that demonstrate the merits of European integration.

The success of the EU's enlargement project will ultimately determine the success of the EU's Common Foreign and Security Policy (CFSP). The EU's influence over its periphery stems from the attraction of future membership of the club. Whatever military capability the EU may develop, it will be a trivial source of influence in comparison to the carrot of membership. It follows that whether or not the EU will be taken seriously as a foreign policy actor will depend on its ability to bring stability and democracy to its immediate periphery—the Western Balkans.

---

[50] 'Council adopts Rapid Reaction Mechanism, Commission now in Position to Intervene Fast in Civilian Crisis Management', IP/01/255, at 1.

7

The Impact of Enlargement: External Policy and External Relations

MARISE CREMONA

1. INTRODUCTION

All prospective EU Member States have existing external policies that are likely to be affected by European Union membership. The increased level of EC and EU activity over the last decade, as well as developments in the nature of that activity, means that the effects on existing policies of new Members in the fifth enlargement are likely to be more far-reaching than they were at the time of earlier enlargements in the 1970s or 1980s. This is yet another area of the *acquis* which appears to be a moving target for pre-accession adjustment.

External policy was included in the Commission's original *avis* (Opinions) on the candidate states' applications, and it has featured since then in the annual progress reports. Whereas the Opinions[1] and initial reports subdivided the subject matter into Trade and International Economic Relations, Development, Customs, and Common Foreign and Security Policy (CFSP), the 2000 and 2001 reports divide the topic according to the negotiating chapters, on the Customs Union, External Relations, and the CFSP.[2]

In the first part of this Chapter we will examine the scope of the obligations imposed on new Member States as they adapt their external policies— international agreements, trade instruments, foreign policy—to Community and Union policy and practice. The first section will consider the Community-law based obligation on Member States (new and existing) to conform their prior international treaty obligations to the EC Treaty. We will then turn to the external policy *acquis* and its impact on new Members' external

---

[1] Commission Opinions on applications for membership, July 1997, COM(97)2001–2010, section 3.8, 'External Policies'.

[2] Regular Reports from the Commission on Progress towards Accession by each of the candidate countries: 4 Nov. 1998, section 3.8; 13 Oct. 1999, section 3.8; 8 Nov. 2000, 13 Nov. 2001, and 9 Oct. 2002, section 3.1, chapters 25 'customs union', 26 'external relations', and 27 'common foreign and security policy'.

policies. However, although there is no real debate over derogations or transitional periods in the external policy context, the effects of enlargement are not all one way. External policy is certainly one aspect of the Union's activities which will be considerably affected by enlargement, and the second part of this Chapter turns to this dimension as the external becomes internal. Inevitably, it has not been possible to examine the impact of enlargement on every aspect of external policy, and the external dimension of Justice and Home Affairs, for example, is mentioned only briefly.[3] The focus is on the two aspects of external policy which may be said between them to exemplify the developing international identity of the European Community and the European Union: trade policy and foreign policy. What obligations will the enlarged Union have towards the WTO in terms of the enlargement of the customs union? How will enlargement affect the management and orientation of the Community's trade policy more generally? And how will enlargement impact on the Union's common foreign and security policy, especially its relations with its near neighbours? Of course, we are here dealing in trends and likelihood, rather than firm prediction. Nevertheless it is clear that enlargement will pose challenges for the Union's external policy which will affect the nature and identity of the Union itself.

2. THE EFFECT OF ACCESSION ON THE EXTERNAL POLICIES OF THE NEW MEMBERS

A. Adaptation of New Members' Existing Agreements

New Member States join the EU with an array of existing international treaty commitments. How are these affected by the new commitments represented by EU membership? The subsequent conclusion by one treaty partner of a second treaty with a third party does not, in the event of any conflict between the two agreements, absolve the former from liability in international law for any failure to comply with its obligations under the earlier treaty.[4] In addition, a subsequent agreement (especially one establishing a regional integration arrangement) may expressly preserve the rights of third parties under earlier treaties. Accession to the EU does not produce any automatic

[3] See further Council Report to the European Council at Santa Maria da Feira, June 2000, 'European Union Priorities and Objectives for External Relations in the Field of Justice and Home Affairs' (doc. 7653/00); Conclusions of the European Council, Seville, 21–22 June 2002, at paras. 33–36. Eisl, 'Relations with the Central and Eastern Countries in Justice and Home Affairs: Deficits and Options', 2 *European Foreign Affairs Rev.* (1997) 351; Zielonka, 'How New Enlarged Borders Will Reshape the European Union', 39 *Journal of Common Market Studies* (2001) 507; see also chapter 6 note 37.

[4] Vienna Convention on the Law of Treaties, 1969, Art. 30.

effects in relation to prior treaty commitments of the new Member State towards third states.[5] There is no automatic requirement that earlier treaty obligations must be revised or denounced.[6] However, they will need to be examined, in order to see how their implementation may be affected by EU membership, and it may become necessary to renegotiate or even to denounce them.

The EC Treaty deals expressly with Member States' prior treaty obligations towards third states in Article 307 (formerly Article 234). The relevant Act of Accession will make an express reference to the applicability of this provision.[7] Article 307 does two things. In the first paragraph (amplified by the third paragraph) it confirms the rights of third states in respect of prior agreements. In the second paragraph it imposes an obligation on Member States to take the necessary steps to eliminate any incompatibility between such earlier agreements and the EC Treaty. Article 307 is of general scope and applies to any international agreement, irrespective of subject matter, which is capable of affecting the application of the Treaty.[8]

The rights and obligations arising from agreements concluded before 1 January 1958 or, for acceding states, before the date of their accession, between one or more Member States on the one hand, and one or more third countries on the other, shall not be affected by the provisions of this Treaty.

To the extent that such agreements are not compatible with this Treaty, the Member State or States concerned shall take all appropriate steps to eliminate the incompatibilities established. Member States shall, where necessary, assist each other to this end and shall, where appropriate, adopt a common attitude.

[5] As regards the Member States' prior Treaty obligations towards *each other*, the Court of Justice confirmed in Case 10/61, *Commission v. Italy*, [1962] ECR 1, in the context of the GATT, that 'in matters governed by the EEC Treaty, that Treaty takes precedence over agreements concluded between Member States before its entry into force, including agreements made within the framework of GATT'. Cf. Vienna Convention on the Law of Treaties, 1969, Art. 30(3).

[6] Even trade agreements; see Council Decision 97/351 authorizing automatic renewal and continuing in force of provisions governing matters within the common commercial policy contained in friendship, commerce and navigation treaties between Member States and third states, OJ 1997 L 151/24.

[7] See, e.g., Act concerning the conditions of accession of the Kingdom of Norway, the Republic of Austria, the Republic of Finland and the Kingdom of Sweden and the adjustments to the Treaties on which the European Union is founded, OJ 1994 C 241/9, Art. 6. For other Acts of Accession, see Act of Accession relating to Denmark, Ireland, Norway and United Kingdom, OJ 1972 L 73/5; Act of Accession relating to Greece, OJ 1979 L 291/9; Act of Accession relating to Spain and Portugal, OJ 1985 L 302/9. The amendment to Art. 307(1) introduced by the Treaty of Amsterdam (see below note 9) may remove this necessity by making explicit the application of Art. 307 to newly acceding states.

[8] Case 812/79, *Attorney General v. Juan C. Burgoa*, [1980] ECR 2787, Rec. 6; Case C–158/91, *Ministère Public v. Levy*, [1993] ECR I–4287, Rec. 11; Case C–62/98, *Commission v. Portuguese Republic*, [2000] ECR I–5171, Rec. 43.

In applying the agreements referred to in the first paragraph, Member States shall take into account the fact that the advantages accorded under this Treaty by each Member State form an integral part of the establishment of the Community and are thereby inseparably linked with the creation of common institutions, the conferring of powers upon them and the granting of the same advantages by all the other Member States.[9]

The first paragraph has been said to be merely declaratory of the general international law principle of *pacta sunt servanda*, by which the Member States and Community are bound.[10] At an early stage it was established that the 'rights and obligations' referred to in Article 307(1) meant the *rights* of third countries and the *obligations* of the Member State(s). Member States cannot thus use this provision to justify giving priority to rights they may have under a prior agreement over their EC Treaty obligations. In *Commission v. Italy*, the Court dismissed an Italian argument defending its application of a particular rate of duty on products from other Member States (during the EEC's transitional period) on the basis of its entitlements under the GATT. The Court agreed with the Commission's argument:

that the terms 'rights and obligations' in Article 234 refer, as regards the 'rights', to the rights of third countries and, as regards the 'obligations', to the obligations of Member States and that, by virtue of the principles of international law, by assuming a new obligation which is incompatible with rights held under a prior treaty a state *ipso facto* gives up the exercise of these rights to the extent necessary for the performance of its new obligations.[11]

This identification of the primary purpose of the Article with the preservation of the rights of non-Member States was confirmed in the *Burgoa* case, on the application of the London Fisheries Convention which came into force in 1966, and which created rights and obligations relating to fisheries between Spain (at the time of the case not a Member State) and Ireland.[12] The Court in this case went on to identify as a corollary a duty on the part of the Community institutions:

Although the first paragraph of Article 234 makes mention only of the obligations of the Member States, it would not achieve its purpose if it did not imply a duty on the part of the institutions of the Community not to impede the performance of the obligations of Member States which stem from a prior agreement. However, that duty of the Community institutions is directed only to permitting the Member State

---

[9] Art. 307 EC. The first para. was amended by the Treaty of Amsterdam to make it absolutely clear that the provision applies not only to pre-1958 agreements but also to those concluded by new Member States before the date of their accession.

[10] Case C–62/98, *Commission v. Portuguese Republic* [2000] ECR I–5171, Opinion of AG Mischo at paras. 56–57.

[11] Case 10/61, *Commission v. Italy*, [1962] ECR 1. Art. 234 has become Art. 307.

[12] Case 812/79, *Attorney General v. Juan C. Burgoa*, [1980] ECR 2787.

concerned to perform its obligations under the prior agreement and does not bind the Community as regards the non-Member country in question.[13]

We have here a somewhat different relationship between the prior treaty and the Community institutions from that explored by the Court in respect of the GATT in the *International Fruit Company* case.[14] The Community is not here in any sense substituting itself for the Member State in the performance of its obligations, and the duty of the institutions arises under Community law; the Community has no international law obligation towards the third-country parties. In no sense, then, does the prior agreement become 'an integral part of Community law', and thus Community law cannot 'alter the nature of the rights which may flow from such agreements' or determine the issue of whether or not they might create directly effective individual rights.[15]

The Court in *Burgoa* did not determine the compatibility of the Community's fisheries conservation regime (which *inter alia* imposed restrictions on fishing within Member State waters applicable to Spanish-registered vessels) with the earlier London Fisheries Convention. It simply stated that the Community measure, although autonomous, had been adopted in 1978 against the background of a reciprocal renegotiation of conditions of access to fisheries between the Community and Spain and that this new 'framework of relations' had been 'superimposed on the regime which previously applied in those zones'.[16]

What does the duty not to impede mean? First, it may give the affected Member State a justification for failing to comply with Community-law obligations, if doing so would be inconsistent with its obligations to a third state under a prior agreement. In the *Levy* case, for example, the Court held:

the national court is under an obligation to ensure that Article 5 of Directive 76/207 is fully complied with by refraining from applying any conflicting provision of national legislation, unless the application of such a provision is necessary in order to ensure the performance by the Member State concerned of obligations arising under an agreement concluded with non-member countries prior to the entry into force of the EEC Treaty.[17]

Whether the application of a provision of national law was 'necessary' in order to fulfil obligations imposed by an international agreement (in this case, ILO Convention No.89 on night work for women in industry), and in particular the scope of the obligation, and whether the provisions of that

---

[13] Ibid., Rec.9.
[14] Cases 22–24/72, *International Fruit Company*, [1972] ECR 1219. The AG in *Burgoa* explores this distinction more fully.
[15] Case 812/79, *Attorney General v. Juan C. Burgoa*, [1980] ECR 2787, Rec.10.
[16] Ibid., Rec.24.
[17] Case C–158/91, *Ministère Public v. Levy*, [1993] ECR I–4287, Rec.22; see also Case C–13/93, *Office Nationale de l'Emploi v. Minne*, [1994] ECR I–371.

Convention had been superceded by later agreements was a question to be determined by the national court, not the Court of Justice.

However, we cannot say that accession to the Community leaves earlier agreements unaffected; Community membership will have an effect on the earlier agreement as it is applied by the new Member State. As we have seen, the duty not to impede is limited to the performance of its *obligations* by a (new) Member State; it does not extend to the exercise of its rights. Nor does it provide a justification for an action which the Member State is empowered but not required to do by the earlier agreement, if that would entail a breach of Community-law obligations.[18] The third paragraph of Article 307 requires Member States to take account of their Community membership, and the particular characteristics of this intensive commitment to integration, in applying the prior agreement.

In addition, the *Burgoa* case illustrates that the 'duty not to impede' does not appear to prevent the development of the Community regime in a direction that will lead to problems in implementing an earlier agreement, and will thus raise the issue of a renegotiation based on Article 307(2). In a case a year later also in the context of the Community fisheries policy, the Court applied similar reasoning to a bilateral agreement entered into by a Member State, not before its accession to the Community, but prior to the exercise of Community competence in the field.[19]

These cases show that even though a prior agreement may not conflict with Community law at the time of accession, Community law and policy may develop subsequently to the point that an incompatibility arises. In either case, Article 307(2) *requires* the Member State(s) concerned to 'take all

---

[18] Case C–324/93, *R. v. Secretary of State for Home Department, ex parte Evans Medical Ltd and Macfarlan Smith Ltd*, [1995] ECR I–0563, Rec.32: 'when an international agreement allows, but does not require, a Member State to adopt a measure which appears to be contrary to Community law, the Member State must refrain from adopting such a measure'. See also Joined Cases C–364/95 and C–365/95, *T. Port GmbH & Co. v. Hauptzollamt Hamburg-Jonas* [1998] ECR I–1023, Rec.61: 'for a Community provision to be deprived of effect as a result of an international agreement, two conditions must be fulfilled: the agreement must have been concluded before the entry into force of the Treaty and the third country concerned must derive from it rights which it can require the Member State concerned to respect'.

[19] Case 181/80, *Procureur général près la Cour d'Appel de Pau and others v. José Arbelaiz-Emazabel*, [1981] ECR 2961. In this case, the agreement at issue was a bilateral fisheries agreement between France and Spain concluded within the framework of the London Fisheries Convention. The Court held, following Joined Cases 3, 4 & 6/76, *Cornelis Kramer and others*, [1976] ECR 1279, that under Community law France was able to enter into the Convention and the bilateral agreement, but that its effects had been superseded by subsequent Community policy, including internal Regulations on fisheries conservation and the negotiation and conclusion of a Community agreement on fisheries with Spain. It is also of interest that the Court here does not merely assert the obligation to renegotiate the agreement; it requires the national court not to apply the prior agreement, to the extent that it conflicts with the Community Regulation: see Case 181/80, *Arbelaiz-Emazabel*, Rec.29–31.

appropriate steps to eliminate the incompatibilities established'. Member States are to assist each other to this end and, where appropriate (for example where more than one Member State is a party), adopt a common attitude. This obligation, which can be seen as part of the Member States' obligation to apply the Community *acquis*, may require a renegotiation, or even a denunciation, of the earlier agreement.

A group of recent cases has illustrated the extent of this obligation imposed upon Member State parties to prior agreements. These cases all concerned the impact of a Council Regulation on maritime transport, which applies to maritime transport not only between Member States but also between Member States and third countries.[20] Under this Regulation, cargo-sharing arrangements contained in existing bilateral agreements concluded by Member States with third countries were to be 'phased out or adjusted', at the latest by 1 January 1993. The first case does not involve Article 307, as it concerned a post-accession agreement between Belgium and Zaire; here the obligation to 'phase out' or adjust the agreement derived directly from the Regulation.[21] The Court held that where negotiated adjustment had not proved possible within a reasonable time and the time limit set by the Regulation had expired, the Member State is under a Community law obligation to denounce the agreement. Political difficulties in the third state are not a reason to delay:

The existence of a difficult political situation in a third state which is a contracting party, as in the present case, cannot justify a failure to fulfil obligations. If a Member State encounters difficulties that make it impossible to adjust an agreement, it must denounce the agreement.[22]

The Court adopted the same approach—this time in the context of Article 307—in two further cases concerning bilateral *pre-accession* agreements between Portugal and Angola[23] and Portugal and the Federal Republic of Yugoslavia[24] respectively (referred to rather confusingly by the Court as 'pre-Community conventions'). In neither case had negotiations with the third countries concerned yet led to a formal amendment of the agreement and the Commission brought infringement actions against Portugal. Portugal put forward a number of arguments in its defence relating to the scope of the Article 307(2) obligation, and its relationship to the first paragraph of that Article.

---

[20] Council Regulation 4055/86/EEC applying the principle of freedom to provide services to maritime transport between Member States and between Member States and third countries, OJ 1986 L 378/1.
[21] Case C–170/98, *Commission v. Belgium*, [1999] ECR I–5493.
[22] Case C–170/98, *Commission v. Belgium*, [1999] ECR I–5493, Rec.42–43.
[23] Case C–62/98, *Commission v. Portuguese Republic*, [2000] ECR I–5171.
[24] Case C–84/98, *Commission v. Portuguese Republic*, [2000] ECR I–5215.

168 *Marise Cremona*

In Portugal's view, by requiring 'appropriate steps' Article 307(2) EC 'does not impose the obligation to achieve a specific result in the sense of requiring [the Member States], regardless of the legal consequences and political price, to eliminate the incompatibility'. Portugal argued that denunciation should be used only in extreme situations; it is appropriate only where it is clear that the third country does not wish to renegotiate the agreement: '[m]ere difficulties, political or otherwise, in adjusting the agreement are not sufficient to require denunciation'.[25] This argument was based in part upon a link drawn between the first and second paragraphs of Article 307. In order to respect the third country's rights under the agreement (paragraph 1), measures taken to eliminate incompatibilities (paragraph 2) should be limited to the minimum necessary. Denunciation, as an extreme measure, should rarely be required. Significantly, in linking the measure of 'appropriateness' of the required action with the concept of proportionality, Portugal also relied in particular on the balance which (it argued) is reflected in Article 307 between 'the interests linked to Portuguese foreign policy as compared with the Community interest'.

The Court starts by denying a link in the sense suggested by Portugal between the first and second paragraphs of Article 307. If the agreement expressly envisages denunciation as an option, as was the case here, then it cannot be argued that to denounce the agreement is to curtail the third state's rights under the agreement (there is no right not to have the agreement denounced). The duty to denounce where the situation is such that adjustment is not possible then follows from the earlier *Commission v. Belgium* case.[26] The Court does not reject completely the Portuguese argument that denunciation should be resorted to only as an exceptional measure; it merely points to the fact that under the Regulation applicable in this particular case a clear obligation is imposed to 'phase out or adjust' certain existing bilateral agreements within a specified time limit. The choice of 'appropriate steps' granted in Article 307 has thus been circumscribed by the *lex specialis* in the specific Regulation. The Court is thus able to side step the Portuguese contention that Article 307(2) does not require elimination of the incompatibility 'regardless of the legal consequences and

[25] Case C–62/98, *Commission v. Portuguese Republic*, [2000] ECR I–5171, Rec.24–25. As regards the interpretation of Art. 307 the arguments of both Portugal and the Commission and the findings of the Court are substantively identical in the two cases.
[26] See the passage from *Commission v. Belgium* cited above at note 22; whereas the Court in this passage refers simply to the impossibility of renegotiation, in Cases C–62/98 and C–84/98 the Court links the obligation to denounce the agreement to the impossibility of meeting the time limit imposed by the Regulation: Case C–62/98, *Commission v. Portuguese Republic*, [2000] ECR I–5171, Rec.33–34. See Hillion, 'Case note on Case C–62/98, *Commission v. Portuguese Republic*, [2000] ECR I–5171 and Case C–84/98, *Commission v. Portuguese Republic* [2000] ECR I–5215', 38 *CML Rev.* (2001), 1269.

political price', although the tenor of the judgment suggests that this is indeed required. The Court also accepts by implication that Article 307 reflects a 'balance between the foreign-policy interests of a Member State and the Community interest', but takes the view that within Article 307 this is incorporated in the balance between the first and second paragraphs. Member State interests are protected by allowing them to continue to honour their earlier treaty obligations, and by giving them a certain choice in how to resolve incompatibilities—subject to the proviso that these incompatibilities must be resolved in favour of the predominance of Community law and policy:

although, in the context of Article 234 of the Treaty [now Article 307], the Member States have a choice as to the appropriate steps to be taken, they are nevertheless under an obligation to eliminate any incompatibilities existing between a pre-Community convention and the EC Treaty. If a Member State encounters difficulties which make adjustment of an agreement impossible, an obligation to denounce that agreement cannot therefore be excluded.[27]

In each of these cases, the Member States claimed that the incompatibility was formal only, in that the agreements were not in fact being *applied* in contravention of Community law. This defence is simply ignored by the Court; whether under the 1986 maritime transport Regulation or under Article 307 itself, the obligation is to remove the source of the incompatibility. Merely failing to apply an incompatible agreement is not good enough.[28] However there is one important constraint on the Member State's ultimate obligation to denounce an agreement under Article 307(2); the Court recognized that it is incumbent on the Member State concerned to denounce the agreement 'in so far as denunciation of such an agreement is possible under international law'.[29] In these specific cases, there was no obstacle as the bilateral agreements contained provision for denunciation. In the absence either of such a provision or of agreement with the third country concerned, international law may present an obstacle to compliance with Community law. Advocate General Mischo has taken the view that in such cases international law must prevail, 'a Member State which finds it impossible under public international law to release itself from a previous

---

[27] Case C–84/98, *Commission v. Portuguese Republic*, [2000] ECR I–5215, Rec.58. The Court here thus accepts the argument of the Commission, supported by AG Mischo, that Art. 307(2) imposes an obligation of result rather than merely an obligation to make best efforts.

[28] Cf. Case 167/73, *Commission v. France*, [1974] ECR 359; Case C–96/95, *Commission v. Germany*, [1997] ECR I–1653. Within an internal context, it is no defence to an action for breach of Community obligations that an incompatible law is in fact not applied, or is applied consistently with Community law.

[29] Case C–84/98, *Commission v. Portuguese Republic*, [2000] ECR I–5215, Rec.40.

commitment made to a non-member country cannot be accused of a failure to fulfil its [Community] obligations'.[30]

These cases emphasize that Article 307(2) is a particular application of the loyalty principle enshrined in Article 10 EC. It should be remembered that Article 307 applies to any international agreement, irrespective of subject matter, which is capable of affecting the application of the Treaty. It is not limited to areas of external policy that are within exclusive Community competence (such as trade); it applies to agreements that are in themselves within Member State competence or shared competence. The Community obligations of new Member States are not limited to adoption of the Community's own external policy *acquis*, and include the duty to align the whole of their external policy so that it does not conflict with Community policy (internal and external).[31] Article 307 is central to this aspect of enlargement.

In some cases, it will be necessary for a new Member State to withdraw from earlier Agreements and the Act of Accession will provide explicitly for such withdrawal. This is usually the case where there is an existing *Community Agreement* with the particular third country to which the new Member State will be bound as from accession. A good example is the need for the EFTA states to withdraw from EFTA at the time of the 1994 enlargement. Relations between the Community and the EFTA states are governed by the EEA, to which the new Member States were already parties (on the EFTA side), so the actual effects of this change as far as trade is concerned were minimal. The provision in the 1994 Act of Accession relating to Sweden illustrates, however, that other preferential trade agreements may also be affected:

With effect from 1 January 1995, the Kingdom of Sweden shall withdraw, inter alia, from the Convention establishing the European Free-Trade Association signed on 4 January 1960 and from the Free-Trade Agreements signed with Estonia, Latvia and Lithuania in 1992.[32]

Among the current candidate states, many of the central and eastern European states are members of the Central European Free Trade Agreement

---

[30] Case C–62/98, *Commission v. Portuguese Republic*, [2000] ECR I–5171, Opinion of AG Mischo at para. 62. On denunciation in cases where there is no provision in the agreement itself, see Vienna Convention on the Law of Treaties, 1969, Art. 56.

[31] Cf. Joined Cases 3, 4 and 6/76, *Cornelis Kramer and others*, [1976] ECR 1279.

[32] Act concerning the conditions of accession of the Kingdom of Norway, the Republic of Austria, the Republic of Finland and the Kingdom of Sweden and the adjustments to the Treaties on which the European Union is founded OJ 1994 C 241/9, Art. 130. The Act also provided in Art. 131 that if replacement trade agreements between the Community and the Baltic states had not entered into force by the date of accession, 'the Community shall take the necessary measures to allow on accession the continuation of the prevailing level of access to the Swedish market of products originating in those Baltic states'.

(CEFTA) and will need to withdraw from this arrangement on accession.[33] However the CEFTA agreements are designed to mirror the trade provisions of the Europe Agreements, and it is a condition of joining CEFTA that the country has an association agreement with the Community; the disruption caused by one or more CEFTA states acceding to the EU will thus be minimized.[34] Likewise, the bilateral FTAs between the central and eastern European states and EFTA will be replaced by the EEA as these states accede to the EU. Not all cases will be so straightforward; Estonia, for example, has a free trade agreement with Ukraine, whereas the EC does not.[35] Slovenia originally requested a ten-year transitional period with respect to its existing preferential trade commitments towards the countries of the former Socialist Federal Republic of Yugoslavia (SFRY) (Croatia, FYROM, and Bosnia and Herzegovina);[36] however as the EU has since concluded free trade agreements with Croatia and FYROM this issue is less problematic and the request has been withdrawn.

One external relationship may cause particular problems, depending on the timing of the accessions. Currently the Czech Republic and Slovakia operate a customs union. This is not a full EC-type customs union: although they share a common external tariff, goods from third countries do not circulate freely between them, and rules of origin are therefore necessary even within the customs union. In the context of the accession negotiations the Czech Republic has requested the maintenance of this customs union should it accede before Slovakia. In the Commission's view, 'this would inhibit the uniform implementation of the common external tariff, prevent the free movement of goods within the Internal Market, lead to distortions of competition and would disrupt the functioning of the Common Agricultural Policy'.[37]

In practical terms the candidate states are under some pressure to conclude new trade agreements only with those countries with which the Community already has a trade agreement, and to limit the extent of the trade preferences

[33] The Agreement establishing the Central European Free Trade Area (CEFTA) was signed by its founding members (the then Czechoslovakia, Hungary, and Poland) in Krakow, Poland in 1992 and came into force in 1993. Its current members are Poland, Hungary, the Czech Republic, the Slovak Republic, Romania, Bulgaria, and Slovenia; that is, all the non-Baltic CEEC applicant states; Lithuania is seeking membership.

[34] e.g., if Hungary accedes to the EU before Romania, their mutual trade relations will alter from being governed by the CEFTA, modelled on the Europe Agreements, to the EC–Romania Europe Agreement.

[35] The EC has a Partnership and Cooperation Agreement with Ukraine (OJ 1998 L 49/1) which is based on most favoured nation (MFN) and which envisages the possibility of progression to a free trade agreement, but without a timetable or obligation on either side.

[36] Negotiating Position of the Republic of Slovenia on Chapter 26, 'External Relations and Development Aid', 18 Dec. 1998.

[37] Commission's regular progress report for 1999.

contained in such an agreement to those offered by the Community, thus minimizing the need for adjustment after accession. The Commission has even suggested that any new Free Trade Agreements (FTAs) entered into by accession states should contain an express clause agreeing to withdrawal from the agreement on accession without compensation.[38] It has also stated that candidate states will be expected to adjust their prior treaty commitments *before* accession (thus minimizing the need to resort to Article 307):

[the candidate states] should keep the Union fully informed about existing trade agreements or negotiations aimed at the conclusion of any new trade agreements with a third country. Any international agreement which is incompatible with the obligations of membership will have to be renegotiated or renounced prior to accession.[39]

As these examples show, there is in practice a close link between the prior agreements of a new Member State and the need to align itself to the Community *acquis*, including existing Community agreements. Let us now turn to the adoption of the Community and Union's external policy *acquis*.

B. Adoption of the External Policy *Acquis*

In acceding to the EU, the candidate states will accede to the Community and Union external policy *acquis*. This external policy *acquis* can be conveniently divided into three elements: first, the autonomous policy instruments, including trade instruments; second, the contractual *acquis*: treaty-based policy, including preferential trade, development cooperation, and association agreements; third, the CFSP *acquis*. In each case, for different reasons, there is little flexibility in the Community's approach to the enlargement negotiations, and in fact no transitional arrangements have been accepted. As far as autonomous policy instruments are concerned, there is little scope for flexibility as a result of the need for uniformity in external trade policy, although, as we shall see, the Community's own policy instruments may need adjustment in the light of enlargement. The contractual *acquis* involves the rights and interests of third countries, and it is difficult for the new Member States to do more than accept the previously agreed arrangements. The CFSP *acquis* has proved to be the least problematic for the candidate states; in this case too, however, no policy change would be agreed by the Union as a condition of accession. This is not to say that Union external policy will be unaffected by accession, and the implications of this will be explored in

---

[38] EP Briefing Report No.37, 'Enlargement and External Economic Relations', 8 Sept. 1999, at 16 The question of possible compensation will be discussed below.

[39] Commission Progress Reports for 2001, note 2 above, sect. 3.1, chap. 26.

section 3 of this Chapter; it is rather that the Community will not readily agree special conditions within these negotiating chapters.[40]

1. Autonomous Policy Instruments

The autonomous policy instruments that fall within the Community's *acquis* include:

- the Community Customs Code (encompassing the common customs tariff, together with rules *inter alia* on nomenclature, valuation, and origin);
- autonomous trade preferences, in particular the Generalized System of Preferences (GSP), but also including trade preferences such as those applicable to certain states of South-East Europe;
- other trade policy instruments such as the Anti-Dumping and Trade Barriers Regulations, legislation on the import of counterfeit and pirated goods, export controls such as those applying to dual-use goods, and instruments on standards and product safety, and trade and environmental measures;
- non-trade measures, such as the financial and technical assistance programmes (PHARE, TACIS, CARDS, MEDA).
- measures concerning third countries which are contained within other internal Community legislation, such as the Banking and Procurement Directives.

Under the Acts of Accession, the 'original Treaties' and the acts adopted by the institutions before accession are binding on the new Member States.[41] Thus, these autonomous instruments will be automatically applicable. The Acts of Accession provide in Annexes for the necessary amendments to these measures.[42] In addition, specific provision is made relating to aspects of external policy, in particular dealing with transitional arrangements. For example, Annex VI of the Act of Accession 1994 deals with transitional arrangements for the application of customs legislation, including rules of origin:

Evidences of origin properly issued by third countries in the framework of preferential agreements concluded by the Republic of Austria, the Republic of Finland, ... or the Kingdom of Sweden with those countries or in the framework of unilateral

---

[40] It is not impossible however; e.g., Hungary has been granted a three-year transitional period for the import of aluminium.

[41] See, e.g., Act concerning the conditions of accession of the Kingdom of Norway, the Republic of Austria, the Republic of Finland and the Kingdom of Sweden and the adjustments to the Treaties on which the European Union is founded (hereafter Act of Accession 1994) OJ 1994 C24/91, Art. 2.

[42] Ibid., Art. 29 and Annex I; Arts. 54, 73, 97, and 126 and Annex VI.

national legislation of the new Member States shall be accepted in the respective new Member States, provided that:
—the evidence of origin and the transport documents have been issued the day before accession at the latest;
—the evidence of origin is submitted to the customs authorities four months after accession at the latest.

Specific provision may also be made for transition/adaptation in relation to the Community's quantitative restrictions regime:

The Republic of Austria may, until 31 December 1996, maintain with respect to the Republic of Hungary, the Republic of Poland, the Slovak Republic, the Czech Republic, Romania and Bulgaria, the import restrictions which it applied on 1 January 1994 in respect of lignite falling under code 27 02 10 00 of the Combined Nomenclature. The necessary adaptations will be made to the Europe Agreements and, where applicable, to the Interim Agreements concluded with those countries in accordance with Article 76.[43]

In the forthcoming enlargement process, two factors will ease the process of alignment to the *acquis*.

The first is the fact that all candidate states are WTO members; Lithuania was last to join on 31 May 2001. As EC trade policy is itself designed to comply with WTO commitments, this means that in many areas EC policy and accession state policy will be compatible and indeed similar, and may need relatively little adjustment to the legislation itself. This is not to say that accession will have no impact on the way those policies are used. For example, Community Regulations will replace national rules on trade defence measures such as anti-dumping and safeguard measures. Another example is the GSP system; most of the candidate states have an existing preferential import regime for imports from developing countries that comply with WTO rules,[44] but adjustments will be needed in relation to coverage and preferences.[45]

The second factor is the pre-accession process itself, whereby the accession states are consciously aligning themselves to EU instruments already. This applies, for example, to customs legislation and origin rules. Alignment with Community product and environmental standards will also assist. Other

---

[43] Ibid., Art. 74.

[44] The GATT Contracting Parties agreed on an 'enabling clause', in June 1971, originally for a period of ten years, and subsequently renewed on 28 Nov. 1979 for an indefinite period; this clause allows for non-reciprocal trade preferences for developing countries as an exception to MFN.

[45] e.g., in the WTO Trade Policy Review carried out for Poland in June 2000, the Polish Government's report recognized that '[t]he adoption of the EU preferences system for DEV and LDC will extend substantially the number of countries eligible for tariff preferences' (currently 45 and 49 respectively; within the EC, by contrast, GSP preferences apply to 146 independent countries and 25 dependent or administered territories).

areas of Community external policy, such as technical assistance measures including the MEDA and TACIS programmes and development policy, are naturally not subject to this process of pre-accession alignment.

The accession states have already aligned or are in the process of aligning their customs legislation with that of the EU. This is part of the process of pre-accession approximation and is provided for in both the Europe Agreements[46] and in the Commission's White Paper of 1995.[47] For example, from 1992 Romania has operated a customs tariff based upon the internationally-based standard of the Harmonized Nomenclature,[48] approximated at the eight-digit level with the Combined Nomenclature of the European Union. In 1997 Romania adopted a new Customs Code designed to be fully harmonized with the EC's Customs Code. In 1997, as part of the process of harmonizing its trade policy regulations with those of the EU, Hungary introduced the European system of cumulation of origin, so that Hungary now applies the same rules of origin as the EU.

More problematic has been the question of institutional capacity, relating especially to the management of customs. A comment made in the Opinion on Poland in 1997 is typical:

Poland's capacity fully to apply the *acquis* presupposes the possibility to adopt and implement the Community legislation; and the existence of an adequate level of infrastructure and equipment, in particular in terms of computerisation and investigation means and the establishment of an efficient customs organisation with a sufficient number of qualified and motivated staff showing a high degree of integrity.[49]

In general the Commission's regular reports since 1997 have evidenced progress in adopting Community standards in relation to customs management. The candidate countries are developing 'policies, systems, procedures, technologies and instruments compatible with the EU requirements and standards',[50] including detection equipment and computerized revenue collection and information systems.

Full alignment with the common external tariff, with preferential tariffs, and with the Community's system of quotas for agricultural and textile products will not take place until accession itself. Generally speaking, the common external tariff is lower than both the candidate states' existing

[46] e.g., the Europe Agreement with Poland, Arts. 69 and 91.
[47] Commission 'White Paper' on Preparation of the Associated Countries of Central and Eastern Europe for Integration into the Internal Market of the Union, COM(95)163 final, 3 May 1995.
[48] See Convention on Harmonized Nomenclature System, OJ 1987 L 198/3, implemented within the EC by Regulation 2658/87, OJ 1987 L 256/1.
[49] Commission Opinion on application for membership, July 1997, COM(97)2002, sect. 3.8, at 99.
[50] Commission report on progress of negotiations on chapter 25, 17 Jan. 2002.

bound tariffs and their applied tariffs. The EC's weighted average MFN tariff for industrial products is 3.6 per cent.[51] Rates for agricultural products are much higher at a simple average of 16.2 per cent (although tariff quotas provide access at zero or reduced rates on high-tariff items for WTO Members, as well as for imports from preferential trading partners).[52] This compares for example with Romania's average MFN tariffs for industrial products for 1999 of 16 per cent (applied) and 35 per cent (bound). Applied tariffs on agricultural products are higher, even though they were reduced in 1997, bringing the average on such products from 134.1 per cent in 1995 to 33.9 per cent in 1999. In Hungary, the rates for industrial products and agricultural products were 7.1 per cent and 31 per cent respectively in 2001. In Poland the weighted average MFN tariff in 2001 for industrial products was 9.9 per cent and 34 per cent for agricultural products.

As the above figures for Romania show, some states, unlike the EC, maintain a considerable gap between bound and applied rates, so accession will result in greater transparency (and reduced flexibility).[53]

It should also be borne in mind that for many candidate states the impact on their domestic industry of the lowering of customs duties implied by accession will be lessened as a result of the prior effects of the trade provisions of the Europe Agreements (for all these states, trade with the EC accounts for a significant proportion of imports).

This picture—of an overall lowering of tariffs on accession—is not universal. Estonia, for example, applies an average tariff of 3.2 per cent on agricultural imports and does not apply any import tariffs to industrial products. It will thus need to engage in a process of introducing customs duties as well as the considerable necessary infrastructure.[54] The implications of this from a WTO perspective are considered further in section 3.A below.

2. The Contractual Acquis

Joining the European Union is not only a matter of accepting the level of economic integration that exists between its Member States. The new Member States will also be acceding to a wide variety of regional integration agreements to which the EC is a party. They will, for example, become members of the EEA as well as the EC and a network of other free trade and

[51] Figures taken from the Commission's Progress Reports of 13 Nov. 2001.
[52] WTO Trade Policy Review: Report on the EC and its Member States, July 2000.
[53] Under WTO rules, a Contracting Party which agrees on a particular 'bound' tariff rate (as set out in its tariff bindings schedule) may not exceed this maximum; however the actual tariff applied may be lower than the bound rate, thus allowing a certain flexibility in managing tariff policy.
[54] Varblane, 'Trade Policy Implications of EU Membership for Estonia', 2 *Baltic Journal of Economics* (1999) 249, at 251.

other cooperation agreements including those with the Euro-Mediterranean states, the states of the former Soviet Union, South Africa, Mexico, MERCOSUR, and other Latin American states. They will also need to accede to the WTO plurilateral agreements to which the EU and its Member States are party, such as the Agreement on Government Procurement and the Agreement on Trade in Civil Aircraft.

The mechanisms whereby the new Member States become bound by these agreements vary according to whether the Agreement is one to which the Community only is a party, or whether it is a mixed agreement. We are in this section concerned with prior *Community* Agreements (for prior Agreements of the accession states see section 2.A of this Chapter).

Where the Community alone is a party (the Free Trade Agreement with Switzerland of 1972, for example, or the Cooperation Agreement on Partnership and Development with India of 1994, or the Mutual Recognition Agreements with Australia and the USA), then the new Member State will become bound by the Agreements directly on the basis of Article 300(7) EC and specific provisions of the relevant Acts of Accession.[55]

A general provision in the Act of Accession refers to Community agreements:

The agreements or conventions concluded by any of the Communities, with one or more third states, with an international organization or with a national of a third state, shall, under the conditions laid down in the original Treaties and in this Act, be binding on the new Member States.[56]

In addition, specific sectoral Agreements may be mentioned, especially those relating to textiles,[57] fisheries,[58] and agricultural products.[59]

Where the existing Agreement is 'mixed' (concluded by both the Community and the Member States) the position is more complex. The new Member States will need to accede to each Agreement. At the time of the 1994 accession, for example, this was required in respect of the Europe Agreements. The provision in the 1994 Act of Accession is typical:

The new Member States undertake to accede, under the conditions laid down in this Act, to the agreements or conventions concluded by the present Member States and any of the Communities, acting jointly, and to the agreements concluded by those

---

[55] In what follows, the Act of Accession 1994 is cited as the most recent example; earlier Acts of Accession have contained substantively identical provisions, and thus provide a reliable guide to what may be expected in the forthcoming enlargement treaties.

[56] Act of Accession 1994, OJ 1994 C 241/9, Art. 5(1).

[57] Ibid., Art. 75 (Austria; similar articles provide for the other new Member States). This includes bilateral agreements and the WTO Agreement on Textiles and Clothing.

[58] Ibid., Art. 124 (Sweden).

[59] Ibid., Arts. 76 and 77.

states which are related to those agreements or conventions. The Community and the present Member States, in the framework of the Union, shall assist the new Member States in this respect.[60]

The final sentence recognizes that this commitment will require negotiation with the EC's partner(s). The EEA expressly provides for accession by new EU Member States in Article 128 EEA. The Europe Agreements also contain provisions relating to accession by a third country to the EU.

In the case of both simple Community Agreements and mixed Agreements, it may be necessary to negotiate adjustments to these treaties to take account of the accessions; in particular, preferential tariff quotas (such as those operating for agricultural products) will need to be increased. Agreements with trade provisions will be applied by the new Member States from the date of accession; meanwhile adjustment protocols are to be negotiated. For example, the Act of Accession of 1994 stipulated:

Article 128:
1. As from 1 January 1995, the Kingdom of Sweden shall apply the provisions of the Agreements referred to in Article 129.
2. Any adjustments shall be the subject of protocols concluded with the co-contracting countries and annexed to those Agreements.
. . .

Article 129:
Article 128 shall apply to:
—the Agreements concluded with Andorra, Algeria, Bulgaria, the former Czech and Slovak Federal Republic and its successor states (the Czech Republic and the Slovak Republic), Cyprus, Egypt, Hungary, Iceland, Israel, Jordan, Lebanon, Malta, Morocco, Poland, Romania, Slovenia, Switzerland, Syria, Tunisia and Turkey and to other Agreements concluded with third countries and concerning exclusively trade in the products listed in Annex II to the EC Treaty;
—the fourth ACP/EEC Convention, signed on 15 December 1989;
—other similar agreements which might be concluded before accession.[61]

The new Member States will also agree to 'adjust their position' within international organizations (such as the UN, OECD, or UNCTAD) and in the context of other international agreements to which the Community and/or other Member States are also parties (such as the WTO), to take account of the rights and obligations arising from their accession to the Union.[62]

---

[60] Ibid., Art. 5(2). The new Member States also agree to accede to the internal agreements concluded by the present Member States for the purpose of implementing these mixed agreements.

[61] Ibid., Arts. 128 and 129. See also Art. 127(2) in relation to the conclusion of protocols to textile agreements in order to adjust quantitative limits on imports of textiles to take account of existing trade flows between the new Member States and the relevant third country.

[62] Ibid., Art. 5(4).

What will be the impact of these commitments in the context of the forthcoming enlargement?

All the accession states are WTO members and are beginning to align themselves to EC positions within the WTO framework (for example, discussion on the New Round). As part of this process, the EC is encouraging the accession states to accede to the plurilateral agreements to which the EC is a party if they have not yet done so. The degree to which this alignment has taken place is commented on in the Commission's regular reports on progress in satisfying the pre-accession (Copenhagen) conditions.

Many of the accession states already have free trade agreements with the EC's free trade partners, especially those within Europe itself.[63] Although the degree of trade liberalization reached by the EC's free trade agreements may differ, there is therefore no fundamental change in direction. We have already seen that the six central and eastern European states (Czech Republic, Slovakia, Hungary, Poland, Romania, and Bulgaria) are members of CEFTA; they all have free trade agreements with each other modelled on the Europe Agreements. Likewise the Baltic states (BAFTA). Romania and Bulgaria will be part of the network of free trade agreements envisaged for the South-East European states.[64]

Among the European Community's network of free trade agreements, the EEA has distinctive characteristics, not least its multilateral character and highly developed institutional framework. The central and eastern European states and the Baltic states already have free trade agreements with the EFTA states. On accession, these will be replaced by the EEA. As the EEA substantively replicates aspects of the internal market, any transitional arrangements negotiated in respect of these provisions will need to apply to the EEA as well, and will ultimately need to be agreed by the EFTA parties. The EEA–EFTA states are working towards a simultaneous enlargement of the EU and the EEA, which will require specific negotiations and the adjustment of the EEA agreement. In a recent meeting, the EEA Council stressed:

the common objective of simultaneous accession of new members to the EU and to the EEA, in order to secure the homogeneity and the good functioning of the European Economic Area. The EEA Council ... underlined the need for these countries to apply for membership in the EEA (Article 128) and negotiate their

---

[63] Malta is an exception; according to the Commission's progress report of Nov. 2001, it does not have free-trade agreements other than with the EC itself.

[64] Under the Memorandum of Understanding on Trade Liberalization and Facilitation, agreed in the framework of the Stability Pact for South Eastern Europe on 27 June 2001, Bulgaria and Romania will conclude a network of bilateral free-trade agreements by 2002 with the five other signatories (Albania, Bosnia-Herzegovina, Croatia, the Federal Republic of Yugoslavia, and FYROM).

accession thereto within a timeframe that ensures simultaneous accession to both the EU and the EEA.[65]

In general, the EFTA states and the existing EU Member States are likely to regard the same issues, such as labour mobility, as sensitive.[66] However, there will inevitably be differences: fisheries, for example, will need specific attention. The existing agreements between the EFTA states and the candidate states of central and eastern Europe are more liberal as regards EFTA fisheries exports than the EEA. The EFTA states will want to see a re-evaluation—at least—of the fisheries regime under the EEA. As the Work Programme of the Icelandic Chairmanship for 2002 states: '[t]he EFTA side expects that the EU will at the very least respect the "no-step-back" principle, which implies that the Communities should not rebuild tariff barriers in Europe'.[67]

A further aspect of the EU–EFTA relationship poses questions for the candidate states. Under the original EEA a financial mechanism, funded by the EFTA partners, was designed to reduce social and economic disparities within the EEA and benefited Greece, Ireland, Northern Ireland, Portugal, and Spain. This mechanism extended over five years, but following its expiry the EU and EFTA states negotiated a new financial instrument designed to make a total of 119.6 million euros available to the same beneficiary countries between 1999 and 2003.[68] Although the new instrument was finally agreed, the EFTA states did not accept that they were under an ongoing obligation to continue this support. A target first-wave enlargement date of 2004 will raise the question of the possible negotiation of a similar financial instrument in the context of the accession of the new EU Member States to the EEA, and difficult questions over its extension to the new EU members are likely. Unlike the 1994 enlargement, those joining the EU will be potential beneficiaries rather than contributors to the financial instruments.

Under the terms of its customs union with the EC, Turkey undertook to align itself not only with the common external tariff, but also with the EC's preferential trade regime, both autonomous and contractual. A specific

---

[65] EEA Council Conclusions, 12 Mar. 2002, para. 4. Under Art. 128(1) of the EEA, 'Any European state becoming a member of the Community shall . . . apply to become a party to this Agreement'. The application is made to the EEA Council, and the terms and conditions will be the subject of an agreement between the existing EEA members and the new member. See also Traavik, 'EFTA and Enlargement', *EFTA Bulletin* 2–2001, Dec. 2001.

[66] European Parliament, Task Force 'Enlargement', Briefing Paper No. 32, *The EEA and the Enlargement of the European Union*, 17 Nov. 1998 at 10.

[67] Standing Committee of the EFTA states, Work Programme of the Icelandic Chairmanship for the first half of 2002; available on the EFTA website at: http://secretariat.efta.int/news/Ice%20work%20programme.doc.

[68] EEA Joint Committee Decision 47/2000 of 22 May 2000 on the EEA financial instrument.

commitment to 'negotiate agreements on a mutually advantageous basis with the countries concerned', included in the customs union Decision, encompasses the Europe Agreements, the EEA, and Agreements with the Mediterranean states and the ACP states. Turkey currently has free-trade agreements with the CEFTA parties, with the Baltic states (thus all the Europe Agreement states), the EFTA states, FYROM, and Israel, and is negotiating agreements with a number of the other Euro-Mediterranean states and Croatia.

As far as Europe is concerned, therefore, accession to the EC's network of contractual preferential agreements will amount to a continuation of an existing policy for the acceding states. This is no accident: in this sense enlargement is a large step towards integration within Europe, but one that has been foreshadowed by existing contractual relationships, not only between the candidate states and the EU but between themselves and with other European states. The CEFTA was deliberately designed to assist in this aspect of integration with Community policies. Taking on board the Community's wider preferential commitments (such as the Cotonou Convention, the Economic Partnership, Political Coordination and Cooperation Agreement with Mexico, the Agreement on Trade, Development, and Cooperation with South Africa, and the anticipated free trade agreement with MERCOSUR) will be more of a challenge, however. As we have already seen, the Commission argues that, in view of the need to align contractual relations, it should be informed of any agreements negotiated or concluded by the candidate states, and that all agreements incompatible with the obligations of membership should be renegotiated, or renounced, prior to accession.[69]

3. Common Foreign and Security Policy Acquis: The Acquis Politique

Membership of the European Union entails acceptance of the CFSP *acquis* as well as the EC external *acquis*. The so-called 'Copenhagen criteria' established, in June 1993, the requirements for accession and amplified the rather bare provision of what is now Article 49 TEU.[70] In addition to the political and economic criteria, prospective Member States must demonstrate 'the ability to take on the obligations of membership including adherence to the aims of political, economic and monetary union'. In addition, accession is now to the *Union*, not only the Community, and entails acceptance of the whole of the TEU, including its second and third pillars.

---

[69] See text *supra* at note 39.
[70] Conclusions of the European Council, Copenhagen, June 1993, *Bull. EC* 6–1993, point 1.13. On the Copenhagen criteria, see Chapter 5; see also Cremona, 'Accession to the European Union: Membership Conditionality and Accession Criteria', 25 *Polish Yearbook of International Law* (2002) 256.

Unlike other aspects of the Community external policy *acquis*, the nature of the CFSP instruments as intergovernmental measures means that no formal transposition will be necessary on accession, although some—for example those relating to sanctions—may require specific implementation. Rather, it will be a case of affirming support for and a willingness to be bound by existing foreign and security policy positions and actions. The 1994 enlargement was the first post-TEU accession in which the content of the CFSP was an issue. In the 1994 Act of Accession, the new Member States agree to be bound by 'the provisions of the original Treaties and the acts adopted by the institutions before accession' (Article 2), and the original Treaties are defined to include the TEU as well as the EC, ECSC, and Euratom Treaties and supplementing and amending acts (Article 1). CFSP decisions, such as Common Positions and Joint Actions, will thus be covered. In addition, provision is made in respect of decisions of the Member States concerning the EU, and other non-binding acts of the institutions:

The new Member States accede by this Act to the decisions and agreements adopted by the Representatives of the Governments of the Member States meeting within the Council. They undertake to accede from the date of accession to all other agreements concluded by the present Member States relating to the functioning of the Union or connected with the activities thereof.

. . .

The new Member States are in the same situation as the present Member States in respect of declarations or resolutions of, or other positions taken up by, the European Council or the Council and in respect of those concerning the Communities or the Union adopted by common agreement of the Member States; they will accordingly observe the principles and guidelines deriving from those declarations, resolutions or other positions and will take such measures as may be necessary to ensure their implementation.[71]

This formulation covers such CFSP initiatives as public statements and declarations made on behalf of the Union.

In addition, attached to the 1994 Act of Accession was a joint Declaration on the CFSP that links this aspect of Union policy with the political objectives of the Treaties:

1. The Union notes the confirmation by . . . Austria, Finland and Sweden of their full acceptance of the rights and obligations attaching to the Union and its institutional framework, known as the 'acquis communautaire', as it applies to present Member States. This includes in particular the content, principles and political objectives of the Treaties, including those of the Treaty on European Union.

The Union and . . . the Republic of Austria, the Republic of Finland and the Kingdom of Sweden agree that:

---

[71] Act of Accession 1994, OJ 1994 C 241/9, Art. 4(1) and (3).

—accession to the Union should strengthen the internal coherence of the Union and its capacity to act effectively in foreign and security policy;

—the new Member States will, from the time of their accession, be ready and able to participate fully and actively in the Common Foreign and Security Policy as defined in the Treaty on European Union;

—the new Member States will, on accession, take on in their entirety and without reservation all the objectives of the Treaty, the provisions of Title V thereof, and the relevant declarations attached to it;

—the new Member States will be ready and able to support the specific policies of the Union in force at the time of their accession.

2. With regard to Member States' obligations deriving from the Treaty on European Union concerning the implementation of the Union's Common Foreign and Security Policy it is understood that on the day of accession the legal framework of the acceding countries will be compatible with the 'acquis'.

The provisions on political dialogue were an innovative feature of the Europe Agreements and have provided a framework for participation in CFSP policy-making with meetings held at different levels: ministers, political directors, and experts. As part of the 'structured dialogue' established by the European Council at Copenhagen and Essen in June 1993 and December 1994, political dialogue extends to Cyprus and Malta as well. This process has contributed to what has been called the 'socialisation effect' of the CFSP.[72] On the other hand, the dialogue has been criticized as a monologue (on both sides) with no real exchange of views or debate,[73] and there may also be some understandable resistance from the accession states to pressure from the EU to speak with one voice, particularly in advance of accession. Those accession states that are members of NATO (the Czech Republic, Hungary, Poland, and Turkey) are able to take part in discussion in that forum relating to security and defence issues. Others are part of the Partnership for Peace initiative and Euro-Atlantic Partnership Council. Candidate states are participating in discussion on the development of the European Security and Defence Policy (ESDP) and within the 'EU + 15' (the EU and its Member States, the non-EU European Members of NATO, and the candidate states). A number of candidate states have made commitments to European crisis management and peacekeeping operations including the Rapid Reaction Force.

As part of the pre-accession alignment of policy, the candidate states have in recent years frequently been invited to associate themselves formally with

[72] Allen, 'Wider but Weaker or the More the Merrier? Enlargement and Foreign Policy Cooperation in the EC/EU' in J. Redmond and G. Rosenthal (eds), *The Expanding European Union: Past, Present, Future* (1997)107, at 115.

[73] Klau, 'Tackling the Structural Monologue', *European Voice* 2 (22–28 Feb. 1996), cited by Allen, *supra* note 72, at 115. See also the discussion of the structured dialogue by Maresceau in Chap. 2.

EU foreign policy positions, and have done so. During 1999, for example, Poland associated itself with 11 EU common positions, including three on the Federal Republic of Yugoslavia. Common Positions and Joint Actions supported in this way have included those on the arms export code, Yugoslavia, Rwanda, and Myanmar. The Declaration by the Presidency on behalf of the EU on the announcement of presidential elections in Belarus is a recent example:

> The Central and Eastern European countries associated with the European Union, the associated countries Cyprus, Malta and Turkey, and the EFTA countries, members of the European Economic Area align themselves with this declaration.[74]

As this example shows, it is not only candidate states that will align themselves to Union policy in this way. Furthermore, even among candidate states, this alignment is not automatic. Turkey, for example, did not align itself with a recent Presidency Declaration welcoming the abolition of the death penalty in Chile.[75] In 1999 the Czech Republic decided not to support the EU's declaration on UNIDO (UN Industrial Development Organization) based on its critical view of the work of UNIDO.[76]

In addition, alignment will not be appropriate where the Declaration relates essentially to EU policy; in May 2001, for example, the EU Presidency welcomed the conduct of local elections held in Croatia, as a sign that Croatia is 'on the path to integration into European structures' and affirming that '[t]he EU stands ready to assist Croatia on her way to full implementation of the newly initialled Stabilisation and Association Agreement'.[77] Neither the candidate states nor the EFTA states aligned themselves to this Declaration.

3. THE EFFECT OF ACCESSION ON THE EXTERNAL POLICIES OF THE EUROPEAN COMMUNITY AND EUROPEAN UNION

It has been argued that enlargement is both a cause and an effect of EU external policy.[78] It is an effect in the sense that enlargement is itself a part of that external policy. Enlargement is one way in which the EU may achieve its foreign-policy goals, especially those of increased security and stability within

---

[74] Press release of 11 June 2001, 9751/01.

[75] Press release of 1 June 2001, 9294/01.

[76] Commission's regular progress report for 2000.

[77] Press release of 22 May 2001, 8859/01.

[78] Ginsberg, 'The Impact of Enlargement on the Role of the European Union in the World' in Redmond and Rosenthal (eds), *supra* note 72 at 213; Smith, 'The Conditional Offer of Membership as an Instrument of EU Foreign Policy: Reshaping Europe in the EU's Image', 8 *Marmara Journal of European Studies*, (2000) at 33.

Europe and support for democratization and market reform in transition countries.[79] It is also an effect in the sense that EU external policy activity is one of the factors influencing prospective members to apply for membership. On the positive side, the ability to benefit from the EC's weight as a trading power and (particularly for the current applicants) the security dimension of its CFSP are powerful incentives. On the more negative side, the experience of the EEA demonstrates that a closely integrated but 'external' relationship with the EU will inevitably be one-sided, making demands on the associated country without the direct involvement in decision-making that full membership would entail.[80]

But of course enlargements have also had, and will have, an influence on the future development of EU external policy. There is a basic sense in which the sheer increase in size of the EC/EU has increased not only its influence and the reach of its external policies, both economic and political, but also the expectations of third countries.

One of the effects of enlargement, discussed above, is the need to renegotiate or reshape existing trading relations, contractual and otherwise. In addition, the character and interests of specific new members have influenced the direction of EU policy. The first accessions in 1972, for example, prompted the conclusion of free-trade agreements with the remaining EFTA states, as well as an increased engagement with the Nordic states through Denmark's membership, and with the ACP states and the USA through the UK's membership. The Spanish and Portuguese accessions stimulated the development of EC policy towards Latin America in the late 1980s and the Mediterranean in the 1990s. The effect of the 1994 enlargement is being felt, *inter alia*, in the development of the Northern Dimension to external policy, and particular interest in the Baltic states and Russia, as well as influencing the direction of the development of European security and defence policy.

In addition to policy-orientation, it is also possible to trace the effects of prospective or recent enlargements in some of the changes that have been made to the institutional aspects of EU external policy, particularly in the gradual institutional development of the EPC/CFSP. However, we should take care not to see every development of external policy as somehow related to the latest enlargement: there are other explanations for the periodic

[79] Sjursen and Smith, 'Justifying EU Foreign Policy: The Logics Underpinning EU Enlargement', Arena Working Papers, No.01/1; http://www.arena.uio.no/.

[80] Vachudova, 'The Leverage of International Institutions on Democratising States: Eastern Europe and the European Union', Working Paper, European Forum, European University Institute, 29 Mar. 2001, at 7–8, citing the burden borne by Bulgaria and Romania as a result of the EU economic sanctions against FRY, over which, as non-Member States of the EU, they had no real bargaining power.

outbursts of external activity in the mid-1970s, the later 1980s and the 1990s, for example.[81]

What will be the consequences for the European Union itself of the 'external' becoming the 'internal', in the context of its external policy? Within the framework of this Chapter it is of course not possible even to try to forecast the future direction of every aspect of EU external policy in the post-enlargement period. In attempting to identify at least some of the issues that will emerge from this process, even if not providing many answers, we will make a very broad distinction between, first, trade and external economic policy, and, secondly, the Union's emergent foreign policy.

A. Trade and External Economic Policy

The EC, as a member of the WTO, a customs union, and an economic integration organization, is required to comply with Article XXIV of GATT 1994 and Article V of GATS. Compliance is relevant in two contexts. On the one hand, the Community's own new preferential agreements either must comply with Article XXIV GATT (and Article V GATS[82]) conditions, or a waiver must be sought, as has been done with the Cotonou Convention.[83] On the other hand, accessions to the EU/EC involve the extension of the customs union and thus an extension of the exception to the fundamental GATT principle of MFN represented by that customs union. In aligning its customs tariffs to the existing common external tariff, a new member may need to increase (at least some of) its bound rates; accession may also affect the new member's trade policy in relation to tariff quotas. Thus, the extended customs union must itself satisfy Article XXIV conditions. It is this aspect of Article XXIV that directly concerns us here.

The WTO rules on customs unions and free-trade areas 'both allow and contain preferential trade'.[84] The increased liberalization between the members of a customs union or free trade area (a regional trade agreement, or RTA) is offset by the selective nature of these preferences; an RTA does

[81] Cremona, 'External Relations and External Competence: The Emergence of an Integrated External Policy for the European Union' in P. Craig and G. de Búrca (eds), *EU Law: An Evolutionary Perspective* (1999).

[82] In what follows, I will focus on Art. XXIV of GATT 1994, as much of the debate on compatibility issues has centred around that provision. We should not, however, forget the need to ensure GATS compliance as well.

[83] Mathis, 'The Community's External Regional Policy in the WTO' in P. van Dijck and G. Faber (eds), *The External Economic Dimension of the European Union* (2000). The waiver for the Cotonou Convention with respect to Art. I para. 1 of the GATT 1994 (MFN obligation) until 31 Dec. 2007 was agreed by a decision of the WTO Ministerial Conference at Doha on 14 Nov. 2001, WT/MIN/(01)/15.

[84] Cottier, 'The Challenge of Regionalisation and Preferential Relations in World Trade Law and Policy', 2 *European Foreign Affairs Rev.* (1996) 149.

not, by its nature, observe the unconditional MFN obligation contained in Article I of GATT 1994 and Article II of GATS. The exceptions to MFN thus contained in the GATT and GATS are subject to conditions designed to minimize the trade diversionary effects of the regional discrimination represented by the RTA. Article XXIV(4) expresses this objective:

the purpose of a customs union or of a free trade area should be to facilitate trade between the constituent territories and not to raise barriers to the trade of other contracting parties with such territories.

The conditions set by Article XXIV are therefore not limited to ensuring a high level of liberalization between the members of the RTA. Article XXIV(5), while confirming that the provisions of the GATT 'shall not prevent' the formation of an RTA, requires that the 'duties and other regulations of commerce' applicable by the customs union as a whole (or by each constituent territory of a free trade area) to products from third countries 'shall not on the whole be higher or more restrictive' than the duties applied before the establishment of the RTA.[85]

It is against this background that we need to examine the effect of enlargement on the EU's trade and external economic policy. The EU and the new Member States will desire to demonstrate compliance with Article XXIV, and the impact on specific policies (tariff rates, agricultural trade, and trade protection, for example) will be influenced by WTO disciplines. In what follows, we cannot undertake a complete analysis; instead, we will pick out a number of issues in EC trade policy that are of particular practical importance.

1. The Overall Balance: Trade Creation or Trade Diversion?

Article XXIV GATT strikes a balance between regional and multilateral trade liberalization:

According to paragraph 4 [of Article XXIV], the purpose of a customs union is 'to facilitate trade' between the constituent members and 'not to raise barriers to the trade' with third countries. This objective demands that a balance be struck by the constituent members of a customs union. A customs union should facilitate trade within the customs union, but it should *not* do so in a way that raises barriers to trade with third countries.[86]

---

[85] According to the 'Understanding on the Interpretation of Article XXIV of GATT 1994', agreed during the Uruguay Round, the general incidence of duties applied by a customs union shall be calculated for this purpose on the basis of weighted average tariff rates based on applied rates of duty: Marceau and Reiman, 'When and How is a Regional Trade Agreement Compatible with the WTO?', 28 *Legal Issues of Economic Integration* (2001), 297.

[86] *Turkey—Restrictions on Imports of Textile and Clothing Products*, Appellate Body Report WT/DS34/AB/R, 22 Oct. 1999, at para. 57.

Getting that balance right is a key to WTO compliance, and it is therefore of concern to the EC and its partners in considering the new enlargements.

Since 1995, the WTO has carried out Trade Policy Reviews for a number of the pre-accession states as well as for the EU, and these give a picture of current trade policy against which background an assessment as to the likely impact of accession can be made.[87]

The Community institutions have presented enlargement as having a net positive (trade-creating) effect, as a result not only of a lowering of tariffs through adoption of the EC's common external tariff, but also of the creation of a wider integrated market, and the economic development envisaged for the accession states as a result of EU membership. A European Parliament study in 1999 failed to identify significant trade-diversionary effects affecting Latin American, South-East Asian, or Mediterranean exports to the EU in favour of the accession states as a result of Europe Agreement-based preferences.[88]

In its 1999 Composite Report on progress towards accession, the Commission specifically addressed the effects of enlargement on third countries, and in particular neighbouring states.[89] It presents enlargement in an entirely positive light. As far as general trade-related issues are concerned, the Commission argues that the economic development of candidate countries and their alignment to EC regulatory policy will benefit third country exporters as well as domestic operators:

Enlargement will bring an internal market of over 500 million consumers and an open, border-free area where goods and services can circulate freely. Instead of having to deal with many different rules and regulations non-EU manufacturers and service providers will only need to comply with EU standards to sell their goods and services throughout the expanded internal market.

An enlarged EU will, the Commission argues, assist in forming international consensus about key transnational issues such as environmental pollution, the fight against organized crime, and corruption and illegal trafficking. To put this another way, the EU 'bloc' will be bigger, more powerful, and more able to promote its own policy agenda. Thirdly, enlargement will support WTO-based moves towards greater liberalization; it will be 'a force for opening

---

[87] Trade Policy Reviews were carried out under the WTO Trade Policy Review Mechanism, for Slovakia (1995 and 2001), Czech Republic (1996 and 2001), Cyprus (1997), Hungary (1998), Romania (1999), Poland (2000), and Slovenia (2002). Reviews of EC trade policy were carried out in 1995, 1997, and 2000.

[88] European Parliament, Task Force 'Enlargement', Briefing Paper No. 37, *Enlargement and External Economic Relations*, 8 Sept. 1999, at 11.

[89] Commission's regular progress report for 1999, *supra* at note 2, Composite Paper, sect. V, 'The Enlargement Process and Neighbouring Countries', part 1. 'Overall Benefits of Enlargement'. These points are reiterated in the regular report for 2000, *supra* note 2, sect.1, part 5.

markets and ensuring non-discriminatory rules for trade and investment and reinforces the efforts undertaken within the WTO to further liberalize trade in goods and services'.

The accession states themselves, not surprisingly, also take a positive view. The Cyprus government's comment is typical:

Regarding Cyprus' preparations for joining the EU, the application of the EU common external tariff would result in tariffs lower than the rates bound in the WTO by Cyprus, hence in more favourable conditions. No new quotas or other trade barriers would result from the customs union; all quantitative restrictions had been lifted from 1 January 1996, with a tariff quota system introduced on various products, including textiles. On trade related policies and objectives, the representative of Cyprus saw no conflicts between acceptance of the EU *acquis communautaire* and WTO objectives.[90]

Certainly, the degree of trade liberalization represented by accession to the EU is not limited to free trade within the enlarged EU itself, or even to alignment with the custom external tariff (to the extent that this represents a reduction in customs duties). It includes an opening up of the new members' markets to imports from third countries with which the EC has preferential agreements.

However, the WTO Secretariat Reports and other WTO members have expressed some reservations. First there is the question of trade creation and trade diversion. On the one hand, external trade is already, for the accession states, heavily weighted towards the EC and their CEFTA and BAFTA partners, as a result of the free-trade agreements already in existence. For example, between 1988 and 1998 imports into the EU from seven central and eastern European states (Albania, Bulgaria, Czech Republic, Hungary, Poland, Romania, Slovakia) increased fourfold; in the same period, imports from the whole of Latin America doubled.[91] About the same proportion of the central and eastern European states' trade is with the EU as is that of the existing Member States. To that extent the additional trade diversion towards EC Member States as a result of accession may not be that great. On the other hand, accession will accentuate and perpetuate that trade 'bias' towards the existing Member States. The effect will be most noticeable in cases where a new Member State has free-trade commitments towards a third state which the EC does not, as is currently the case for Estonia with respect to Ukraine.

In the discussion over Hungary's Report to the WTO Trade Policy Review, the issue of trade diversion was debated:

Questions were raised on possible trade diversion stemming from preferences, and there was a considerable debate on this issue and its systemic implications. In

[90] WTO Trade Policy Review of Cyprus, June 1997, Government Statement.
[91] European Parliament, Task Force 'Enlargement', note 88 above, at 8.

response, the representative of Hungary stressed that WTO rules and commitments had been, and would be, thoroughly observed during the whole process of integration into the European Union. He rejected allegations that European integration had diverted trade to the disadvantage of third countries; on the one hand, trade flows had moved in favour of western markets, following the collapse of the CMEA, and before the introduction of EU preferences; on the other, imports from non-European trade partners, both in North America and in the Pacific region, had grown faster than those from EU sources.[92]

The shift in trading patterns resulting from enlargement is not just a case of potential diversion in favour of fellow EU Member States. In previous enlargements the new members' relations and trade ties with particular third countries have encouraged the development of EC preferential trade relations with particular third countries. However, the major shift in trading patterns following 1989 which has already been noted makes this less likely to be the case with the CEES enlargements. They have already reoriented their trade towards the EU and EFTA. They are not former colonial powers and there are no obvious other third countries whose specifically trade interests the accession states will be supporting,[93] although the reorientation of external policy in a broader sense is likely to affect trading patterns.

2. Quotas and Support: Textiles and Agricultural Trade

Apart from the general assessment of levels of tariffs and possible trade diversion, the direction of specific EC policy regimes may be contentious. The EC's trade policies, particularly in relation to agriculture and textiles, are not always more liberal than those of the potential new members.

As we have seen, Acts of Accession have in the past made express provision for alignment to Community policy on textiles, and in particular to its programme of reducing restrictions under the Agreement on Textiles and Clothing.[94] Some of the accession states, such as Poland, the Czech Republic, and Estonia, do not currently maintain quantitative restrictions on any textile or clothing products. On accession the Community textiles policy would be extended to the new Member States with a resulting imposition of quotas. Existing Community restrictions will require adjustment by an appropriate amount to take account of the accessions. Although not arising out of an enlargement, the complaint brought by India against Turkey in relation to the textile quota introduced as a result of Turkey's customs union agreement with the EC illustrates the problems that may

[92] WTO Trade Policy Review of Hungary, July 1998, Chairperson's Conclusions.
[93] Grabbe and Hughes, 'The Impact of Enlargement on EU Trade and Industrial Policy', in Redmond and Rosenthal (eds), *supra* note 72, 125 at 143.
[94] See text *supra* at note 57.

arise.[95] Here, the WTO Appellate Body rejected a view of Article XXIV that would place customs unions (and free-trade areas) within the meaning of Article XXIV outside the reach of GATT disciplines. Rather, the Appellate Body insisted that Article XXIV must be interpreted in line with its particular purposes and taking into account the fact that it provides an exception to fundamental GATT principles. The Appellate Body accepted that 'Article XXIV may justify a measure which is inconsistent with certain other GATT provisions'.[96] However, this defence is available only when it is demonstrated by the member imposing the measure *first* that 'the measure at issue is introduced upon the formation of a customs union that fully meets the requirements of sub-paragraphs 8(a) and 5(a) of Article XXIV' and *secondly* that 'the formation of that customs union would be prevented if it were not allowed to introduce the measure at issue'.[97] Trade in textiles is in a transitional phase under the Agreement on Textiles and Clothing, and the process of enlargement will require a convergence between Community and accession state policy on textile imports while respecting existing levels of liberalization. Recent Commission Progress Reports indicate that as far as the Commission is concerned, the closer the pre-accession alignment, the fewer problems will arise on accession:

As regards the Agreement for Textiles and Clothing, Poland needs to use the third stage of integration under the ATC to align its integration programmes with those of the EC, while notably avoiding integrating products not yet integrated by the EC.[98]

Agricultural policy is proving to be one of the most difficult aspects of enlargement negotiations, and this affects not only the internal dimension (the application of Common Agricultural Policy (CAP) mechanisms to the new Member States) but also the external trade dimension. The WTO Report on Poland in June 2000 identified agricultural trade as an aspect of EC trade policy which might call into question the overall trade-creating effects of enlargement. As it noted:

[95] *Turkey—Restrictions on Imports of Textile and Clothing Products*, Appellate Body Report, WT/DS34/AB/R, 22 Oct. 1999. For comment see von Bogdandy and Makatsch, 'Collision, Co-existence or Cooperation? Prospects for the Relationship between WTO Law and European Union Law' in G. de Búrca and J. Scott (eds), *The EU and the WTO: Legal and Constitutional Issues* (2001), 131, at 136–143.

[96] *Turkey—Restrictions on Imports of Textile and Clothing Products, supra* note 95, at para. 58.

[97] *Ibid.* In this particular case, the formation of a GATT-compatible customs union would not be prevented were Turkey to refrain from introducing the relevant textile quota and the EU to maintain the resulting necessary origin checks. Art. XXIV(8)(a)(i) requires only that duties and other regulations of commerce be eliminated with respect to 'substantially all trade' between the members of the customs union, and this does not preclude controls of this nature.

[98] Commission Progress Report on Poland, 2000. Similar statements are made in other Reports.

the impact on net trade creation of Poland's possible EU accession is not completely clear. While Polish most-favoured-nation (MFN) tariffs would fall on average by almost two-thirds (based on 1999 levels) following adoption of the EU's Common External Tariff, agricultural assistance is likely to increase significantly.

For Hungary, too, agricultural policy will be affected: '[c]hanges in agricultural policy as a result of adaptation to EU policy, however, could well lead to a less liberal trade regime as, at present, Hungary's support to agriculture, as measured by the producer subsidy equivalent (PSE), represents only about one-quarter of the EU's overall level of support'. Changes have already taken place: Hungary withdrew from the Cairns Group (of which it was a founding member) in 1998, following the opening of EU accession negotiations. Estonia will need to 'completely change' its agricultural policy, including increased tariffs and support.[99] At the time of writing, the negotiations on the agriculture chapter have not been concluded and the Community's proposals are proving highly contentious to the accession states, especially Poland. Although the outcome is by no means settled, the Commission claims that its proposals, including the phasing in of direct support over ten years, are compatible with the EC's WTO commitments.[100] The WTO context here includes not only the EC's and the accession states' commitments under the Agreement on Agriculture, concluded as part of the Uruguay Round, but also the current round of negotiations on agriculture launched at Doha in 2001. The Commission says that its position paper on agricultural policy has been drafted so as to reflect the Community's negotiating proposal on agriculture for the new round. Draft schedules of commitments are due to be tabled by 2003 with a view to concluding negotiations in 2004, so this negotiating period will coincide with the first wave of accessions. The EC and the accession states will thus need to coordinate their negotiating position within the WTO, and the EC's position will certainly be affected by the imminent enlargement, as well as influencing the terms of the Community's position in the enlargement negotiations themselves. Agricultural trade will also give rise to negotiations for compensatory adjustment under Article XXIV(6) of GATT 1994, and it is to this aspect of trade and enlargement that we will now turn.

3. Compensatory Adjustment

Under Article XXIV(4) of GATT 1994, it is the overall balance which is important, but within that overall picture individual tariff rates may rise as a member (or new member, in the case of an accession) aligns its tariffs

---

[99] Varblane, *supra* note 54, at 260.
[100] Commission Issues Paper, 'Enlargement and Agriculture: Successfully Integrating the New Member States into the CAP', SEC(2002)95 final, 30 Jan. 2002, at 22–23.

to the common external tariff applied by the customs union. In Article XXIV(6) provision is made for 'compensatory adjustment' where the entry into force (or enlargement) of a customs union requires a WTO member to modify its scheduled commitments by increasing a bound rate of duty. Where, on the other hand, the alignment results in a *reduction* of duty by one of the new customs union members, this does not create any obligation on the part of other WTO members to provide compensatory adjustment for the customs union members.[101] Such benefits are one of the beneficial results of a customs union, justifying the exception they have from MFN obligations. The negotiation process for compensatory adjustment is essentially political and non-objective in character: should agreement not be possible within a reasonable period, the customs union may go ahead anyway, with the affected third countries 'free to withdraw substantially equivalent concessions in accordance with Article XXVIII'.[102] Failure to reach agreement does not therefore create a legal barrier to conformity with Article XXIV, although the requirement of 'good faith' in paragraph 5 of the *Understanding* suggests that failure even to enter into negotiations may do so.

Compensatory adjustment will be 'satisfactory' where it has been agreed between the parties.[103] There is no legal standard of what must be provided, other than a provision that account should be taken of compensation afforded by reductions in the equivalent duty by other acceding members of the customs union. In other words, the overall picture must be taken into account. In the past, the extent of this overall picture has been controversial as far as the EC is concerned; the EC has argued that the reduction in duties between existing EC Member States should be included and not merely changes affecting trade with the accession states.[104]

In the wake of the 1986 enlargement which brought Spain and Portugal into the Community, compensation negotiations with the United States

---

[101] Understanding on the Interpretation of Art. XXIV of GATT 1994, para. 6.

[102] Ibid., para. 5.

[103] In Case C–352/96, *Italy v. Council*, [1998] ECR I–6937, Rec. 23, the Court of Justice held that 'if the parties themselves have reached agreement on the question of mutually satisfactory compensatory adjustment, the requirement referred to in Article XXIV:6 of GATT must be regarded as fulfilled and cannot therefore serve as a basis for examining the legality of the Regulation'. The Regulation in question implemented agreements entered into by the EC with Thailand and Australia consequent upon the accession of Austria, Finland, and Sweden: Council Decision 95/592/EC, OJ 1995 L 334/38. Exporting countries were compensated by the introduction of new tariff quotas so that specified quantities (of rice, in this case) could be imported at a zero tariff: Council Regulation 1522/96/EC opening and providing for the administration of certain tariff quotas for imports of rice and broken rice, OJ 1996 L 190/1.

[104] Lal, 'Trade Blocks and Multilateral Free Trade', 31 *Journal of Common Market Studies* (1993) 349.

proved difficult. The issue was the raising of Spanish import levies on corn and grain, in order to meet the EC's external tariff, together with a substantial Community preference in access to Portugal's grain market (15.5 per cent of which was reserved to EC suppliers). The USA was not happy with the EC's offer of compensation. After threats of retaliation and counter-retaliation, an agreement was eventually reached which involved a removal of the Community preference on the Portuguese market, and a tariff quota in relation to Spanish grain imports.[105]

Article XXIV(6) applies to changes to *bound rates*. Where therefore a party to an FTA with a third country joins a customs union such as the EU, compensation to other FTA parties is not required under GATT because the preferential rates applied inside the FTA are not bound in GATT terms. Nevertheless, the Commission has suggested that any new FTAs entered into by accession states should contain an express clause agreeing to withdrawal from the agreement on accession without compensation. This approach is directed not only at the international (WTO-based) process of compensatory adjustment but also, as we have seen, at the protection offered by Article 307 of the EC Treaty to the rights of third countries under prior agreements.

4. Trade Defence Measures

Under the WTO Agreement on Safeguards, safeguard measures may be imposed by a customs union either in respect of the customs union as a single unit or in respect of only one Member State; in each case the measures are adopted by the customs union as such.[106] The Agreement does not preclude *per se* the introduction of safeguard measures by one member of a customs union on its own account.[107] Within the EC, such unilateral measures are not permitted, either against other Member States or against third-country imports. All safeguard measures are imposed by the EC itself, although there does exist a possibility for the EC to adopt such measures in respect of a specific

---

[105] Ginsberg, 'The Impact of Enlargement on the Role of the European Union in the World' in Redmond and Rosenthal (eds), *supra* note 72, at 209.

[106] Agreement on Safeguards, footnote to Art. 2(1). Under Art. XIX of GATT 1994 and the Agreement on Safeguards, safeguard measures may be imposed where a product is being imported in such quantities and under such conditions as to cause or threaten to cause serious injury to domestic industry producing like or directly competing products.

[107] *Argentina—Safeguard Measures on Imports of Footwear*, Report of Panel, 25 June 1999, WT/DS121/R; Report of Appellate Body, 14 Dec. 1999, WT/DS121/AB/R. In such a case, however, where the state concerned (here, Argentina) had taken account of imports from all sources including those from other customs union members in order to assess injury, it was obliged under Art. 2(2) of the Agreement on Safeguards to impose measures on *all* imports from whatever source, including those from other members of the customs union.

region of the Community.[108] On accession, therefore, existing national safe-guard measures will have to be abrogated. Two questions in particular arise. First, whether safeguard measures in existence in a new Member State at the time of accession could be transmuted into an EC safeguard measure, whether for the whole EC or not. Secondly, whether the EC can merely extend the operation of any existing EC safeguard measures to new Member States.

The answer to the first question is simpler in legal terms, but likely to be of practical significance to the new Member States. On accession, competence in the trade sphere (including trade defence) will transfer to the Community. National trade defence legislation, whether general or specific, will have to be repealed, and will be replaced by Community-level measures. Existing spe-cific national safeguard or anti-dumping measures will therefore disappear. However their replacement by Community-level measures will require that Community procedures are followed and criteria applied. Although the criteria (such as serious injury) will be the same (because both the EC rules and those of the accession states are based on WTO rules) their application is likely to be very different when the entire Community market is investigated. This may be an occasion for the use of 'regional' safeguard measures under Article 18 of the common import Regulation, a provision not yet used.

Extension of an existing EC safeguard measure to a new Member State might be problematic under the Agreement on Safeguards in the absence of any evidence of serious injury to the industry of that state. Under that Agreement, Article 2(1), footnote 1, where a customs union applies a safe-guard measures as a single unit then 'all the requirements for the determin-ation of serious injury or threat thereof . . . shall be based on the conditions existing in the customs union as a whole'. It may well be, therefore, that accession will require a reassessment of the conditions taking into account the extension of the customs union.

The same is true of anti-dumping duties. As the Commission has said:

> Experience from previous accessions has shown that the automatic extension of existing anti-dumping measures to new member states prompts third countries to raise problems in terms of the compatibility of this approach with relevant WTO provisions.[109]

This need for reassessment may not only be a matter of formal procedures. It will bring into focus the question of EC trade policy post-enlargement. Put crudely, will the EC become more protectionist? Will enlargement affect the

---

[108] Council Regulation 3285/94/EC on the common rules for imports, OJ 1994 L 349/53; under Art. 18, safeguard measures may be adopted in respect of one or more regions of the Community.

[109] Commission's Opinion on Poland's application for membership, sect. 3.8; similar statements were made in the other *avis*.

EC's current pro-liberalization stance both in multilateral fora such as the WTO and in its regional and bilateral trade policy? Within the WTO the rhetoric of the accession states is towards liberalization and support for the WTO, and there is no doubt that—in part as the result of the pre-accession process—the accession states are serious about their free-trade credentials. In most cases, for example, they are avoiding the use of trade-protection measures and are increasing their GATS commitments (for example, by signing the Information Technology Agreement). However, whatever the policy orientation of the new members, the EC may become more inward-looking as it sorts out its own cohesion and structural/consti-tutional problems in the wake of enlargement (and we should not forget that 'enlargement' will not take place all at once and may be spread over several years, even decades if we include South-East Europe in the overall picture).

5. Increased Transparency and Homogeneity

For third countries trading into the EC, the change from dealing with a multiplicity of trading arrangements, including varieties of FTA, to one customs union with a common external tariff and common commercial policy—including trade defence measures—will be considerable. The nature of the EC market as an export market for its trading partners depends not just on its external policy, however. As the accession states adopt the *acquis* in areas such as standards, competition policy, and indirect taxation, the market will become more homogeneous as well as bigger. As the Commission argues, enlargement should increase the transparency of trade relations, as well as (in most cases) reduction of the barriers themselves. The Commission has particularly stressed the benefits to the neighbouring states within the Stabil-ization and Association Process for the Western Balkans, the Barcelona process for the Mediterranean, and the Partnership and Cooperation frame-work for Russia, the Ukraine, and the other CIS states. These are all engaged in a process of trade liberalization and alignment to EU regulatory standards, which will encourage trade and investment from the EU and elsewhere.[110] The European Parliament has also taken a positive view of the trade effects of enlargement, arguing that the resulting trade liberalization (between the accession states and the EU as well as between the accession states and other EU trading partners) will have 'a positive impact on trade and invest-ment flows' and that the more homogeneous market will encourage foreign investment in the new Member States.[111]

Although the enlarged Union will become a bigger and more homoge-neous market as far as trading rules are concerned, in the medium term it will

[110] Commission Strategy Paper, 'Making a Success of Enlargement', 13 Nov. 2001, 7.
[111] European Parliament, Task Force 'Enlargement', *supra* note 88, at 7.

be less homogeneous than it is at present in terms of its economic development and ability to compete in a liberal trade environment. The diversity of interests among 20 or 25 Member States will be even more evident than it is now among the 15. The effects of becoming an even bigger bloc within the WTO and other negotiations may be offset by the increased difficulty in reaching consensus.[112] In this context, it is of significance that the Treaty of Nice will extend majority voting under Article 133 EC to external policy areas such as services and trade-related intellectual property issues. However such a change would not itself be sufficient to ensure that the existing broad consensus on trade policy issues that has allowed the EU to exercise a leadership role within the WTO will continue.

B. Enlargement and the Common Foreign and Security Policy (CFSP)

1. Enlargement as part of the CFSP

Every enlargement has had a strong political dimension, and this is perhaps especially true of the current fifth enlargement. Since the European Council in Copenhagen in June 1993, enlargement to include the countries of central and eastern Europe has been at the centre of Union foreign policy, a way of achieving its CFSP objectives, including regional stability and security.[113] The political conditionality attached to enlargement that crystallized at Copenhagen and has developed since reflects these objectives. At Madrid in December 1995 the European Council, under the heading 'A Europe open to the world, enjoying stability, security, freedom and solidarity', declared that enlargement 'will ensure the stability and security of the continent and will thus offer both the applicant states and the current members of the Union new prospects for economic growth and general well-being'. This perspective is also reflected in the Commission's Agenda 2000 which refers to the impact of enlargement 'far beyond the new frontiers of an enlarged Europe', since 'it will increase Europe's weight in the world, give Europe new neighbours and form Europe into an area of unity and stability'.[114] From this perspective, it is significant that what we have been calling 'enlargement' will not be a single event. Twelve countries are currently in the process of accession negotiations, the EU side has indicated that of these, ten may be ready to join in 2004, subject to the successful completion of negotiations. Even assuming that

---

[112] Rollo, 'EU Enlargement and the World Trade System', 39 *European Economic Review* (1995) 467.

[113] The CFSP objectives, as stated in Art. 11(1) TEU, include safeguarding the independence and integrity of the Union, strengthening the security of the Union, preserving peace, and strengthening international security.

[114] Commission, Agenda 2000, Vol. I 'For A Stronger and Wider Union', Part One, section IV 'The Union in the World', COM(1997)2000.

these ten do all join at once, Romania and Bulgaria will still be completing negotiations and negotiations have not yet been opened with Turkey, a candidate state. Further applications, from some of the South-East European states, are likely by 2004–2005. Enlargement, and in particular the role of the EU in shaping the political evolution of Europe will continue as a centrally important issue for the CFSP for at least the next decade and probably beyond. To that extent, although the adhesion of the candidate states to existing CFSP policies has not been a particularly controversial aspect of the pre-accession process or the negotiations,[115] enlargement may still be seen as a challenge for the maturing CFSP, both in terms of its institutional capacity and in terms of its policy development.

2. Institutional Issues

The conclusions that may be drawn as regards the effect of enlargement on the institutional aspects of the CFSP will be influenced by the view taken of the development of the CFSP itself. If this is seen as an essentially intergovernmental process based on inter-state bargaining, then no doubt this process will be more difficult with more players. The European Parliament, for example, which has advocated a consolidation of all Union external powers under the Community 'pillar', argues that 'the CFSP's present lack of coherence will worsen' in a Europe of 27 or 28 Member States.[116] The European Parliament has also been very critical of the failure to move towards a greater acceptance of majority voting within the CFSP, especially in light of enlargement.[117] Constructive abstention is possible since the Treaty of Amsterdam amendments,[118] and enhanced cooperation between a sub-set of Member States will be possible under the Treaty of Nice revisions, both options designed to lessen the risk of stagnation in an enlarged consensus-based CFSP at some (unquantifiable) risk to cohesion. The case has not really been made that the requirement of consensus is hindering active and effective policy-making. However it can be argued that enlargement will necessarily exacerbate the existing problems of coherence, coordination with both national and other elements of Union external policy, and effective decision-making within the CFSP.

If on the other hand the emergence of a CFSP is seen as an organic process, developing out of an interaction between national and European-level policy-making, a gradual socialization into a shared community of

---

[115] European Parliament, Taskforce 'Enlargement', Briefing Paper No.30, *The CFSP and Enlargement of the EU*, 14 Mar. 2000.
[116] Ibid., 7.
[117] Ibid. at 9; see also Commission, *supra* note 114, at 44.
[118] Art. 23(1) TEU.

values,[119] then the numbers game becomes less important than the pre-accession policy alignment. This suggests that enlargement may be seen as one aspect of a process of Europeanization of foreign policy which is not necessarily limited to the EU's existing Member States and within which consensus is an important part of policy formation.

From this perspective, the effect of enlargement on the existing balance within the EU between states with long and powerful foreign-policy and diplomatic traditions and smaller states without such a tradition is ambiguous. More of the latter will be joining. However it is not clear whether this will dissipate and weaken the stature and identity of the EU in foreign-policy terms, encouraging states such as France and the UK to maintain and even prioritize their own independent national policies, or whether, on the contrary, a willingness on the part of the accession states to identify national foreign-policy interest with that of the EU will encourage the development of a distinctively 'European' foreign and security policy. As Lamy has accepted, the impact of enlargement in this respect is a 'major uncertainty'.[120]

The role of the smaller states within the CFSP is often linked to the function of the rotating Presidency. Assuming the Presidency means not only taking on a leadership and organizational role with respect to the EU's internal affairs, but also playing a primary part in projecting the presence of the EU to the world.[121] Will the smaller candidate states be able to manage the burden of the Presidency, especially the multiplicity of political dialogues with non-members and the lead responsibility for implementation of CFSP initiatives? In practice this often-mooted problem has not proved intractable with the current smaller Member States, and the 'new-style troika' of Presidency, the High Representative for the CFSP, and the External Relations Commissioner helps to provide continuity and institutional support.

3. Policy Issues

It is, if anything, even more difficult to predict the effects of enlargement on policy development within the CFSP, not least because the existing interests of the accession states are likely to be affected and changed by membership, at least to some extent. Earlier enlargements have been seen in terms of creating new special relationships for the EU: the UK with the Commonwealth and the USA, Denmark with the Nordic states, Spain and Portugal with Latin

[119] Sjursen, 'Enlargement and the Common Foreign and Security Policy: Transforming the EU's External Policy?', Arena Working Papers, 98/18, http://www.arena.uio.no/.

[120] He puts the question thus: 'Will the new members have a strong desire that the EU punches its weight at the international level? Or will they give priority to gaining US protection through NATO?': Lamy, 'Europe's Role in Global Governance: The Way Ahead', speech at Humboldt University, Berlin, 6 May 2002.

[121] Cf. Art. 18 TEU.

America and the Mediterranean, Sweden and Finland with the Baltic, and Austria with Hungary. This enlargement will create new neighbours for the EU, such as Russia and Ukraine, and the new Member States will have their own 'special interests', including Polish and the Baltic states' interest in Russia, Ukraine, and Belarus,[122] Bulgarian interests in the Balkans and the Black Sea region,[123] and Cyprus's relations with Turkey. To take one example, the accession of Sweden and Finland in 1994 has led to an increase in EU interest in northern Europe, as evidenced by the adoption of the Northern Dimension Action Plan at Feira in June 2000.[124] This focus will be supported and extended by the role played by the Baltic states and Poland in the Baltic Sea region and the Council of Baltic Sea states.[125]

However these interests play themselves out in practice, these examples reveal one particular characteristic of the fifth enlargement. Rather than turning the EU's attention towards a more distant region of the world, this enlargement is likely, for a variety of reasons, to keep in the forefront of Union policy its relations with its nearer neighbours, and in particular the states of the Stabilization and Association Process (SAP) in the Western Balkans, the Mediterranean states within the Barcelona process, and the Partnership and Cooperation states to the east, including Russia and Ukraine.[126]

For each of these geopolitical areas, security and regional issues are an important aspect of their relations with the EU and an increased focus on these areas will thus have an impact on the EU's emerging security and defence policy (CESDP) and its relationship with NATO.[127] Security has

[122] E.g., in a speech in Feb. 2000, the Lithuanian President Valdas Adamkus said 'Stability in the region is one of the main priorities of Lithuania, and that will be one of the qualities, which they will bring the EU. Close links to Russia and Belarus will be a part of the agenda, links which otherwise will be hard to find anywhere else.' Source: http://www.president.lt/eng/eng10295.htm.

[123] The Black Sea Economic Cooperation Pact includes Albania, Armenia, Azerbaijan, Bulgaria, Georgia, Greece, Moldova, Romania, Russia, Turkey, and Ukraine.

[124] Action Plan for the Northern Dimension in the External and Cross-Border Policies of the European Union 2000–2003, endorsed by the European Council, Feira, June 2000. The Northern Dimension geographical area extends from Iceland on the west across to North-West Russia, from the Norwegian, Barents, and Kara Seas in the North to the Southern coast of the Baltic Sea; it involves the EU and the non-EU Northern Dimension partner countries Estonia, Iceland, Latvia, Lithuania, Norway, Poland, and Russia.

[125] See, e.g., the statement by Toomas Hendrik Ilves, Minister of Foreign Affairs of Estonia, at the meeting of Nordic-Baltic Foreign Ministers with Russia, 15 May 1999, St. Petersburg; source: http://www.vm.ee.

[126] Regular Report from the Commission on Progress towards Accession by Each of the Candidate Countries, 13 Oct. 1999, Composite Paper, sect. V. 'The enlargement process and neighbouring countries', part 2. Neighbours of the Enlarged Union.

[127] Teunissen, 'Strengthening the Defence Dimension of the EU: An Evaluation of Concepts, Recent Initiatives and Developments', 4 *European Foreign Affairs Rev.* (1999)

been one major reason for the countries of central and eastern Europe to join the EU.[128] Hungary, Poland, and Czech Republic are currently members of NATO and other accession states are candidates. The other seven central and eastern European candidates are WEU Associate Partners; membership of the EU will allow for the possibility of full WEU membership, and as a result the WEU (insofar as it still retains a role) will become less 'western' and more fully 'European'. However, membership of the EU does not necessarily mean enlargement of NATO, and thus, whereas existing Member States rely on NATO for their defence and security, new members may be more reliant on the CESDP.[129] Both the current candidates and the Union itself are confident that enlargement will enhance stability and security for the EU's non-member partners as well as its (new) members; to avoid polarization the EU is likely to try hard to include Russia and Ukraine (and other CIS states) in a wider security framework, possibly building on the Partnership for Peace (all the central and eastern European states are Members of NATO's Partnership for Peace created in January 1994) and the OSCE.[130]

As this indicates, the impact of enlargement on the CFSP raises the huge question of the political impact of the reunification of Europe. This enlargement will not just be a question of moving the EU's borders further East. As Sjursen argues, the enlarged EU will contribute to the drawing of new institutional, political, and economic boundaries in Europe.[131] Its relations with its neighbours will not just be influenced by the fact that a number of the new Member States will have particular interests and priorities (essentially the same process as earlier enlargements but with different inputs). The enlarged EU will be engaged in a process of reshaping Europe as a whole and redefining its borders in political and economic as well as geographical terms. The Commission has reiterated that 'the future borders of the Union must not become a new dividing line'.[132] However, in discussing

327; Duke, 'CESDP: Nice's Overtrumped Success', 6 *European Foreign Affairs Rev.* (2001) 155; Missiroli, 'European Security Policy: The Challenge of Coherence', 6 *European Foreign Affairs Rev.* (2001) 177.

[128] Allen, 'Wider but Weaker or the More the Merrier? Enlargement and Foreign Policy Cooperation in the EC/EU', in Redmond and Rosenthal (eds), *supra* note 72. In 1997, the Polish National Strategy for Integration stated, 'Only membership in the EU, NATO and WEU can, under present conditions, guarantee our sense of security, long-term balanced development and the opportunity to participate in the making of decisions which are important from the point of view of Poland's interests. From the Polish perspective, security is an indivisible concept, which includes economic and military security.'

[129] European Parliament, Taskforce 'Enlargement', *supra* note 115, at 26.

[130] Ginsberg, *supra* note 78, at 213.

[131] Sjursen, *supra* note 119. See also White, McAllister, and Light, 'Enlargement and the New Outsiders', 40 *Journal of Common Market Studies* (2002) 135.

[132] Commission Strategy Paper, 'Making a Success of Enlargement', 13 Nov. 2001, at 7.

the enlarged Union's relations with its neighbours, strategy documents refer in vague terms to 'deep relationships' and 'distinctive strategic partnerships'.

It is not yet clear how this 'proximity policy', as the Commission has started to call it, will develop or how it will reflect the interests of the EU's neighbours. In its 2000 Report,[133] the Commission recognizes that neighbouring countries are concerned about enlargement and that 'the EU needs to explain these benefits to its neighbours and to discuss the impact of enlargement so that both they and the Union take full advantage of the new opportunities. Some issues will need sensitive handling.' Among these will be the way in which the interests of the 'first wave' of new members will affect the position, positively or negatively, of the second wave and other potential members such as the SAP states or Ukraine. However, enlargement negotiations are a matter between the EU and the accession states, and there is no room for third-country input directly; all the Commission commits to is to provide 'detailed explanations of the changes which will take place'.

For each of the three main neighbouring groups (the Western Balkans, the Mediterranean, and the eastern states) the Union has developed a framework for relations which, although based upon a specific type of agreement (Stabilization and Association Agreements,[134] the Euro-Mediterranean Agreements,[135] and the Partnership and Cooperation Agreements,[136] respectively), extends beyond the Community-based agreements and includes an explicit wider political and regional dimension. These have distinctive objectives and will follow different paths (only the SAP, for example, has a clear accession objective), although the Commission has stated that the enlarged EU 'is likely to see an interest in linking together common elements' of these three geographic policies.[137] Specific aspects of these policies are likely to increase in importance, especially their regional dimension, migration, and border management.

[133] Commission's Strategy Report for 2000, Part I 'The Overall Context', sect. 5, 'The Enlargement Process and Neighbouring Countries'.

[134] Commission Communication on the Stabilization and Association Process for Countries of South-Eastern Europe', 26 May 1999, COM(99)235. See further Cremona, 'Creating the New Europe: The Stability Pact for South-Eastern Europe in the Context of EU-SEE Relations', II *Cambridge Yearbook of European Legal Studies* (1999) 463.

[135] Barcelona Conference Declaration and Work Programme, 27–28 Nov. 1995, *Bull. EU* 11–1995; Common Strategy on the Mediterranean, adopted by European Council at Feira, 20 June 2000; Euro-Med Association agreements with Tunisia, Morocco, and Israel are in force; agreements have been signed with Jordan (November 1997), Egypt (June 2001), Algeria (December 2001), Lebanon (January 2002).

[136] Partnership and Cooperation Agreements (PCAs) have been concluded with Russia, Ukraine, and Moldova. The PCA with Belarus was signed in Apr. 1995 but is not yet in force. PCAs have also been concluded with Armenia, Azerbaijan, Georgia, Kazakhstan, Kyrgyz Republic, and Uzbekistan.

[137] Commission Strategy Paper, 'Making a Success of Enlargement', *supra* note 132, at 7.

For the countries of the Western Balkans further enlargement will be a central concern. The European Council at Feira in June 2000 agreed that all of the countries in the region are 'potential candidates' of the Union. This indeed follows from the commitment given in the Stability Pact for South-East Europe,[138] and is confirmed in the preambles to the SAAs concluded with FYROM and Croatia, which 'recall' their status 'as a potential candidate for EU membership on the basis of the Treaty on European Union and fulfilment of the criteria defined by the European Council in June 1993, subject to successful implementation of this Agreement, notably regarding regional cooperation'. Regional cooperation, international and regional peace and stability, and the development of good neighbourly relations are distinctive objectives of the Agreements and of the SAP as a whole,[139] and are likely to form a basis for the forthcoming Common Strategy for South-East Europe as well as for future decisions on further enlargement. It is worth noting in this context that in June 2001 seven states in South-East Europe (Albania, Bosnia-Herzegovina, Bulgaria, Croatia, Romania, FYROM, and FRY; Moldova is also expected to join) signed a memorandum of understanding on trade liberalization and facilitation within the framework of the Stability Pact for South-East Europe, under which the aim is to establish a network of bilateral free-trade agreements liberalizing substantially all trade within a transitional period of six years. Alongside its emphasis on the regional dimension of relations with South-East Europe—an emphasis which is not wholly welcome to the countries of the region themselves—the EU also insists that relations with each country will develop at a bilateral level in line with that country's individual development (and desires).[140] Combining the two will require subtlety on both sides.

Relations with the EC's eastern neighbours take place within the context of the Partnership and Cooperation Agreements and the Common Strategies on Russia and Ukraine. In its Enlargement Strategy Paper for 2000 the Commission highlighted the need to discuss enlargement issues with Russia, and proposed the use of the PCA institutions as a mechanism for doing this, rather than the creation of new committees. In addition to some specific

---

[138] 'The EU will draw the region closer to the perspective of full integration of these countries into its structures . . . this will be done through a new kind of contractual relationship taking fully into account the individual situations of each country with the perspective of EU membership, on the basis of the Amsterdam Treaty and once the Copenhagen criteria have been met.' Stability Pact for South-East Europe, adopted in Cologne, 10 June 1999, para. 20.

[139] See SAA with FYROM, COM(2001)90 final, OJ 2001 C 213/ 23, Arts. 1, 3, and 4; SAA with Croatia, COM(2001)371 final, OJ 2001 C 332/2, Arts. 1, 3, and 4; Commission's First Annual Report on The Stabilization and Association process for South East Europe, 4 Apr. 2002, COM(2002)163, 11.

[140] Commission's First Annual Report on the Stabilization and Association Process for South East Europe, 4 Apr. 2002, COM(2002)163, 14.

issues raised by enlargement,[141] in October 2001 the EU–Russia Summit agreed to intensify dialogue on political and security issues and to establish a High Level Group which is to develop the concept of a Common European Economic Space and define its core elements.[142] Russian and Ukrainian participation in the CESDP has been discussed.[143] Unlike the SAP states, there is no mention by the EU of future membership in relation to these countries, although it is discussed in the Ukraine, and Ukraine and Moldova have been invited to participate in the European Conference.[144]

Relations with the southern neighbours are structured around the Barcelona Process and based on the Euro-Mediterranean Association Agreements and the Common Strategy on the Mediterranean adopted in June 2000. Again, the security dimension is an important feature of the relationship, alongside support for economic transition and integration. Progress towards establishing a regional free-trade area has been slow, but the mere fact of regular dialogue has been a valuable aspect of the Barcelona Process. Three of the southern participants (Cyprus, Malta, and Turkey) are candidate states, and so the fifth enlargement will not be entirely northern and eastwards. There will be pressure from the existing Mediterranean states, and likely too from Cyprus and Malta, to give more attention to the Mediterranean, although the relative overall weight of the Mediterranean Member States may decrease.[145] Unlike some

[141] Following the accession of Poland and Lithuania, for example, Kaliningrad will be surrounded by the EU and a strategy of regional cooperation will be needed; see Commission Communication to the Council, 'The EU and Kaliningrad', COM(2001)26 final; Commission Communication to the Council, 'Kaliningrad: Transit', COM(2002)510 final; Conclusions of the European Council, Seville, June 2002; Report from the Presidency to the Council on Kaliningrad, 21 Oct. 2002, 13345/02; Conclusions of the European Council, Brussels, Oct. 2002.

[142] EU–Russia Summit meeting, 3 Oct. 2001, para. 7. The concept of a Common European Economic Space (or Area—both terms are used) is not defined. In terms of Annex 2, 'The task of the High-Level Group is to elaborate a concept for a closer economic relationship between Russia and the EU, based on the wider goal of bringing the EU and Russia closer together. The High-Level Group will consider the opportunities offered by greater economic integration and legislative approximation and assess options for further work.'

[143] Feira European Council, June 2000, Annex I, Presidency Report on Strengthening the Common European Security and Defence Policy. See also Nice European Council, Dec. 2000, Annex VI, Presidency Report on European Security and Defence Policy.

[144] The European Conference was established by the Luxembourg European Council in Dec. 1997 as a forum for including applicant states which could not yet be considered as 'candidates', in particular Turkey (paras. 4–9 and 31–36); it has now been extended to the SAP and EFTA states (Conclusions of the European Council at Nice, Dec. 2000, para. 12) and Ukraine and Moldova, countries which are not yet applicants (Göteburg European Council, June 2001, para. 13). On attitudes towards possible future membership of the EU: see White, McAllister, and Light, *supra* note 131, at 143.

[145] Tovias, 'On the External Relations of the EU21: The Case of the Mediterranean Periphery', 6 *European Foreign Affairs Rev.* (2001) 375, at 380.

earlier examples, this development of the CFSP will have to take place without the possibility of offering membership as part of the package.[146]

In assessing these three geographical policy dimensions, the Commission has said that 'these policies foresee the creation of a free trade area encompassing the EU and its neighbours in which democracy and respect for human rights and the rule of law prevail'.[147] This statement is significant not only for the way in which it links the EU's neighbouring regions, but also in linking economic, free-trade, and political 'values' as an objective of Union external policy in the context of enlargement. The EU proposes itself as a model for conflict resolution and prevention and reconciliation.[148] The inevitable concentration of focus, attention, and resources on its own regional neighbourhood will thus take the form of promoting its own values and itself as a model of political and economic integration.

4. CONCLUSIONS

What conclusions can we draw as to the impact of enlargement on the trade policy of the EU and its new members? First, although the EU will of course become a larger trading block, of about 500 million people, the relatively undeveloped nature of the new Member States' economies will mean that the impact on trade will be felt in the medium and longer term rather than short term.[149] Secondly, just as the developing countries felt the impact of the extension of EU preferences to central and eastern Europe during the 1990s, so they are likely to be more affected by enlargement than the economies of the developed world. With their preferential margins in access to the wealthy markets of the existing EU Member States further weakened by the incorporation of the new members, developing countries will be affected by such trade diversion as does occur. An enlarged EU will mean that a larger group of countries will have preferential access to their markets under EU preferential agreements such as the Cotonou Convention. There is also a risk of diversion of foreign direct investment of both Community and third country origin from developing countries into the new

[146] Allen, 'Wider but Weaker or the More the Merrier? Enlargement and Foreign Policy Cooperation in the EC/EU' in Redmond and Rosenthal (eds), *supra* note 72, M. Maresceau and E. Lannon (eds), *The EU's Enlargement and Mediterranean Strategies: A Comparative Analysis* (2001).

[147] Commission Strategy Paper on Enlargement, *supra* note 132, at 7.

[148] Commission Communication to the Council and European Parliament on the Stabilization and Association Process for Countries of South-Eastern Europe, 26 May 1999, COM(1999)235.

[149] The accession of the 12 states currently negotiating membership of the EU would add approximately 100 million to the EU's population (30%), but only 4% to the EU's GDP.

Member States. At the same time, developing countries' export markets will be extended, as the EC market—to which they have preferential access—is enlarged, and we have seen that the overall effect is likely to be a reduction in tariff barriers.

Further, the questions we have posed and the conclusions we have reached—the increased regulatory homogeneity of the enlarged market, the increased economic diversity of its Member States, the likely preoccupation with the EC's own underdeveloped regions, potentially divergent rather than convergent trade and economic policy interests among the Member States, and the increased difficulty of achieving a consensus—all these factors are particularly and acutely relevant to the future of the Community's trade and development policy.[150] What is at issue here is the effect of enlargement on the priorities and orientation of Community external policy. Although most of the accession states have had only limited trade policies towards developing countries, adaptation to the Community level of GSP and participation in its development cooperation programmes are unlikely to be controversial in themselves.[151] However, the EU will be less uniformly a highly developed trading partner and we may see a shift of emphasis away from development outside the EU and towards internal development (such as cohesion policy).

For the new Member States, adjustment of external economic and trade policy is likely to pose the greatest difficulty, including as it does the extensive existing EU trade preference regime, both contractual and non-contractual. Some aspects of EU trade policy, such as customs legislation, can be aligned before accession, but full adoption of the *acquis* in relation to levels of customs duties and application of trade-protection measures will wait until enlargement. Existing relationships of both the new Member States and the EU itself, such as those with the EFTA states, will need adjustment and this may require the renegotiation, or even denunciation, of prior treaties.

These factors also point to a more general conclusion. There will be an even greater need to adopt a more systematic approach to the requirements of the EC's external economic policy. Unlike either development cooperation policy or the common foreign and security policy, external economic policy lacks any treaty-based binding statement of principles. This applies to the fundamental principles of the common commercial policy, including uniformity, liberalization, and non-discrimination, as well as the extent to which they should, or can, be applied to areas, such as trade in services or competition policy, outside the 'traditional' common commercial policy.[152] The

---

[150] J.A. McMahon, *The Development Cooperation Policy of the EC* (1998).

[151] See text *supra* at note 44.

[152] Cremona, 'The External Dimension of the Single Market: Building (on) the Foundations' in C. Barnard and J. Scott (eds), *The Law of the Single European Market* (2002).

greater inherent diversity within an enlarged EU will mean there is a greater need for an explicit position on how much uniformity in external policy is required. The tensions that currently exist between liberalization in external trade and the needs of internal policy objectives are likely to be sharpened. The enlarged Community will have to demonstrate compliance with WTO disciplines, especially those on regional trade agreements, while taking into account the specific needs of both its new members and its preferential trading partners. In order to fulfil its potential as a powerful and effective player within the multilateral context, able not only to establish its own agenda for global trade policy, but also to exercise leadership over issues such as global governance and sustainable development, the EU will need to develop a coherent set of principles and strategies in the light of its own internal market objectives. It is precisely the greater degree of diversity resulting from enlargement—a diversity of both economic development and interests—which will make this process both more necessary and more difficult.

However, the greatest challenge of the enlargement for EU external policy is likely to lie, not in preserving a liberal trade agenda or the further development of economic integration initiatives or the defence of trade interests within the WTO, but rather in the need to reshape EU policy towards the rest of Europe and its immediate neighbours. Initiatives such as the Northern Dimension and the Stabilization and Association Process, encompassing both EU members and non-members and both bilateral and regional initiatives, will be important here. They indicate that alongside economic integration measures, important though these are, we are likely to see a growing emphasis on other dimensions of external policy, including environmental protection, security issues, border-control policy and other 'justice and home affairs' issues, including crime control and migration policy. Underpinning these and other external policies, and legitimizing specific external policy initiatives as well as membership conditionality, will be an emphasis on the values—especially those of democracy, respect for human rights, the rule of law, a market economy, and regional cooperation— with which the Union identifies.

There is no real evidence that the institutional development of the CFSP and its decision-making processes will be obstructed by enlargement to an extent greater than policy-making within the EC pillar.[153] In both cases, the larger and more diverse membership will pose challenges for the development of common policies, and in both cases there will be a risk that the internal needs of the Union will divert attention inwards, resulting in a Union which is ever more preoccupied with its own future constitutional and economic

---

[153] For further discussion of the impact of enlargement on the decision-making capacity of the EU, see Chap. 8 in this volume.

development. In practice, however, the direction of the EU's development depends more than anything on the Union's place in the world, and in particular within its own continent. The enlarged Union will define itself in the way in which it engages with its partners at every level. The enlarged EU will not have the luxury of time to 'put its own house in order' before turning to the restructuring of its political and trade relationships. On the contrary, its ability to contribute to wider global debate such as the Doha Development Agenda within the WTO,[154] and to the reconstruction of non-EU Europe (or EU-rope[155]), is a fundamental part of the essential process of self-definition which will face the enlarged European Union.

[154] The timeframe for the Doha Development Agenda Work Programme, envisaging completion of negotiations by 1 Jan. 2005, overlaps with the projected accession date of 2004: WTO Ministerial Conference Declaration, Doha, 14 Nov. 2001, WT/MIN(01)/DEC/1.
[155] T. Garton Ash, *History of the Present* (1999), 180.

8

The Impact of Enlargement on the Constitution of the European Union

BRUNO DE WITTE

1. INTRODUCTION: ENLARGEMENT AS CONSTITUTIONAL AGENDA-SETTER FOR THE EUROPEAN UNION

Unlike most of the other Chapters of this book, that deal with the *relations* between the European Union and the candidates (or potential candidates) for EU membership, this Chapter adopts the 'inside' perspective to enlargement, by presenting some of the main implications of the pending accessions for the constitutional fabric of the *European Union itself*.

Previous enlargements of the European Communities first, and the European Union later, have also acted as catalysts for constitutional change, or at least for rethinking the political and institutional course of the European integration process. However, the successive accession treaties themselves were fairly modest in this respect. Article 49 EU specifies that accession treaties may make 'adjustments' to the existing treaties upon which the EU is based, and accession treaties have not gone further, so far, than making rather minor adjustments to the existing rules, such as providing for the representation of the new Member States in the Council, the Parliament, and the other institutions. Further-reaching changes were excluded, on the basis that the acceding countries should accept the entire *acquis communautaire*, subject only to narrowly defined transition phases in specific policy areas.

This time round, it was clear from the start that the *acquis*-cum-transition mix of earlier enlargements was an insufficient response, not so much for the candidate countries as for the European Union itself. The probable accession of an unprecedented number of new states, at a time when the EU already suffers from a crisis of legitimacy, called for institutional responses of unprecedented sophistication. The tone was set by the Copenhagen European Council of June 1993, at which the enlargement process was officially started by the European Council and the general conditions for accession were laid down. It also was a defining moment in setting the agenda of enlargement-related constitutional reform of the Union. In this Chapter, I consider three broad strands of this enlargement-related constitutional agenda:

—An eye-catching aspect of the Copenhagen conclusions, namely the un-precedented formal imposition of so-called *political conditions* for member-ship (democracy, fundamental rights, rule of law, and protection of minorities)[1] helped to stimulate the debate on whether the European Union itself should take these basic constitutional values more seriously by entrenching them more firmly in its own legal order. Democracy and fundamental rights concerns were part of the agenda of the 1996 IGC and the Amsterdam Treaty involved important Treaty changes in this respect. Further, though limited, attention was given to these questions during the 2000 Intergovernmental Conference (IGC), and they have become very prominent again in the post-Laeken reform debate.

—The Copenhagen European Council of 1993 further specified that acces-sion would depend not only on the political and economic performance and state of preparation of the candidate states, but also on the institutional state of preparation of the European Union: '[t]he Union's capacity to absorb new members, while maintaining the momentum of European integration, is also an important consideration in the general interest of both the Union and the candidate countries'.[2] Thereby, internal reform of the decision-making cap-acity of the Union became a precondition for enlargement. The IGC of 1996 was, in part, devoted to this question, and the IGC of 2000 was almost entirely devoted to it. However, the Treaty of Nice that resulted from the latter does not constitute a convincing response to the problem. Apart from the fact that the reforms were limited to only some institutional questions and omitted others, the solutions found were often inappropriate. Moreover, it is still highly uncertain, at the time of writing, whether the Nice Treaty will enter into force at all. For all these reasons, the question of making the EU's decision-making machinery more robust is still very much on the political and constitution-making agenda today.

—A third strand of the constitutional-reform debate is less immediately apparent from the Copenhagen Conclusions, but 'Copenhagen' indirectly formed a watershed also in this respect. Until 1993, attempts had been made to devise innovative forms of institutional linkage between the European Union and the central and eastern European countries that would closely associate the latter to the EU but without offering them full membership. Such forms of asymmetrical integration based on advanced methods of international cooperation were definitively discarded by the Copenhagen European Council. Full membership of the European Union became the

---

[1] For discussion of political conditionality see Chap. 5.

[2] European Council of Copenhagen (June 1993), Conclusions of the Presidency, *Bull. EC* 12–1993.

sole option for the future. At the same time, this decision to take concrete steps towards full membership and a major enlargement of the Union fuelled discussion on whether membership of the EU could be accompanied by more radical forms of differentiation of rights and obligations between states than had hitherto been the case; while asymmetrical relations would no longer be pursued as part of the EU's *external relations* with Central and Eastern Europe, they might be put in place as part of its *internal constitution*. The debate on 'flexibility' and 'closer cooperation' took off in earnest in the summer of 1994, and the prospect of enlargement has greatly contributed to keeping it on the EU's constitutional reform agenda ever since.

This Chapter considers only the three constitutional dimensions of enlargement mentioned above. Other institutional or policy challenges posed by enlargement, such as the future budgetary arrangements or the reform of agricultural and structural policies, will not be dealt with. Nor will I examine the whole spectrum of reform topics whose character was first described as being 'constitutional' in the scholarly literature of the mid-1990s,[3] and finally acknowledged to be 'constitutional' by all the Member State governments in the *Laeken Declaration* adopted by the European Council in December 2001. This Chapter deals, more narrowly, with the *intersection* between the two legal-political questions that have occupied the minds of the EU institutions and Member States in the past decades: anticipating the consequences of enlargement and proceeding with the overall constitutional reform of the EU.

2. DECISION-MAKING CAPACITY

A central goal of recent and upcoming institutional reforms of the Union is to prevent the EU from becoming paralysed by a brutal expansion of its membership. This issue has been variously defined as that of 'efficiency'[4] or of

---

[3] For a synthetic account written during that (pre-Amsterdam) period, see Walker, 'European Constitutionalism and European Integration', *Public Law* [1996] 266; for a full-length study from that same period, see J. Gerkrath, *L'émergence d'un droit constitutionnel pour l'Europe* (1997).

[4] See, for instance, the Laeken Declaration of Dec. 2001, stating that one of the questions to be addressed in the post-Laeken debate would be 'how we can improve the *efficiency* of decision-making and the working of the institutions in a Union of some thirty Member States': Laeken Declaration on the Future of the European Union, Annex I to the Conclusions of the Laeken European Council, 14 and 15 Dec. 2001, emphasis added. For an earlier example of the use of the term 'efficiency of the institutions', see *The Institutional Implications of Enlargement* (Report to the Commission of the 'Three Wise Men', von Weizsäcker, Dehaene, and Simon, 18 Oct. 1999, at 6, (http://europa.eu.int/igc2000/repoct 99_en.pdf).

'effectiveness'[5] of the institutions. I prefer to describe it, fairly narrowly, as the issue of the Union's *decision-making capacity*, whereby capacity is understood as being 'the probability that a political system, given the diversity of interests to which it is exposed, will be able to take decisions'.[6] As the diversity of political interests increases with the accession of new Member States, the capacity to act of the EU institutions is likely to decrease, unless the decision-making rules are modified so as to promote the 'ease of action'.

The accession of new states affects the functioning of the institutional system in several ways. The new states are represented in each of the institutions of the EU. Accession of new states makes the overall number of members of each institution grow, with the risk of exceeding the appropriate size allowing for effective deliberation. In addition, accession of new states has a specific impact on the functioning of the Council of Ministers, the institution composed of representatives of Member State governments. The Council decides according to two main modes, depending on the policy area: unanimity or qualified-majority voting. It is clear that unanimous decision-making becomes more difficult to achieve with increasing numbers of national delegations possessing a veto power. Qualified-majority voting, on the other hand, is based on a mathematical formula whereby states are given a number of votes in remote accordance with their population, and decisions are carried when they are approved by a given percentage (somewhat more than 70 per cent) of the total vote. So, accession by new states to the Union does not necessarily make qualified-majority decision-making more difficult: the new states are given a number of additional votes, but the percentage needed for a qualified majority can be kept constant. However, the addition of new members complicates the game of coalition-building for the purpose of assembling a qualified majority. It also means, in most cases, the addition of new official languages of the Union, which creates higher translation costs and forms a new source of communication failures in the decision-making process. Each new Member State also brings new practices of political and administrative culture, which again complicates (at least in a first period of adaptation) the informal patterns of EU decision-making.

One might wonder, at first sight, whether this issue can truly be qualified as a 'constitutional question'. It is arguable, however, that the capacity to take effective action is a primary constitutional value since it represents the

---

[5] See, for instance, Art. 2 EU (as enacted by the Treaty of Maastricht): 'The Union shall set itself the following objectives: . . . to maintain in full the acquis communautaire and build on it with a view to considering to what extent the policies and forms of cooperation introduced by the Treaty may need to be revised with the aim of ensuring the *effectiveness* of the mechanisms and institutions of the Community' (emphasis added).

[6] Kerremans, 'The Political and Institutional Consequences of Widening: Capacity and Control in an Enlarged Council', in P.H. Laurent and M. Maresceau (eds), *The State of the European Union*, Vol. 4: *Deepening and Widening* (1998) 87, at 87.

original *raison d'être* of the European Communities (which remains as vital in the European Union today) namely to provide an institutional apparatus that can perform more effectively certain common tasks that the Member States can no longer adequately perform themselves. Maintaining or improving the institutions' capacity to act thereby enhances the 'performance legitimacy'[7] of the European Union. Moreover, if one accepts that the allocation of powers among the political institutions and the rules of operation of these institutions are a central element of the constitution of a state, then the efforts to reform these matters in the European Union context can also be qualified as constitutional. This does not mean that improving the ease of action of the EU institutions is an independent value. Indeed, 'improving the capacity to act does not necessarily improve the substantive merit of the ultimate action'.[8] Speedier decision-making by Council, Parliament, and/or Commission, with reduced possibilities for vetoes and blockage, may allow for *more* decisions to be adopted, but does not necessarily mean *better* EU law and policies.[9] It does not directly address the concern that the European institutions are remote and undemocratic, nor does it guarantee that the policies thus decided will be effectively applied by the Member States and private actors. Thus, in constitutional terms, promoting the capacity to act of the EU institutions is a means for achieving other ends—but an essential means nevertheless.

A. General Evolution of the Debate on Decisional Capacity

The most important EU institutions (the Commission, the Council of Ministers, the European Parliament, and the European Court of Justice) were conceived in the 1950s for a European Community of six Member States. The division of powers between these institutions has been changed several times since. However, their composition and internal organization have not been radically modified since those early days. The ineluctable question is whether this institutional framework, conceived for a small international organization of six members, and already coping uneasily with the increased membership and growing agenda of the EU, will be able to function as the EU expands eastwards and southwards to include, eventually, 27 or more states.

[7] For this expression, see Walker, 'Constitutionalizing Enlargement, Enlarging Constitutionalism', 8 *European Law Journal* (2003), forthcoming.

[8] Lebessis and Paterson, 'Developing New Modes of Governance', in O. De Schutter, N. Lebessis, and J. Paterson (eds), *Governance in the European Union* (2001) 259, at 262.

[9] See R. Dehousse, 'European Governance in Search of Legitimacy: The Need for a Process-based Approach', ibid., at 169, who distinguishes (at 177) between *decision-making efficiency* (defined as 'the ability to take decisions when needed') and *substantive efficiency* (defined as 'the ability to take the right decisions').

There have been debates before on the consequences that enlargement of the European Union would have on its internal operation. Already at the time of the first enlargement, with the UK, Denmark, and Ireland, there was considerable anxiety that the addition of these three newcomers would negatively affect the functioning of the European Community's institutions. Similar concerns were expressed when Greece joined and, later in the 1980s, Spain and Portugal. From 1989 onwards, with the immediate prospect of the accession of Austria, Finland, and Sweden (and also Norway according to expectations at that time), and the long-term prospect of the accession of a host of other countries further east, it became fashionable to put the future of the European Union in terms of a dilemma between 'deepening' and 'widening'.[10]

Overall, one can say that the Union's *widening* has so far been accompanied by some degree of *deepening* of the integration process. Successive reforms of the European treaties which took place through the Single European Act, the Treaty of Maastricht, and the Treaty of Amsterdam all led to an extension of the range of common policies and also introduced reforms of the institutional system. In the areas of internal market and social regulation, there was a marked shift away from unanimity towards qualified-majority voting in the Council and a major increase in the role of the directly elected European Parliament, which developed into a co-legislator with the Council. In other areas of EU policy, such as the common foreign and security policy and justice and home affairs, the institutional approach was rather different, with decision-making power concentrated in the hands of the Council and with its decision-making mode in the Council being that of unanimity rather than majority voting.

So, when looking at these two decades of widening and deepening in combination, it appears that the threat to the EU's institutional capacity that could *prima facie* result from increasing numbers of Member States was addressed in some areas of European policy-making by easing the conditions for making decisions, but this did not happen in other areas. Institutional reform continued to be a constant preoccupation for the states and for the EU institutions themselves all through this period, and new urgency was lent to this preoccupation when a new process of enlargement, of an unprecedented scale, was set in motion in the mid-1990s. Internal institutional reform of the European Union became so closely wedded to its new eastward enlargement, that the two successive intergovernmental conferences leading to the Treaty of Amsterdam (1997) and the Treaty of Nice (2000) were expressly mandated to grapple with this problem.

---

[10] For one of the first uses of these expressions see H. Wallace, *Widening and Deepening: The European Community and the New European Agenda* (1989).

Already in its 1992 report on 'Europe and the Challenge of Enlargement', written shortly after the adoption of the Treaty of Maastricht, the Commission stated the following:

In the perspective of enlargement, and particularly of a Union of 20 or 30 members, the question is essentially one of efficacy: how to ensure that, with an increased number of members, the new Union can function, taking account of the fact that the responsibilities would be larger than those of the Community, and that the system for two of its pillars is of an inter-governmental nature. In that perspective, how can we ensure that 'more' does not mean 'less'?

This challenge was thus defined, to put it in simple terms, as 'dealing with numbers'.[11] If membership of an extra 12 states were accomplished through a mechanical adjustment of the existing institutional rules (as had been the case, by and large, with previous enlargements), it would cause a major increase in the *absolute number* of members of the principal EU institutions: it would lead to a European Parliament of close to 1,000 members, to a European Commission of some 35 members (as compared to 20 now), and to a Council of Ministers with 27 delegations deliberating on legislative texts, subject, in many cases, to the requirement of reaching a unanimous agreement. Mechanical adjustment would also lead to an awkward issue of *relative numbers*, in that it would increase the existing imbalance between the voting power in the Council of the small and the large countries, to the detriment of the latter.

The Turin European Council of 29 March 1996, when formally launching the post-Maastricht Intergovernmental Conference, was quite explicit about the important consideration to be given to the effects of enlargement: '[t]he Union must also preserve its decision-making ability after further enlargement. Given the number and variety of the countries involved, this calls for changes to the structure and workings of the institutions'.[12] During that Intergovernmental Conference, which took place for most of 1996 and half of 1997, and which was to lead to the adoption of the Treaty of Amsterdam, there gradually developed a triangle of sensitive enlargement-related institutional questions which were considered to be intimately linked, so that a compromise could only emerge, it appeared, on a package covering each of these three issues: the size and composition of the Commission; the weighting of the votes of states when acting within the Council of Ministers; and the extension of qualified-majority voting (rather than unanimity) to further fields of EU policy. According to a close observer

---

[11] Wallace, 'Flexibility: A Tool of Integration or a Restraint on Disintegration?', in K. Neunreither and A. Wiener (eds), *European Integration After Amsterdam: Institutional Dynamics and Prospects for Democracy* (2000) 153, at 179.

[12] European Council of Turin (Mar. 1996), Conclusions of the Presidency, *Bull. EC* 3–1996.

of the Amsterdam European Council, a settlement there and then of these sensitive institutional questions was not beyond the reach of the heads of government.[13] Instead, they gave up during the final hours of the summit, and postponed a decision on these points; they agreed instead on the text of a Protocol to the newly agreed Treaty of Amsterdam, in which they expressed a commitment to resolve the outstanding institutional issues at a follow-up Treaty revision conference, the date of which was, however, not fixed.[14]

In fact, only one month after the entry into force of the Amsterdam Treaty (which took place on 1 May 1999), the European Council of Cologne agreed that a new Intergovernmental Conference, which it directed to concentrate its efforts on the three institutional 'left-overs' of Amsterdam, was going to convene in early 2000.[15] The Commission and the European Parliament called upon governments to use this opportunity for a more comprehensive reassessment of the institutional machinery of the European Union, but to no avail. The Intergovernmental Conference of 2000 had, like the previous one of 1996–1997, the overarching ambition of preserving the efficacy of the European Union's institutional machinery after the upcoming massive expansion of EU membership. Unlike in Amsterdam, though, this ambition was not mixed with other major reform aims: the agenda of the IGC of 2000 was deliberately limited to the three institutional left-overs from Amsterdam, as if a negotiated solution of these three issues were the only key to a successful institutional adaptation to the coming enlargement. By focusing on these relatively narrow questions, negotiations quickly became reduced to 'bargaining over relative power, instead of constructive compromise in the common interest'.[16] In the end, the Treaty of Nice embodied some kind of compromise agreement on each of these three Amsterdam left-overs; and it also decided, less controversially, several measures to facilitate the working of the European Court of Justice in view of its growing workload, as well as a modification of the regime of

---

[13] B. McDonagh, *Original Sin in a Brave New World. An Account of the Negotiation of the Treaty of Amsterdam* (1998), at 193.

[14] Sedelmeier, 'East of Amsterdam: The Implications of the Amsterdam Treaty for Eastern Enlargement', in *European Integration after Amsterdam, supra* note 11, at 224.

[15] See para. 52 of the Presidency Conclusions of the European Council meeting of Cologne, June 1999: 'In order to ensure that the European Union's institutions can continue to work efficiently after enlargement, the European Council confirms its intention of convening a Conference of the Representatives of the Governments of the Member States early in 2000 to resolve the institutional issues left open in Amsterdam that need to be settled before enlargement.' The following para. of the Conclusions spells out which are these 'institutional issues left open'.

[16] Best, 'The Treaty of Nice: Not Beautiful but It'll Do', *Eipascope* (2001) 1, 1, at 2.

closer cooperation which was also inspired by the pending enlargement of the Union.[17]

The intra-EU condition for accession now appears to be fulfilled, at least according to the Heads of State and Government of the EU countries. At the Nice European Council of December 2000, they agreed on the text of the Treaty of Nice and stated, in an annexed *Declaration on the future of the Union*, that 'with ratification of the Treaty of Nice, the European Union will have completed the institutional changes necessary for the accession of new Member States'.[18] At the time of writing, this process of ratification of the Nice Treaty by each of the 15 Member States has not been completed, and the Irish ratification seems seriously compromised after the 'No' vote at the popular referendum held on 7 June 2001. However, whatever the fate of the Nice Treaty, the candidate countries have now received the assurance that their EU accession depends on their own economic and political perform-ance, and on the willingness of the EU states to recognize the quality of this performance, but no longer on the question whether the Union itself man-ages to put its own house in order. That housekeeping exercise, so the Nice Declaration tells them, has now been successfully completed.

Some doubt could be cast on this optimistic perspective by the fact that the very same *Declaration on the future of the Union* launched a new round of public debate on EU institutional reforms whose scope is unprecedently large as it is dealing, among other things, with the delimitation of powers between the EU and the Member States, the incorporation of a bill of rights in the European Treaties, the role of national parliaments in the European insti-tutional system, and the question of democratic legitimacy in the EU. Thereby, the whole institutional system of the European Union is now subject to a complete review. However, when starting this new reform process, the Nice Declaration emphatically added that this debate on future EU treaty reform 'shall not constitute any form of obstacle or pre-condition to the enlargement process'.[19] At the time of writing, the official scenario is

---

[17] Relevant aspects of the Nice reforms will be addressed in later sections of this Chap. For general overviews of the Nice institutional reforms see, among others: D. Galloway, *The Treaty of Nice and Beyond—Realities and Illusions of Power in the EU* (2001); Bradley, 'Institutional Design in the Treaty of Nice', 38 *CMLRev.* (2001) 1095; Shaw, 'The Treaty of Nice: Legal and Constitutional Implications', 7 *European Public Law* (2001) 195; Van Nuffel, 'Le traité de Nice. Un commentaire', *Revue du droit de l'Union européenne* (2001) 2, 329; Yataganas, 'The Treaty of Nice: The Sharing of Power and the Institutional Balance in the European Union—A Continental Perspective', 7 *European Law Journal* (2001) 242; Favret, 'Le traité de Nice du 26 février 2001: vers un affaiblissement irréversible de la capacité d'action de l'Union européenne?', 37 *Revue trimestrielle de droit européen* (2001) 271; Piris, 'The Treaty of Nice: An Imperfect Treaty but a Decisive Step towards Enlargement', 3 *Cambridge Yearbook of European Legal Studies* (2000) 15.

[18] OJ 2001 C 80/85, point 2.

[19] OJ 2001 C 80/85, point 8.

that the (first) accession treaty will be signed and ratified by all the present and future Member States prior to the formal start of the IGC of 2004 which is supposed to crown the ongoing constitutional reform debate—but it is not unlikely that some *accident de parcours* will delay the enlargement process so that it could overlap and collide with the final stages of the EU's constitutional reform.

After Nice, 'the policy of Eastern enlargement appears to be safely locked in and effectively shielded from the "fallout" of the tough bargaining on internal reforms'.[20] This political consensus among EU governments leaves open the question whether the rather modest institutional reforms agreed at Nice will equip the European Union with the practical capacity to act after enlargement and whether it has strengthened its constitutional fabric.[21] There is, in fact, a striking contrast between the bold way in which successive European Council meetings have opened the way for accession negotiations with an ever growing number of states (without awaiting the approval of the Member State parliaments for these momentous decisions), and their very timorous approach to the question of internal reform of the European Union, where heads of government have constantly invoked the real or imagined reservations of their national parliaments or domestic public opinion as a justification for blocking some sensible institutional reform proposals.

As a result of this, the question of 'decision-making capacity' is still solidly on the EU's institutional reform agenda today. In the Laeken Declaration, the European Council reiterated once more the eternal *leitmotif* when stating that one of the questions for the post-Laeken debate would be 'how we can improve the efficiency of decision-making and the working of the institutions in a Union of some thirty Member States'. The Laeken Declaration coyly omitted to recall that the Nice Treaty had precisely aimed at solving this question 'once and for all'. In the following section, I will address in somewhat more detail why the Nice Treaty failed, even in the view of the heads of state and government that authored it, to deal adequately with this question.

B. The Nice Treaty's Attempt to Improve EU Decision-making Capacity

Two of the Amsterdam 'left-overs' dealt directly with questions of decisional capacity: the issue of the size and composition of the Commission and the

[20] Schimmelfennig, 'The Community Trap: Liberal Norms, Rhetorical Action, and the Eastern Enlargement of the European Union', 55 *International Organization* (2001) 47, at 76.

[21] Sharply contrasting views on this point can be found in the commentaries of the Nice Treaty mentioned *supra* in note 17.

question of replacing unanimous decision-making by qualified-majority decision-making in the Council. The way the IGC of 2000 and the Nice Treaty dealt with these two matters will be examined in this section. In addition, the question of the capacity of the European Court of Justice and the European Central Bank was also addressed in the IGC. The third of the Amsterdam 'left-overs', namely the weighting of votes in the Council, bears, on a closer view, no direct relationship with the capacity to act of the Council, but is an expression of the relations of power and influence among the states—this matter will therefore be dealt with in the part of this Chapter dealing with the differentiation theme.

In recent years, there have been mounting doubts whether the *European Commission* is sufficiently equipped to deal with its many important functions in the European integration process. Particularly after the somewhat accidental downfall of the Santer Commission in early 1999, immediately following the publication of the first report of Independent Experts on the (mis)management of the Commission, a process of internal reform was launched relating to staff management, rules of behaviour, and administrative structure. This process is still under way at the time of writing.[22] At the level of treaty reforms, however, the Commission was mainly looked at from two specific angles: that of its size and composition, and that of the authority of its President over its members. The former issue is most directly related to enlargement. The European Commission was created as a 'collegial body', meaning that all decisions of any political relevance are taken by the Commission acting collectively, at one of its weekly meetings.[23] The gradual increase in the number of commissioners after each enlargement made this collegial interaction more cumbersome, increased the scope for internal conflicts and misunderstandings, and made it increasingly difficult to find sufficiently weighty and consistent policy portfolios for each of them. With the latest round of enlargement, the number of commissioners rose to 20, which was considered as a limit beyond which the operation of the Commission would become very problematic. Various options for reform were considered in the academic debate and in the IGC negotiations, both in 1996–1997 and in 2000. The *status quo* solution, whereby the Commission,

---

[22] For views on the events of 1999 and on the way forward see Craig, 'The Fall and Renewal of the Commission: Accountability, Contract and Administrative Organisation', 6 *European Law Journal* (2000) 98; Van Gerven, 'Ethical and Political Responsibility of EU Commissioners', 37 *CMLRev.* (2000) 1; Spence, 'Plus ça change, plus c'est la même chose? Attempting to Reform the European Commission', 7 *Journal of European Public Policy* (2000) 1; Curtin, 'The European Commission in Search of Accountability: From Chamber of Secrets to Good Governance?', in J. Wouters and J. Stuyck (eds), *Principles of Proper Conduct for Supranational, State and Private Actors in the European Union. Essays in Honour of Walter van Gerven* (2001) 5; N. Nugent, *The European Commission* (2001), at 56–61.

[23] See Nugent, *supra* note 22, at 91–101.

in a future Union of 27, would have 33 members (with the six larger countries continuing to have two members rather than one), was rejected by all and the choice was narrowed down to two basic options.[24]

The more conservative option, strongly supported by all the small states, was to keep only one commissioner for each Member State, whether large or small, so that the present number of 20 members would rise only after more than five additional states had joined the Union. Supporters of this option thought it vitally important for the Commission's authority that it should continue to be seen as representing and acknowledging the interests of *all* Member States;[25] it would imply, for instance, that three nationals of the Baltic countries would have a seat on the Commission as against one German. Apart from the problem of skewed representation that this would raise, it might also reduce the authority of the Commission in the eyes of the larger states—whereas a strong Commission is traditionally seen as a guarantee for the interests of smaller states in particular. A further obvious difficulty with this option, of having one commissioner per Member State without a cap on the total number, is that it would eventually render the Commission rather unwieldy, more of an 'assembly' than a 'college'. This problem could be overcome, but presumably only in part, by giving greater authority to the President over his or her fellow commissioners.

The alternative option was to abandon the principle that each Member State should have at least one national in the Commission and to reduce its membership to a fixed and manageable number (between ten and 20), while setting up a rotation system: all the Member States would have their predetermined turn to appoint members of the Commission, but not all would be represented at the same time. The primary drawback of this option is that those countries (whether small or large) which do not have one of their nationals on the Commission could feel that their views are insufficiently taken into account in the Commission's policy.

While these two options were on the conference table right from the start, the IGC did not make any significant progress in reaching a consensus on one of them. This was left for the Nice European Council itself, as this question became inextricably linked with other questions affecting the overall power balance between states, namely the weighting of votes in the Council and the

---

[24] The two options were presented in an intermediate report during the IGC: Presidency Report to the Feira European Council, 14 June 2000, CONFER 4750/00 (accessible on http://db.consilium.eu.int/cig), at 11–12. For a discussion of arguments in favour of and against the various reform options see Bar Cendón, 'The Number of Members of the Commission: A Possible Reform?', in E. Best, M. Gray, and A. Stubb (eds), *Rethinking the European Union. IGC 2000 and Beyond* (2000) 77, and Galloway, *supra* note 17, chap. 3.

[25] This case is vigorously made by Temple Lang, 'How Much do the Smaller Member States Need the Commission? The Role of the Commission in a Changing Europe', 39 *CMLRev.* (2002) 315.

allocation of seats in the European Parliament. At the Nice summit, agreement was reached on the principle that, first, the five larger states will give up their second national commissioner as of 2005, and, secondly, that 'the number of members of the Commission shall be less than the number of member states' as soon as the latter number reaches 27. The specific form and extent of this future reduction of numbers were largely left in the dark. According to Article 4 of the Enlargement Protocol, where this question is dealt with, the states will participate in a rotation system which must be 'based on the principle of equality' so that 'Member States shall be treated on a strictly equal footing as regards determination of the sequence of, and the time spent by, their nationals as Members of the Commission'. At any given moment, the composition of the Commission must reflect 'the demographic and geographical range of all the member States of the Union'.[26] The details of the system will have to be worked out by a decision of the Council, acting unanimously. There are, thus, a number of factors of uncertainty as to whether and when this reform will take place and as to its scope. More particularly, the triggering moment of an EU enlargement up to 27 members is unlikely to occur in the next five to ten years, so that the reform of the Commission's composition may be a very long way from happening (even assuming that the Treaty of Nice enters into force). As a partial compensation for this procrastination, the Nice Treaty decided that the President of the Commission would be given increased powers to ensure the cohesiveness of his large college.[27]

The *Council of Ministers* is probably the EU institution whose functioning is most under threat with expanding membership of the Union. The challenge of 'dealing with numbers' is situated at two different levels as far as the Council is concerned: decision-making in the strict sense (the voting mode in the Council) and the deliberative and decision-shaping techniques at the various echelons of the Council machinery. Only the former question has been dealt with in successive Treaty revision rounds, but the latter question is perhaps equally important and will imperatively have to be addressed in the wake of enlargement. There is also a more diffuse concern that the 'club character' of the Council at its various levels may be vulnerable as numbers grow too much and too rapidly with enlargement, and that the new members may be particularly hard to socialize.[28]

The Council's voting mode depends on the policy area in which the EU acts; technically, it depends on the legal basis for a given measure, that is, the Treaty article defining a certain objective or a certain field of action for the

[26] For some considerations on the meaning of these criteria see Bradley, *supra* note 17, at 1102–1103.

[27] New Art. 217 EC, as amended by the Treaty of Nice.

[28] Wallace, 'The Council: An Institutional Chameleon', 15 *Governance* (2002) 325, at 333.

EC institutions. This Treaty article also indicates the formal procedure to be followed for adoption of the measures, including the decision-making mode which the Council of Ministers must adopt, whether by unanimity or by qualified majority.

It seems to be a plausible hypothesis that, as the number of Member States of the EU increases, and therefore also the number of national delegations taking part in the work of the Council of Ministers, the efficiency of decision-making in that body will be adversely affected. An increase in the number of Member States raises transaction costs among them, if only because the *tour de table* at the start of each Council meeting eats up ever more of the available time. It also raises the likelihood of there being diverging preferences about policy outcomes, as well as the likelihood of a veto by one country in those cases where the Council must decide by unanimity. However, contrary to expectations, statistical analysis shows that the accessions of Greece, Spain, and Portugal had no detrimental effect on decision-making speed. This result leads the author of this analysis to predict that 'a much larger Council, eventually including Central or Eastern European states, might not face the insurmountable collective action problems that many have predicted, regardless of whether or not majority voting rules are extended to the few remaining areas of treaty competence governed by unanimity'.[29] One reason offered for this paradoxical conclusion is that the Council rarely votes and that attempts are systematically made by the Commission and the Council Presidency to reach a consensus among all delegations, irrespective of whether the measure can be adopted by qualified majority or requires unanimity. However, this view, that a shift from unanimity to qualified-majority voting (QMV) is politically irrelevant in the context of enlargement, is not widely shared. It does happen after all, even though not frequently, that Member State delegations are formally outvoted at a Council meeting. Also, and more importantly, insiders confirm that in policy areas subject to QMV, the Council, the Coreper, and the working groups all very much operate 'in the shadow of the vote', so that states that find themselves in an isolated minority position sometimes accept a relatively unsatisfactory compromise proposal for fear of being outvoted.[30] Finally, one may wonder whether this strongly ingrained practice of consensus seeking will continue to hold in a very much larger and politically diversified European Union. The formal veto power wielded by each country might well become a much more unpredictable and obstructive weapon than it is today.

[29] Golub, 'In the Shadow of the Vote? Decision Making in the European Community', 53 *International Organization* (1999) 733, at 760.

[30] The effect of majority voting on the operation of the Council is strongly emphasized by the Council's chief legal adviser: Piris, *supra* note 17, at 24.

Therefore, the conclusion seems warranted that a shift from unanimity to qualified majority in any given policy area is an essential means of maintaining the Union's capacity to act in that area when the number of Member States is growing. At any rate, the Commission, the European Parliament, and the most pro-integrationist countries (the Benelux and Italy) pleaded, during both the Amsterdam and the Nice negotiations, for a systematic move to qualified-majority decision-making for all *ordinary* legislative business of the EU. They proposed keeping unanimity only for a limited number of decisions of *constitutional* importance (including revision of the treaties). In the IGC negotiations, however, bargaining took the usual form of an article-by-article search for general agreement to shift from unanimity to qualified-majority voting.[31] In the end, the Treaty of Nice decided only a limited number of such shifts relating to relatively minor policy areas. Many countries (most prominently the UK, Germany, France, and Spain) each had their own impeccable reasons for insisting on unanimity for particular policy areas that they considered to be of vital interest.[32] Adding up all these policy areas, there is still a large proportion of EU policy decisions that will continue to be subject to a national veto after the entry into force of the Nice Treaty.[33] As a result, the Laeken Declaration on the future of the European Union included, among the many questions it mentioned, that of whether there is a need 'for more decisions by qualified majority'. The IGC of 2004 will thus be the fifth consecutive treaty revision grappling with this question. The Nice Treaty negotiations seem to indicate that, as the number of policy areas subject to unanimity diminishes, finding a consensus for further shifts becomes increasingly difficult. This raises the hitherto taboo question whether treaty revision itself can remain subject to unanimous decision-making (and separate ratification by each state) in a future enlarged Europe.[34]

The capacity to act of the *European Court of Justice* was the object of unprecedented attention during the 2000 IGC. Unlike with the Commission and the Council, what is at stake here is not the capacity to propose and adopt new policies, but rather the capacity to ensure effective control of compliance with EU law by the institutions, the Member States, and private actors. The Nice Treaty puts in place the signposts for a rather significant reform of the

[31] For a good view of the negotiation process on this point, see Galloway, *supra* note 17, chap. 5.

[32] See Favret, *supra* note 17, at 278.

[33] For a detailed analysis of the Nice changes on this point see Dashwood, 'The Constitution of the European Union after Nice: Law-making Procedures', 26 *ELRev.* (2001) 215, at 225–231, and Van Nuffel, *supra* note 17, at 363 ff.

[34] The option of introducing a 'superqualified majority' rule for Treaty revisions (accompanied perhaps by a partial opt-out for countries that would be overruled) is discussed in the report of the Robert Schuman Centre of the European University Institute: *Reforming the Treaties' Amendment Procedures*, 31 July 2000 (http://europa.eu.int/comm/archives/igc2000/offdoc/repoflo_en2.pdf).

judicial structure of the European Union.[35] The principle that there shall be at least one judge from each Member State in the European Court of Justice was confirmed for the indefinite future. This raises the same queries about balanced representation as for the Commission (one German judge as against three from the Baltic countries?), but expanding numbers are, as such, less of a threat to the adequate functioning of the Court than of the Commission, for, unlike the Commission, the ECJ will be able to split up into small chambers of judges for deciding all except the most politically sensitive cases. The Nice Treaty, once it comes into force, will allow for more categories of cases to be moved from the jurisdiction of the ECJ to that of the European Court of First Instance (CFI) and from that of the CFI to new judicial panels hearing appeals in special areas of the law that are of lesser importance for the general evolution of the European Union (such as employment disputes between EU institutions and their staff). As a result, the European Court of Justice will be left to consider only the more important cases. If these reforms are put in place—if and when the Treaty of Nice enters into force—and if, in addition, there is a significant increase in the number of judges of the Court of First Instance, then the European court system should have an increased capacity to deal adequately and in a timely fashion with its workload, including new cases resulting from accession of the candidate states. At the same time, these reforms would enable the ECJ to continue to give principled guidance to the legal and institutional development of the European Union. In this context, one may note that the Nice Treaty negotiators have recognized the importance of the uniform application of EU law by rejecting proposals to create 'decentralized' Community courts and to relax the conditions under which national courts must refer preliminary questions to the ECJ.[36]

With regard to the operation of the *European Central Bank*, the Treaty of Nice has changed next to nothing. The main decision-making organ of the European Central Bank (ECB), the Governing Council, is presently composed of the six appointed members of the Executive Board and the 12 governors of the national banks of the countries in the Eurosystem. A major expansion of membership of the EU and hence, sooner or later, of the ECB will affect the deliberative capacity of the Governing Council, in the same way as it will affect the deliberation dynamics of European Commission meetings and plenary sessions of the European Court of Justice. But in the

---

[35] Among the many early commentaries devoted to this aspect of the Nice Treaty see Shaw, *supra* note 17, at 203 ff.; Johnston, 'Judicial Reform and the Treaty of Nice', 38 *CMLRev.* (2001) 499; Arnull, 'Modernising the Community Courts', 3 *Cambridge Yearbook of European Legal Studies* (2000) 37; Ruiz-Jarabo, 'La réforme de la Cour de justice opérée par le traité de Nice et sa mise en oeuvre future', 37 *Revue trimestrielle de droit européen* (2001) 705.

[36] See Arnull, *supra* note 35, at 62 and 42–43.

case of the ECB, it will have the further effect of radically altering the proportion, within the Governing Council, between the supranational element, represented by the six members of the Executive Board who, in principle, take a common line inspired by the general European interest as they define it, and the national element represented by the governors of the Eurozone states' central banks.[37] It would make it more difficult for the Executive Board to put together a winning coalition within the Governing Council and would thereby make ECB decision-making generally more difficult.[38] The 2000 IGC failed to give sustained attention to this problem, although a last-minute reference was inserted in the Treaty of Nice to the effect that future changes in the composition of the Governing Council will no longer need to be decided at an intergovernmental conference, but in a more straightforward manner, by a unanimous decision of the European Council; a solution of the question was thus postponed.

C. Beyond Nice: Unresolved Challenges to the Effective Operation of the Decision-making System

The questions that were on the official agenda of the two recent treaty revision negotiations (in 1996–1997 and 2000) constitute only the superficial 'high politics' part of the institutional response to the EU's large-scale enlargement. There is a more diffuse, but probably more daunting, side to the question of institutional adaptation to increased membership, which relates to the functioning of the European Union's administrative machinery.

The ongoing reform of the Commission's internal operation was mentioned above.[39] The internal operation of the *Council* is even more directly challenged by enlargement. There are hundreds of *committees and working groups* composed of civil servants of the Member States that assist the Council of Ministers in its legislative task.[40] According to one calculation, up to 1,000 national civil servants are present in Brussels on an average working day to participate in one of these meetings. They do the hard work of negotiating the nuts and bolts of draft legislation proposed by the Commission. After further fine-tuning efforts at the higher level of the Committee of Permanent Representatives, the ministers assembled in the Council meetings can limit

[37] Admittedly, the governors of the national central banks are not 'representatives' of their states in the same way as the members of the EU Council of Ministers; see on this point C. Zilioli and M. Selmayr, *The Law of the European Central Bank* (2001), at 88–89.

[38] R. Baldwin, E. Berglöf, F. Giavazzi, and M. Widgrén, *EU Reforms for Tomorrow's Europe*, Centre for Economic Policy Research, Discussion Paper Series, No. 2623 (2000), at 33–42.

[39] See *supra* note 22.

[40] On their role generally, see F. Hayes-Renshaw and H. Wallace, *The Council of Ministers* (1997), chap. 3.

themselves to approving the compromises reached at these lower levels of the
Council machinery or to striking the final political compromise among the
alternative solutions offered to them. It is hard to envisage how the interaction between these national teams at the lower echelons can meaningfully
proceed with up to 27 or more delegations placed around committee tables.
Already now, an often heard complaint is that an inordinate amount of time
at these meetings is taken up by the presentation of the separate views of the
15 delegations, with little time and energy left for efforts to have a constructive dialogue. A worsening of this situation can only be prevented by fundamentally reconsidering the functioning of these committees, either by
strengthening the guiding role of the Commission or that of the Council
Presidency and the Council Secretariat, or by resorting more often to entirely
written proceedings. Whatever solution is to be adopted (and thinking on
this matter has only started), the European Union's decision-making process
will no longer be the same.

At the highest level, the meetings of the ministers themselves (in the
Council) and the meetings of the heads of state and governments (in
the European Council), the reviewing and streamlining operation has recently picked up steam. In several documents, the latest of which were
adopted at the Seville summit of June 2002,[41] the European Council has
broached issues such as the reduction of the number of different Council
formations, the possible separation between the 'horizontal' and 'foreign
affairs' parts of the activity of the General Affairs formation, the semestrial
rotation of the Presidency (which would become quite problematic in a
Union of 27 members), and the organization of the work of the European
Council.[42] The reform proposals made on all these matters are invariably
presented by their proponents as being urgently needed in order to 'oil the
wheels' of the Council and the European Council in the wake of the Union's
enlargement.

Another preoccupying and as yet unresolved issue is that of the *use of
languages* in the operation of the European Union. The number of official
languages stands, at present, at 11 and, in the Europe of 27 predicted by the
Nice Treaty, there will be an additional ten official languages at least (only

---

[41] See particularly Annex III to the Conclusions of the Helsinki European Council, 10–11
Dec. 1999, *An Effective Council for an Enlarged Union: Guidelines for Reform and Operational
Recommendations*; Annex I of the Conclusions of the Seville European Council of 21–22 June
2002, *Rules for Organising the Proceedings of the European Council*; Annex II to the same
Conclusions, *Measures Concerning the Structure and Functioning of the Council.*

[42] Among other things, the European Council notoriously lacks formal rules of procedure,
even though it occasionally takes (either directly or in the special composition of Heads of
State and Government, without the President of the Commission) formal EU decisions (see
Dashwood, 'Decision-making at the Summit', 3 *Cambridge Yearbook of European Legal
Studies* (2000) 79).

Cyprus and Malta may not add an extra language). Indeed, recognition as an official EU language is such a highly symbolic political question that one cannot expect even the smallest of the applicant countries to agree to renounce that recognition. Owing to the fact that the increase of one-to-one relations between languages rises exponentially when the number of official languages grows, there will inevitably be considerable additional costs of translation and, even more worrying, a further decrease in the possibility for genuine dialogue taking place in the major meetings of the EU institutions. At the lower level of working groups and executive commit-tees, and in the drafting of preparatory and consultative documents, the present practice of privileging English, French, and (to a lesser extent) German as so-called 'working languages' will no doubt have to be re-inforced.[43] But, as this is a very sensitive issue, no official plan on how to tackle the linguistic clogging of the institutional machinery of the European Union has, as yet, been presented.

3. FUNDAMENTAL VALUES

Although, according to the text of Article 6(1) EU, the European Union is founded on the principles of liberty, democracy, respect for human rights and fundamental freedoms, and the rule of law, there is still much controversy about the extent to which the European Union and, indeed, its Member States, effectively comply with these fundamental values in their institutional structure and daily activities. The most obsessive dimension of this debate is the question whether, or to what extent, the European Union provides for sufficiently democratic forms of representation and participation. There is a huge literature on this subject,[44] and the Member States and EU institutions keep affirming the importance of making the EU 'more democratic'.[45] The roles of the European Parliament and of the national parliaments are crucial variables in this debate, but so is the exploration of the many other possible channels of democratic participation in European policy-making.

---

[43] On the distinction between official and working languages, and the practice of language use in the EU institutions more generally, see Goebel, 'The European Union Grows: The Constitutional Impact of the Accession of Austria, Finland and Sweden', 18 *Fordham International Law Journal* (1995) 1092, at 1135 ff.; Milian Massana, 'Le régime linguistique de l'Union européenne', 35 *Rivista di diritto europeo* (1995) 485.

[44] Among the recent contributions (with further references to the literature), see: Lenaerts and Verhoeven, 'Institutional Balance as a Guarantee for Democracy in EU Governance', in C. Joerges and R. Dehousse (eds), *Good Governance in Europe's Integrated Market* (2002) 35; P. Magnette, *L'Europe, l'Etat et la démocratie* (2000); Lord, 'Assessing Democracy in a Contested Polity', 39 *Journal of Common Market Studies* (2001) 641; 'L'Union européenne: une démocratie diffuse?', special issue, 51 *Revue française de science politique* (2001) 859.

[45] See, recently, the Laeken Declaration, *supra* note 4.

So far, no direct connection has been made, in the political debate or in the scholarly literature, between this democracy theme and the enlargement of the Union. Indirectly, enlargement may worsen the alleged democracy deficit by diluting even more the voice of the single citizen in the European decision-making process; it may also make the prospect of the emergence of a true European *demos* more remote than before. On the other hand, the limited improvements of the EU's capacity to act described in the previous section of this Chapter can also be seen as improving democracy and legitimacy; thus, it has been argued that the quasi-elimination of unanimity in the Council is also commendable from a democratic point of view.[46] A specific linkage between democratic representation and enlargement occurred at the Nice summit, where the anomalous and unjustified decision was taken to allocate to Hungary and the Czech Republic a lower number of seats in the European Parliament than existing Member States with comparable populations.[47] This discriminatory treatment will, presumably, be corrected in the accession treaty to be concluded with these countries.

This being said, it is not a pure coincidence that the 'fundamental values' clause of Article 6(1) EU was inserted by the Treaty of Amsterdam, the revision treaty which also aimed at preparing the European Union for the new wave of accessions. Also, some important intra-EU constitutional reforms, particularly in the field of fundamental rights protection, might not have occurred, or at least not in the same form, if it had not been for the EU's strong affirmation of these fundamental values in the pre-accession context. Therefore, subsection A below will deal with the role of political conditionality in this pre-accession context; this subsection is, strictly speaking, outside the scope of the present Chapter (which is about the *internal* EU dimension of enlargement), but it seems a useful prelude to the other subsections of this section, which deal with intra-EU changes that can be understood, to some extent, as efforts to eliminate the 'double standard' used by the EU in respect of the applicant countries.

A. The Policy of 'Political' Conditionality

Article 49 EU, which defines the conditions and procedure of accession to the European Union (and to its component organizations the EC, EAEC, and ECSC) states that 'any European state which respects the principles set out in Article 6(1) may apply to become a member of the Union'. The principles set

---

[46] Justus Lipsius, 'The 1996 Intergovernmental Conference', 20 *ELRev.* (1995) 235, at 258.

[47] Nice Treaty, Declaration on the enlargement of the European Union. The related question of the allocation of weighted votes in the *Council* will be dealt with in the next section of this Chap.

out in Article 6(1) EU are 'the principles of liberty, democracy, respect for human rights and fundamental freedoms and the rule of law, principles which are common to the Member States'.

This reference to basic constitutional principles as underlying and conditioning membership of the Union was inserted only by the Treaty of Amsterdam. The nine countries that acceded earlier on to the European Communities and, later, the European Union, did so without having to comply with this formal 'political conditionality' clause. The original text of the EEC Treaty did not provide for any other substantive condition for membership than that the applicant country had to be 'European'. However, the new text of Article 49 EU is, in fact, the constitutional codification of an existing practice. Already in April 1978, a European Council meeting had affirmed that 'respect for and maintenance of representative democracy and human rights in each Member State are essential elements of membership of the European Communities'.[48] The Commission had proposed this formula to the European Council and used it itself, shortly afterwards, in its opinion on the application for membership of Greece and, also in 1988, in its negative opinion on the 'first' membership bid of Turkey.

In respect of the present candidates for membership, political conditionality was famously imposed by the Copenhagen European Council of June 1993 when it stated that 'membership requires that the candidate country must have achieved stability of institutions guaranteeing democracy, the rule of law, human rights and respect for and protection of minorities'.

The insistent formulation of political criteria for accession by the Copenhagen European Council was preceded by, and can be understood against the background of, two other developments. The first was the policy of admissions of central and eastern European countries to the Council of Europe, which had started immediately after the fall of the Berlin Wall. The Statute of the Council of Europe clearly imposed (and did so from the start) democracy and human rights conditions for accession. In practice, however, the admissions policy of the Council of Europe proved to be rather lax, as was exemplified by the controversial accessions of Croatia, Russia, and countries of the Caucasus region. It is true that the Council of Europe has put in place various devices for post-accession monitoring of human rights and democratic principles, but these cannot easily compensate for the lack of serious scrutiny prior to the accession of certain countries.

The second development preceding and accompanying 'Copenhagen' was the formulation of a general policy of conditionality in the European Community's external relations,[49] which was solemnly affirmed in the conclusions

[48] European Council of Copenhagen, Declaration on democracy, *Bull.EC* 3–1978, 6.
[49] There is an extremely rich literature on this subject. See, among others: F. Hoffmeister, *Menschenrechts- und Demokratieklauseln in den vertraglichen Aussenbeziehungen der*

of the Luxembourg European Council of June 1991[50] and gradually extended ever since. This policy is also, more specifically, reflected in the Europe Agreements concluded in the early 1990s with the states that are now candidates for accession.[51] There are, however, some important legal differences between the recourse to human rights conditionality in external agreements concluded by the European Community (including those with the candidate countries) and in accession negotiations. First: whereas its use in external agreements is subject to the legal limits of EC competence (and the insertion of sweeping human rights clauses may be objectionable from this point of view[52]), accession treaties are formally concluded by the Member States (not the EU), so that there are no competence limits to the use of human rights conditions in these negotiations (even though the EU institutions are actively participating in the negotiations *on behalf of* the Member States). Secondly, in the case of EC external agreements, the only sanction at the disposal of the EC is a suspension of the agreement, whereas in accession negotiations the EU can wave the tasty carrot of membership of the Union.

In the years after 1993, the EU made it clear to the potential applicants for membership that compliance with the political criteria would be required, not only as a condition for *accession* proper, but also as a prior condition for opening accession *negotiations*. In fact, the assessment of the performance of candidate countries in respect of human rights, democracy, and other political conditions became a long-drawn-out process which started in 1997 and has not yet ended. When negotiations come to a successful end with one or, more likely, a batch of candidate countries, full compliance with the membership conditions will be assessed again by the Commission, the European Parliament, the European Council, and, indeed, all the present Member States individually (who will have to sign the accession treaty). The accession

---

Europäischen Gemeinschaft (1998); M. Bulterman, *Human Rights in the Treaty Relations of the European Community* (2001); Brandtner and Rosas, 'Human Rights and the External Relations of the European Community: An Analysis of Doctrine and Practice', 9 *EJIL* (1998) 468; Ward, 'Frameworks for Cooperation between the European Union and Third States: A Viable Matrix for Uniform Human Rights Standards?', 3 *European Foreign Affairs Review* (1998) 505; Youngs, 'European Union Democracy Promotion Policies: Ten Years On', 6 *European Foreign Affairs Review* (2001) 355.

[50] European Council, Luxembourg 28–29 June 1991, Conclusions of the Presidency: 'respect, promotion and safeguard of human rights is an essential part of international relations and one of the cornerstones of European co-operation as well as of relations between the Community and its Member States and other countries'.

[51] See King, 'The European Community and Human Rights in Eastern Europe', 23 *Legal Issues of European Integration* (1996) 83.

[52] For a discussion of these limits to EC competence see Cannizzaro, 'The Scope of EU Foreign Power. Is the EC Competent to Conclude Agreements with Third States Including Human Rights Clauses?', in E. Cannizzaro (ed.), The *European Union as an Actor in International Relations* (2002) 297.

treaty will then have to be ratified by all signatory states, which gives the national parliaments of the present Member States an opportunity to examine once more compliance with the political conditions of membership.

At each of these moments, the political criteria of Copenhagen are taken into the balance together with the economic criteria and the 'compliance with the *acquis*' criterion. The political criteria have played a meaningful, though certainly not dominant, role in this overall assessment process.[53] In the initial Commission opinions of 1997, only one of the ten candidate countries of Central and Eastern Europe, namely Slovakia, was found not to comply with the political criteria. This country was found not to meet the appropriate standard for a variety of reasons, including in particular the malfunctioning of democracy and its problematic record of minority protection.[54] The European Council of Luxembourg endorsed the Commission's view and decided not to include Slovakia among the six countries with which negotiations could be started, because of its failure to comply with the political criteria (whereas the other four countries that were not considered ready for negotiations were sidelined for their failure to comply with the *economic* criteria for membership). However, after the replacement of the Meciar government in 1998, the attitude of both the Commission and the European Council changed quickly and radically. In the Commission's Regular Report of 1999, Slovakia was considered to meet the political criteria, and the Helsinki European Council followed suit and agreed to open accession negotiations with that country.[55]

The only candidate country that is currently not considered to have met the political conditions for accession is Turkey. The country's human rights record is the most important factor explaining this negative assessment by the EU institutions. Since December 1999, when its candidate status was recognized by the European Council at Helsinki, and for presumably several years to come, the political conditions have continued to be an obstacle to the opening of negotiations with Turkey. Although 34 constitutional amendments were adopted by Turkey in October 2001, many of them on human rights matters,[56] the European Commission's Regular Report of November 2001 gave an assessment which, again, was negative on balance: '[d]espite a

[53] For an overall legal analysis of the application of conditionality in the context of enlargement see Cremona, 'Accession to the European Union: Membership Conditionality and Accession Criteria', *Polish Yearbook of International Law* [2002] (forthcoming).

[54] Commission's Opinion on Slovakia, *Bull. EC*, Supplement 9/97.

[55] For a detailed account of the domestic and international dimensions of this evolution see Pridham, 'The European Union's Democratic Conditionality and Domestic Politics in Slovakia: The Meciar and Dzurinda Governments Compared', 54 *Europe-Asia Studies* (2002) 203.

[56] See Avci, 'Putting the Turkish EU Candidacy into Context', 7 *European Foreign Affairs Review* (2002) 91, at 102–103.

number of constitutional, legislative and administrative changes, the actual human rights situation as it affects individuals in Turkey needs improvement. Though it is beginning to make progress in some areas, Turkey does not yet meet the Copenhagen political criteria.'[57]

Leaving aside the special case of Turkey, all 12 countries admitted to the negotiations (the ten Central and Eastern European countries, Cyprus, and Malta) have since 1999 constantly been considered to meet the political conditions. Save for a major political change in one of the candidate countries, due to election results or internal upheaval, this assessment is not likely to change between now and the time when the accession treaties are signed.

Now, one may think that, if the Commission and the European Council consider that a candidate country complies with the required human rights and democracy standards, that should be the end of the examination, and no further comments will be made about the domestic situation in the country concerned until the final assessment upon signature of the accession treaty. Instead, in the current practice of the EU institutions, assessment of compliance has been a continuous process, in which the performance of each of the candidate states in the matters covered by the political conditionality criterion is assessed annually by the Commission's Regular Report on that state, and the causes for concern identified by the Commission (and endorsed by the European Council) are translated into priorities for the Accession Partnership between the EU and the country concerned. Typically, the relevant heading of the Commission's Regular Reports starts with the phrase that the candidate country continues to fulfil the political criteria, but then goes on considering in detail a long list of matters for which further progress should be made. For example, if one reads the Regular Reports of 2001, there is not a single one among the candidate countries in which the human rights situation is considered to be entirely satisfactory, and the accompanying Accession Partnerships all continue to list human rights policy goals among their 'priorities'.[58]

The candidate countries have not protested against this particular interpretation of the political conditionality criterion; indeed, they make an effort to meet the specific requirements and recommendations addressed to them

[57] http://europa.eu.int/comm/enlargement/report2001/tu_en.pdf, at 97. The human rights situation is discussed at 19–30 of the report.

[58] To take just one example: the update of the accession partnership with Slovakia for 2002 lists the following three human rights actions among the priorities of the partnership: 'continue improving the situation of the Roma through strengthened implementation of the relevant strategy..., ensure due implementation of the minority language legislation, ensure that an effective system for redressing police misconduct is established': Council Decision on the principles, priorities, intermediate objectives and conditions contained in the Accession Partnership with Slovakia, OJ 2002 L 44/92, at 94.

each year by the EU institutions. It is therefore correct to say, as the Commission did in its 2001 Strategy Paper, that 'the requirement set by the Copenhagen political criteria, and the Commission's regular assessment of progress achieved in meeting them, have continued to serve as important incentives for the candidate countries'.[59] Whether this has also led to a marked overall improvement of the human rights situation in the candidate countries, as the Commission went on to claim in the same document, is more debatable.[60]

B. Double Standards and EU Constitutional Reforms (I): The Mechanism of Article 7 EU

The policy of political conditionality, delineated in the previous section, is a feature of the 'external' relations between the EU and the candidate countries. However, it has had consequences for the 'internal' constitutional fabric of the European Union itself. It is to these, existing and possible future, consequences that I will turn now. It has often been noted that the EU's political conditionality policy contains various elements of a double standard, in the sense of imposing higher or more detailed requirements on candidates for membership than on the existing Member States. As was argued by Andrew Williams, 'the notion that states may be subjected to a different regime of scrutiny and intervention on the cusp of entry to the Union from that which applies when full membership is achieved, is both dangerous and potentially divisive'.[61] Even after the Nice Treaty reforms, there will still be a marked contrast between the concrete and detailed examination of state practice in the field of human rights in the context of pre-accession and the highly symbolic *ultima ratio* procedure established by Article 7 EU for preventing Member States of the Union from trampling over fundamental rights and values. The first double standard (which will be examined in this section) lies in the *scope of application* of the fundamental values test, whereas the second double standard (to be examined in the next section) lies in the *substantive content of the fundamental values standard.*

---

[59] http://europa.eu.int/comm/enlargement/report2001/strategy_en.pdf, at 12. For further reflections on the effectiveness of membership conditionality, see Chap. 5 of this volume and Smith, 'The Conditional Offer of Membership as an Instrument of EU Foreign Policy: Reshaping Europe in the EU's Image', 8 *Marmara Journal of European Studies* (2000) 33, at 38 ff.

[60] For a note of scepticism on this point see Cartabia, 'Allargamento e diritti fondamentali nell'Unione europea. Dimensione politica e dimensione individuale', in S. Guerrieri, A. Manzella, and F. Sdogati (eds), *Dall'Europa a Quindici alla Grande Europa. La sfida istituzionale* (2001) 123.

[61] Williams, 'Enlargement of the Union and Human Rights Conditionality: A Policy of Distinction?', 25 *ELRev.* (2000) 601, at 602.

The double standard as to the scope of application results from the following situation. The EU institutions, in their annual assessments, check the overall across-the-board compliance of the candidate member states with the principles of democracy, rule of law, and respect of human rights. As regards the current Member States, the situation is rather different. Until the entry into force of the Treaty of Amsterdam, they had a duty only to respect *some* fundamental rights in *some* circumstances: they had the obligation to comply with the few fundamental rights directly contained in the EC Treaty, such as the principle of non-discrimination on grounds of nationality and the principle of equal pay for work of equal value; with the fundamental rights spelled out in acts of secondary EC law, such as the directives on sex discrimination; and with all the rights that are part of the unwritten corpus of general principles of Community law whenever the states implement Community law or enact restrictions of one of the common market freedoms. However, in each of these situations, the human rights standard is linked to a specific competence of the EC or EU, whereas there are still many policy areas in which the Member States act entirely autonomously and are therefore not subject to an EU-based fundamental rights standard. Indeed, many of the matters of concern mentioned in the Commission's Regular Reports on the candidate countries (minority rights, prison conditions, children's rights) are currently outside the scope of the EU's *internal* competence, and, hence, not subject to control mechanisms such as the Commission's right to bring an enforcement action under Article 226 EC.

The idea that the European Union should have a mechanism through which it exercises a *comprehensive* (rather than piecemeal) control of human rights standards in its Member States is not altogether new (the European Parliament had already proposed one in its Draft Treaty of 1984[62]), but the prospect of enlargement gave driving force to its realization. The Amsterdam Treaty made an important contribution to building the Union's 'liberal constitutionalist edifice'.[63] As was mentioned before, it formally included in Article 49 EU a reference to the fundamental principles of Article 6(1), thus constitutionalizing the Copenhagen criteria (to a large extent at least). It also, more directly, entrenched the constitutional values on which the EU is based by setting out, in Article 7 EU, a new procedure for imposing sanctions against Member States not complying with the principles of democracy, human rights, and rule of law proclaimed in Article 6(1) EU. The control mechanism which was put in place by the Treaty of Amsterdam has two stages, each with a different scope and procedure: the first stage is the determination of the existence of a breach,

---

[62] See Arts. 4(4) and 44 of the Parliament's Draft Treaty establishing the European Union, OJ 1984 C 77/53.

[63] Shaw, *supra* note 17, at 198.

and the second stage is the sanction itself, namely the suspension of certain membership rights.[64]

The Amsterdam sanction mechanism—which was based on a common initiative of the Italian and the Austrian foreign ministers Dini and Schüssel during the 1996 Intergovernmental Conference—was hailed as one of the most innovative and prominent outcomes of the 1996 IGC. The mechanism filled a vacuum in the EU legal order, if compared to other international organizations that have longstanding mechanisms for the suspension of membership rights.[65] On the eve of enlargement, it represented an attempt to guarantee the future respect for the EU 'constitutional' principles. However, the mechanism has several major deficiencies. First, the possibility of imposing severe sanctions is not counterbalanced by strict respect for the principle of *audiatur altera pars* and by judicial protection for the Member State in question. Secondly, it is evident that the procedural and substantive thresholds within the mechanism are so high that it is difficult to envisage its actual use. It can be seen as an instrument that is better suited for the prevention of human rights breaches than for redressing such breaches. However, its shortcomings even as a preventive instrument were soon, and very unexpectedly, shown by the so-called 'Austrian crisis' of 2000, which was triggered by the coming to power in Austria of Jörg Haider's FPÖ.[66]

The Austrian case evidenced the lack of a multilateral mechanism for collective and controlled reaction to incidents that do not represent a material breach of Article 6 principles. Article 7 EU was not applicable in the Austrian

---

[64] See Art. 7(1) and (2) EU. The most detailed analysis of the whole mechanism is by F. Schorkopf, *Homogenität in der Europäischen Union—Ausgestaltung und Gewährleistung durch Article 6 Abs. 1 und Article 7 EUV* (2000). See also, for briefer accounts, Verhoeven, 'How Democratic Need European Union Members Be? Some Thoughts after Amsterdam', 23 *ELRev.* (1998) 217; McGoldrick, 'The European Union after Amsterdam: An Organisation with General Human Rights Competence?', in D. O'Keeffe and P. Twomey (eds), *Legal Issues of the Amsterdam Treaty* (1999) 249, at 251 ff.; Nowak, 'Human Rights "Conditionality" in Relation to Entry to, and Full Participation in, the EU', in P. Alston *et al.* (eds), *The EU and Human Rights* (1999), 687; Monjal, 'Le Traité d'Amsterdam et la procédure en constatation politique de manquement aux principes de l'Union', *Revue du Marché Unique Européen* [1998] 69; Schmitt von Sydow, 'Liberté, démocratie, droits fondamentaux et Etat de droit: analyse de l'article 7 du traité UE', *Revue du Droit de l'Union Européenne* (2001) 285.

[65] See in particular Art. 8 of the Statute of the Council of Europe; and see the survey by Hofstötter, 'Suspension of Rights by International Organisations: The European Union, the European Communities and Other International Organisations', in V. Kronenberger (ed.), *The European Union and the International Legal Order: Discord or Harmony?* (2001) 23.

[66] Among the many comments on the Austrian crisis and on the legitimacy of the sanctions from an international and a European law perspective, see Cramér and Wrange, 'The Haider Affair, Law and European Integration', *Europarättslig tidskrift* [2000] 28; Happold, 'Fourteen against One: The EU Member States' Response to Freedom Party Participation in the Austrian Government', 49 *ICLQ* (2000) 953; Hummer, 'The End of EU Sanctions against Austria—a Precedent for New Sanctions Procedures?', *The European Legal Forum* [2000] 77.

case, as it presupposes concrete *action* from a state, so that the Union had no suitable means of control. In contrast, had the 'Austrian' case had occurred for example in Hungary, there would have been an extensive armoury of reactions at the disposal of the EU, especially by putting pressure through the accession-monitoring mechanism described in the previous section of this chapter.[67] On the other hand, the action of the EU states in the Austrian case could also be seen as an unruly 'spill-over' on the intra-EU scene of their habit of exercising discretionary political control over the human rights and democracy standards in applicant countries. However, to end on a positive note, the Austrian crisis has also promoted the Europe-wide public debate on common values and fundamental rights, and furthered the reflection on how a guarantee of such values and rights could be organized at the European level. A first consequence of the latter was the attempted reform of the 'Article 7 mechanism' by the Treaty of Nice.

In the report which put an end to the Austrian crisis, the three 'wise men' proposed the introduction of:

preventive and monitoring procedures into Article 7 of the EU Treaty, so that a situation similar to the current situation in Austria would be dealt with within the EU from the very start. This would underline the fundamental commitment of the EU to common European values. Such a mechanism would also allow from the beginning an open and non-confrontational dialogue with the Member State concerned.[68]

Alongside such a monitoring procedure, the wise men also emphasized the need for flanking policies and institutional arrangements such as:

the creation of a Human Rights office within the Council reporting to the European Council; the appointment within the Commission of a Commissioner responsible for human rights issues; and, particularly the extension of the activities, budget and status of the existing EU Observatory on racism and xenophobia.[69]

While the latter suggestions have not been taken up yet,[70] the Amsterdam sanction mechanism itself was the object of sustained discussion during the Nice IGC, which, however, did not lead to a complete revision of the mechanism.

---

[67] Williams, *supra* note 61, at 616.

[68] Report of the three 'wise men' (Martti Ahtisaari, Jochen Frowein, and Marcelino Oreja), *International Legal Materials* (2001) 1, at 102, para. 117.

[69] Ibid., para. 118.

[70] Notwithstanding the fact that these institutional measures could have been adopted through secondary EU law, without the need for prior Treaty revision. Measures of this kind had been proposed earlier in *Leading by Example: A Human Rights Agenda for the European Union for the Year 2000*, published in P. Alston *et al.* (eds), *The EU and Human Rights* (1999), 921, and, in more detail, by Alston and Weiler, 'An "Ever Closer Union" in Need of a Human Rights Policy: The European Union and Human Rights', in ibid., at 3.

If the Treaty of Nice enters into force, a new paragraph (1) is to be added to Article 7 EU containing a procedural mechanism which will operate prior to the 'breach determination' procedure. This new monitoring procedure will allow one third of the Member States, the Commission, or even the Parliament to submit to the Council a 'reasoned proposal', whereupon the Council, acting by a majority of four-fifths of its members (instead of the unanimity-minus-one that continues to be required in the later stages of the procedure) may determine that there exists 'a clear risk of a serious breach' by a Member State of Article 6(1) EU principles and, additionally, may 'address appropriate recommendations' to that state.[71] Such recommendations will not be legally binding, but may well serve to establish standards against which the future acts of the Member State will be checked.[72]

The establishment of a preventive monitoring procedure at the European level does not mean that the Member States lose their competence to express their own individual concerns about the human rights situation in another state, but it certainly provides an incentive to use in the future this new multilateral framework when situations similar to the Austrian crisis arise. Another positive feature of the Nice Treaty is the fact that it extends the Courts' jurisdiction over Article 7, at least as far as the 'purely procedural stipulations' are concerned.

C. Double Standards and EU Constitutional Reforms (II): The EU Charter of Rights

Although the Copenhagen criteria refer to 'human rights' in general and do not mention the European Convention in so many words, the Convention rights seem to provide a natural core of the human rights standard against which the candidate countries are assessed annually by the Commission. However, it is striking to see that the Commission, in its Regular Reports on progress towards accession, does not use compliance with the ECHR as the sole or even primary indicator of the applicant states' human rights performance. It rather refers to a variety of sources of human rights protection, including other Council of Europe conventions (such as the Framework Convention on National Minorities) and OCSE documents, while leaving open the relative importance it chooses to give to these various instruments in coming to its assessment. The Commission clearly conceives of its role in political rather than quasi-judicial terms, and feels free therefore to use a wide range of substantive human rights standards. By contrast, the European Union institutions themselves (and the Member States acting within the

---

[71] See Art. 7(1) EU as amended by the Treaty of Nice, OJ 2001 C 80/1, at 6.

[72] A far-reaching proposal by the Belgian delegation to permit 'appropriate measures' already in the course of a monitoring procedure was not accepted.

scope of application of EU law) are merely subject to respect for the 'general principles of Community law' which are based on national constitutional traditions and the ECHR but, arguably, do not include other Council of Europe conventions and OCSE instruments.

This particular gap between external requirements and internal human rights policy could be remedied by a recent (though half-hearted) constitutional reform of the EU, namely the proclamation in December 2000 of the Charter of Rights of the European Union. This is not to say that enlargement was a motivating factor for launching the work of the Charter; there are, in fact, no indications of this.[73] Still, the Charter could serve as a common yardstick both for the EU surveillance mechanism of the general human rights record of Member States under Article 7 TEU, and for determining the readiness of a third country for accession.[74] So far, however, the Charter has not been used in either of these two contexts. It has not modified the approach taken by the Commission in its latest Regular Reports on candidate countries' progress in the field of human rights. The Charter would arguably have the advantage of providing a clearly spelled out standard against which the applicant countries' performance could be checked. This standard would be relatively broad and would encompass the existing Commission practice of devoting due attention to economic and social rights.

However, the Charter does not solve the substantive double-standard problem in one important respect, namely by not containing any provisions on *minority protection*. As was mentioned above, the political criteria for membership as formulated by the Copenhagen European Council in 1993 include 'stability of institutions guaranteeing democracy, the rule of law, human rights and respect for and protection of minorities'. This formula does not entirely correspond to the text of Article 6(1) EU which was enacted a few years later for the EU's internal usage: '[t]he Union is founded on the principles of liberty, democracy, respect for human rights and fundamental freedoms, and the rule of law, principles which are common to the Member States'. The formula which was used for the purpose of the enlargement process is more demanding, as it also includes protection of minorities as one of the indispensable premises for membership. Thus, among the political criteria set out by the European Union as conditions for the accession of the candidate states, the insistence on genuine minority protection is clearly the odd one out. Respect for democracy, the rule of law, and human rights have been recognized as fundamental values in the European Union's internal development *and* for the purpose of its enlargement, whereas minority protection is mentioned *only* in the latter context. Therefore, its imposition

---

[73] Sadurski, 'The Charter and Enlargement', 8 *European Law Journal* (2002) 340, at 345.
[74] Von Bogdandy, 'The European Union as a Human Rights Organization? Human Rights and the Core of the European Union', 37 *CMLRev.* (2000) 1307, at 1309.

on other countries may seem rather inconsistent or even somewhat hypocrit-
ical, and the distinctive treatment meted out to them is strangely reminiscent
of the infamous post-World War I minority protection regime, which
collapsed, in part, because it was perceived as a set of unilateral obligations
imposed on the newly created states of Central and Eastern Europe by the
Western victors of that war.[75]

References made by the European Union institutions in their recent
documents addressed to Central and Eastern European countries to minority
protection standards remain very generic. The action expected from these
countries is specified, but the instruments or standards which serve as the
basis of the EU's exigencies are not named, perhaps for fear that they could
return as a boomerang against the EU states themselves. Minority protection
is, then, an ill-defined political requirement with which the candidate countries are expected to comply because of the considerable carrot of accession
offered to them. Once a country will be accepted for membership, this will
ipso facto mean that the minority question is settled as far as the EU is
concerned. And if Central and Eastern European countries join the EU
with a clean slate in respect of their minorities, then there will be no need
for the European Union itself to modify its 'agnosticism' in respect of
minority protection *inside* the Union.

At the present time, there is certainly no consensus among the EU Member
States to include minority protection among the fundamental values listed
in Article 6 EU, nor to enact more modest forms of minority protection.[76]
Various proposals were made to include minority protection provisions in
the Charter of Rights, but to no avail;[77] Article 22 of the Charter merely
makes a generic reference to the values of cultural, religious, and linguistic
diversity.[78] It therefore seems likely that, in the future enlarged EU, ethnic
minority questions will basically remain within the domestic jurisdiction and

[75] See De Witte, 'Politics versus Law in the EU's Approach to Ethnic Minorities', in
J. Zielonka (ed.), *Europe Unbound. Enlarging and Reshaping the Boundaries of the European
Union* (2002) 137, and Pentassuglia, 'The EU and the Protection of Minorities: The Case of
Eastern Europe', 12 *EJIL* (2001) 3.

[76] Recent contributions on the timid emergence of minority protection in 'internal'
European Union law include: Hilpold, 'Minderheiten im Unionsrecht', *Archiv des Völker-
rechts* [2001] 432; Toggenburg, 'A Rough Orientation through a Delicate Relationship:
The European Union's Endeavours for its Minorities', in S. Trifunovska (ed.), *European
Minorities and Languages* (2001), 205 and in *European Integration Online Papers* (2000),
http://eiop.or.at/eiop/texte/2000–016a.htm; Fenet, 'Le droit européen des minorités', in A.
Fenet, G. Koubi, and I. Schulte-Tenckhoff, *Le droit et les minorités* (2000) 115.

[77] See the study by G Schwellnus, 'Much Ado about Nothing? Minority Protection
and the EU Charter of Fundamental Rights', *Constitutionalism Web-Papers* (2001),
http://les1.man.ac.uk/conweb/.

[78] For an analysis of Art. 22 and its possible application to minority groups see Piciocchi,
'La Carta tra identità culturali nazionali e individuali', in R. Toniatti (ed.), *Diritto, diritti,
giurisdizione. La Carta dei diritti fondamentali dell'Unione europea* (2002) 119.

constitutional discretion of the states. A marginal supervision of the performance of all states will be exercised, not by the European Union, but by the Council of Europe through the mechanisms provided under the European Convention of Human Rights and the Framework Convention on National Minorities. It is not to be ruled out, however, that a different constitutional scenario will unfold in which accession of Central and Eastern European countries will gradually make minority questions more prominently present in the institutional system and in the policies of the EU. Once the European Union has let the genie escape from the bottle, through its activist minority policy in the context of the preparation for enlargement, it may be difficult to put it back in after accession. Furthermore, the Union itself may well, in the years preceding the next enlargement, see a greater salience of ethnic minority questions, in respect of both immigrant and territorial minorities. Indeed, there is a certain convergence of 'traditional' ethnic minority issues and issues of multiculturalism arising out of immigration. The reference to 'ethnic discrimination', now inscribed in Article 13 of the EC Treaty after the Amsterdam revision, is a good expression of this convergence, and means that ethnic minority questions will, one way or the other, remain on the European Union's agenda for the years to come. In the years following enlargement, there may be mounting pressure to make the protection of various forms of cultural pluralism a central concern of the European Union.

Beyond the specific case of minority rights, the general 'double standard' problem will lose some of its bite as candidate countries start joining the European Union. Once these countries become full members of the European Union, the pre-accession monitoring of their human rights records will obviously come to a halt. They will then become subject to the same human rights obligations as the other Member States. The paradoxical conclusion could then be that accession will lead to a reduction of the European human rights standards for the candidate countries, and *could* therefore lead to a reduction of their actual respect for human rights. This may be the case in particular for those matters which, although duly examined in the human rights sections of the pre-accession reports, are not evidently within the scope of EC internal competence, such as: the rights of children, prison conditions, and minority protection. Formally speaking, the EU institutions will suddenly have to cease being interested in minority protection in Latvia, children's rights in Romania, and prison conditions in the Czech Republic, once these countries have joined the EU. This is hard to envisage, and one may think that NGOs, but also the EU institutions, will try to find the means of ensuring some continuity between pre- and post-accession.

The question for the future may therefore be whether membership of the European Union will entail a more comprehensive and articulated set of duties for all states to respect human rights and other fundamental constitutional values. The answer to this question will be given by the outcome of the current debate on the formal integration of the Charter of Rights in the EU Treaty, but also, and even more so, by the possible development of a systematic internal human rights 'policy' of the EU, addressing in new and more sophisticated ways the enforcement of the rights to which its institutions and Member States have paid tribute either in the Charter or in the pre-accession monitoring process.[79] Perhaps the aim should be for a middle way regime situated in between the two extremes of today, namely the detailed and across-the-board monitoring applied to the candidates for membership and the very subsidiary control of the performance of states that have become members of the European Union.

4. DIFFERENTIATION

Many observers of the European Union have noted that there is 'an apparent shift in the paradigm of European governance from one of uniformity and harmonisation to one of flexibility and differentiation'.[80] This evolution started prior to, and independently of, enlargement. However, the prospect of enlargement has made differentiation of rights and obligations between the Member States seem more appealing and even ineluctable. It is felt that the increased heterogeneity of the EU's member countries may, or must, also be reflected in a greater heterogeneity of the Union's institutional structures. In the years prior to the Copenhagen European Council of 1993, the alternative option of 'external flexibility', that is, a network of treaty relations with Central and Eastern European countries *without* membership of the Union itself, had been considered for a while (subsection A, below). Once the Copenhagen summit had set the signposts towards full membership, institutional differentiation *within* the European Council became a central constitutional topic (subsection B). In the late 1990s, the prospect of enlargement also prompted a reconsideration of the existing balance of power between large and small Member States, as it is expressed in the system of weighted voting in the Council (subsection C).

---

[79] For a broader discussion of this question, see de Búrca, 'Convergence and Divergence in European Public Law: The Case of Human Rights', in P. Beaumont, C. Lyons, and N. Walker (eds), *Convergence and Divergence in European Public Law* (2002) 131.

[80] De Búrca and Scott, 'Introduction', in G. de Búrca and J. Scott (eds), *Constitutional Change in the EU—From Uniformity to Flexibility?* (2000) 1. The contributions to that collective volume examine a wide range of aspects of this shift, as do the contributions in B. De Witte, D. Hanf, and E.Vos (eds), *The Many Faces of Differentiation in EU Law* (2001).

A. Flexibility Instead of Enlargement: The Short-lived Debate on the 'European Confederation'

In a TV speech of 31 December 1989, that is, very shortly after the fall of the Berlin Wall, the French President Mitterrand proposed the creation of a 'European Confederation' for creating a close institutional link between the EU countries and the countries of Central and Eastern Europe, including Russia. This new organization could, for some of its members, form the first stage on the road towards membership of the EU, but the idea of the Confederation was also presented in some of Mitterrand's statements as a semi-permanent scheme, obviating the need for extending EU membership. France pursued the idea for some years, but the Prague 'Assises' of June 1991, that were supposed formally to launch the project, were a failure. The project had evoked the hostility of the United States, mainly because the Confederation envisaged by Mitterrand included Russia but not the USA, and the Central and Eastern European countries themselves came to see it as a harmful diversion on their way to establishing closer links directly with the European Community.[81]

As a matter of fact, a different form of 'external flexibility' was set up under the Europe Agreements concluded in the early 1990s between the EC and the countries of Central and Eastern Europe. All these Europe Agreements set up their own separate Association Council, in the framework of which the original package deal laid down in the Agreement is gradually being extended and updated. These Association Councils act, as it were, as institutional satellites of the European Union. The EU institutions, as yet unencumbered by the direct participation of the candidate countries, continue to develop new regulatory policies, the content of which is then transposed to the applicant countries either by means of decisions of the Association Council or simply through their voluntary reception of the *acquis communautaire*. This asymmetrical situation, in which the European Union can unilaterally define (and constantly modify) the body of rules which the applicant states then have to accept, is planned to be transitional. It will come to an end with the conclusion of the accession negotiations when the applicants, or at least some of them, join the European Union. They will then be direct actors in the EU institutions on a par with the present 15 Member States. However, it cannot be ruled out that, if the accession negotiations should break down with one or other of these countries or if one or other of these countries failed to ratify the future accession treaty, the 'external flexibility' provided by the

[81] For a recent insider's account of the Confederation plan and of the reasons for its failure see Dumas, 'Un projet mort-né: la Confédération européenne', *Politique Etrangère* [2001] 687; see also Niblett, 'France and Europe at the End of the Cold War: Resisting Change', in R. Niblett and W. Wallace (eds), *Rethinking European Order—West European Responses, 1989–97* (2001) 89, at 91–94.

Europe Agreements' institutional mechanism would continue to apply for longer than expected.[82]

B. The Hesitant Codification of Flexibility and Closer Cooperation

The Treaty of Maastricht introduced major forms of institutional flexibility in the field of Economic and Monetary Union and social policy. These forms of flexibility were presented at the same time as, possibly temporary, exceptions and were not vindicated as a new generally applicable mode of addressing the problem of how to deal with the variety of interests and values of the Member States of the EU. Not long after the entry into force of the Maastricht reforms, the debate on the constitutional codification of a general regime of 'flexibility' began rather abruptly with a series of speeches and papers presented by leading politicians in the summer of 1994. Right from the start, this debate was intimately linked to enlargement, flexibility being seen in some quarters as a means of sidelining unknown and possibly unpredictable newcomers (but also the reluctant 'integrators' among the present Member States).

Three different political positions emerged in the early years. In his William and Mary Lecture given in Leiden in September 1994, John Major, the then British Prime Minister, welcomed the enlargement of the EU to the east and stated that the continuing growth in size and diversity of the Union should lead to greater *à la carte* flexibility, whereby overlapping groups of countries would be allowed to cooperate in specific fields of common interest *outside* the main EU institutional framework.[83] This was, in fact, nothing but the development of a traditional but little-noticed form of flexibility that had been present since the start of the European integration process: in all the policy fields in which the EC had not been granted exclusive competence, the Member States had retained a qualified power to conclude bilateral or multilateral international agreements among themselves.[84]

---

[82] The Europe Agreements are, in turn, one specific mode of cooperation within the broad range of EC external relations that are generally marked by a high degree of flexibility (see Cremona, 'Flexible Models: External Policy and the European Economic Constitution', in de Búrca and Scott, *supra* note 80, 59). A form of cooperation which follows rather closely the Europe Agreements model, and which offers a qualified perspective of eventual EU membership, is that of the Stabilization and Association Agreements that are being concluded with countries of South-Eastern Europe: see Cremona, 'Creating the New Europe: the Stability Pact for South Eastern Europe in the Context of EU–SEE Relations', 2 *Cambridge Yearbook of European Legal Studies* (1999) 463.

[83] Major, 'Europe, A Future that Works' (William and Mary Lecture, Leiden Town Hall), *Agence Europe*, No.6312, 10 Sep. 1994.

[84] De Witte, 'Old-fashioned Flexibility: International Agreements between Member States of the European Union', in de Búrca and Scott, *supra* note 80, at 31.

Other countries, particularly France and Germany, started canvassing, around the same time, the alternative and radically new idea of enabling smaller groups of states, or a permanent inner group of core countries, to cooperate *within* the institutional framework of the European Union. Many other governments saw both options (outside and inside the EU framework) as threats to the cohesion of the European Union, and to the principle of uniform rights and duties of states which had characterized the European integration process so far. The consensus that emerged during the 1996 Intergovernmental Conference, after long and exhausting negotiations, was that some mechanism of institutional flexibility (or of, as it was eventually called, 'closer cooperation') should be put in place, but that it should be encapsulated wthin the existing EU framework and be made subject to rather strict conditions.[85]

In fact, the conditions for closer cooperation imposed by the Amsterdam Treaty were so rigid that, only one year after the Treaty's entry into force and before the new regime had even been tested in practice, the Member State governments started a process of reviewing and, ultimately, redrafting of the relevant rules during the IGC that took place in 2000. Closer cooperation had not been on the initial narrow IGC agenda that was agreed by the Cologne European Council in June 1999, but was put there by the Feira European Council meeting in June 2000. The general willingness of Member State governments to consider a reform of the closer cooperation regime may have been inspired by the references made, in speeches by the German foreign minister, Joschka Fischer, and the French President, Jacques Chirac, held shortly before Feira, to the possible need of creating a 'centre of gravitation' or 'vanguard group' *outside* the EU framework if a more flexible system of closer cooperation *inside* the EU were not in place by the time of enlargement.[86]

General agreement was eventually reached, surprisingly easily (compared to the difficult negotiations on the same subject during the previous IGC), on

[85] For a political analysis of the negotiation of the Amsterdam flexibility regime, see Stubb, 'Negotiating Flexible Integration in the Amsterdam Treaty', in Neunreitner and Wiener, *supra* note 11, 153, and Wallace, 'Flexibility: A Tool of Integration or a Restraint on Disintegration?', in *ibid.*, 175. For a legal analysis of the Amsterdam regime see, among others, Bribosia, 'Différenciation et avant-gardes au sein de l'Union européenne. Bilan et perspectives du Traité d'Amsterdam', *Cahiers de droit européen* [2000] 57; F. Tuytschaever, *Differentiation in European Union Law* (1999); Ehlermann, 'Différenciation, flexibilité, coopération renforcée: les nouvelles dispositions du traité d'Amsterdam', *Revue du marché unique européen* [1997] 53; Kortenberg, 'Closer Cooperation in the Treaty of Amsterdam', 35 *CMLRev.* (1998) 833; Gaja, 'How Flexible is Flexibility under the Amsterdam Treaty?', 35 *CMLRev.* (1998) 855.
[86] See e.g., Louis, 'Post-scriptum: From Differentiation to the "Avant-garde"', in de Witte, Hanf, and Vos, *supra* note 80, at 379.

facilitating recourse to closer cooperation.[87] The Treaty of Nice will, if and when it comes into force, allow for enhanced cooperation initiatives to be launched by a qualified-majority vote in the Council, except in common foreign and security policy where the consensus of all states will continue to be required. The substantive conditions for closer cooperation are also somewhat relaxed compared to the Amsterdam regime. Furthermore, the Treaty of Nice sets out to modify the 'critical mass' of states required to launch a closer cooperation regime. Whereas under the present rules established by the Treaty of Amsterdam cooperation must concern a majority of Member States, the Treaty of Nice modifies this into 'eight Member States'.[88] This number corresponds, at the present time, to a majority of the states, so that the 'critical mass' requirement will not, in practice, change until the first enlargement of the Union. The significance of this reform is, therefore, that it should facilitate closer cooperation *after* enlargement, and the reform's half-hidden agenda may well be that it will allow the *present* Member States to cooperate more easily among themselves if and when the enlargement of the European Union appears to dilute the integration ethos.[89] Still, the possibility thus created of systems of closer cooperation among a minority only of Member States, but allowed to operate inside the framework of the European Union, has some odd consequences: in a Union of 25 or more Member States, it will theoretically allow up to three closer cooperation groups to be created in the same policy field, with all three being allowed to use the organs and mechanisms of the EU. Even if—as one may hope will be the normal case—only one closer cooperation group of eight operates within a specific field of EU policy, it would seem odd to have the European Commission and the European Parliament exercising their normal decision-making powers in their normal composition (that is, with the participation of representatives of *all* the Member States) and spending their limited time and financial resources on policy initiatives benefiting only a minority of eight states. These oddities underline the fact that the decision taken in Nice to facilitate closer cooperation in an enlarged European Union, while it may possibly allow greater flexibility in the development of EU policies (and thereby to some extent compensate for the lack of clear-cut reforms on the other matters discussed at the recent IGC), also contains a danger of institutional fragmentation and policy dilution. However, it could also remain an institutional *fata morgana* which, despite the time and energy invested by

---

[87] For a detailed analysis of the new rules agreed at Nice see Bribosia, 'Les coopérations renforcées au lendemain du Traité de Nice', *Revue du Droit de l'Union Européenne* [2001] 111; Rodrigues, 'Le Traité de Nice et les coopérations renforcées au sein de l'Union européenne', *Revue du marché unique européeen* [2001] 14; Tuytschaever, 'Nauwere samenwerking volgens het Verdrag van Nice', 11 *SEW* (2001) 375.

[88] Text of Art. 43(g) EU Treaty as amended by the Nice Treaty.

[89] Bribosia, *supra* note 87, at 155.

treaty negotiators in formulating its criteria and functioning, will have no practical application. It is not obviously the case that the new members from the East will show a greater propensity either to engage in closer cooperation or to let other states engage in it.[90]

Of possibly greater immediate importance is the place of the aspirant members in the existing (so-called 'predetermined') systems of closer cooperation that were put in place in Maastricht and Amsterdam: economic and monetary union (EMU) and justice and home affairs. In the latter field, the firm expectation is that the new Members States will be full participants in relation to both police and criminal law cooperation (the 'third pillar') and immigration, asylum, and civil law cooperation (Title IV of the EC Treaty), and will not want, or be allowed, to avail themselves of the various opt-outs applying to Denmark, Ireland, and the United Kingdom.[91] As regards economic and monetary union, the picture is rather different. Although the candidate countries do not claim an opt-out position similar to that of Denmark and the UK, they will, for several years, remain outside the Euro zone for failing to comply with the convergence criteria. The EMU chapter of the EC Treaty provides for the partial participation in decision-making of Member States who do not adopt the single currency,[92] and there is some tension about drawing the line between autonomous action of the 'Euro group' countries and joint decisions involving all the Member States of the Union. This tension may be exacerbated if the number of countries remaining outside the 'Euro group' becomes as large, or almost, as that of the 'ins'.

The differentiation that could, in practice, be most prominent after enlargement is the less spectacular but omnipresent kinds of flexibility permitted by recourse to minimum harmonization, soft law and tailor-made opt-outs which are, already, a major characteristic of EC regulatory instruments.[93]

---

[90] Manin, 'Flexibilité et élargissement', in C.D. Ehlermann (ed.), *Multi-Speed Europe—the Legal Framework of Variable Geometry in the European Union* (1999) 141, at 147.

[91] See in particular Art. 8 of the Schengen Protocol to the Treaty of Amsterdam: 'For the purposes of the negotiations for the admission of new Member States into the European Union, the Schengen acquis and further measures taken by the institutions within its scope shall be regarded as an acquis which must be accepted in full by all State candidates for admission'.

[92] See C. Zilioli and M. Selmayr, *The Law of the European Central Bank* (2001), chap. 4, and Louis, 'Differentiation and the EMU', in de Witte, Hanf, and Vos, *supra* note 80, 43.

[93] For views of this kind of differentiation in secondary EU law see e.g., de Búrca, 'Differentiation within the "Core"? The Case of the Internal Market', in de Búrca and Scott, *supra* note 80, 133; Vos, 'Differentiation, Harmonisation and Governance', in de Witte, Hanf and Vos, *supra* note 80, at 145.

C. The Equality of Small and Large Countries and the Question of Voting Power in the Council of Ministers

The EC Treaty strongly affirms and entrenches the principle of equal treatment of the citizens of the Member States, regardless of their nationality. The central embodiment of this principle is Article 12 EC, but there are many other, more specific manifestations of it. In contrast, no explicit mention is made, in the Treaties, of a principle of *equality of the Member States qua* states. However, it may be argued that this is an unwritten constitutional principle of EU law, which is rooted in the international legal principle of sovereign equality of states and finds expression in a large number of EC and EU Treaty norms, such as: the equal representation of all Member States in the Council of Ministers and the European Council, the rotation of the presidency of the Council among all states, the equal availability of the veto right when the Council decides by unanimity, the equal status of all national languages as official languages of the EU, etc.[94]

Whenever the Council of Ministers decides by qualified majority, the Member States' representatives are provided with an unequal number of weighted votes. This device can be considered either as an exception to the principle of equality of Member States; or, alternatively, it can be viewed as a 'formal inequality which aims at bringing about substantive equality, or, at least, aims to reduce the substantive inequality that results from an over-accentuated formal equality of States'.[95]

The system of weighted votes was originally introduced for the European Economic Community, which had only six Member States. The formula adopted then was to grant Belgium and the Netherlands twice the number of votes of Luxembourg, and the three larger Member States (France, Germany, and Italy) twice the number of votes of Belgium and the Netherlands, creating a 4:2:1 ratio in voting strength. The qualified majority was set at 12 out of 17 votes, which was just over 70 per cent of the total number. This crude allocation of votes bore only a dim resemblance to the actual population of each country but expressed a subtle political *rapport de forces* and proved to be very stable.[96] Both the proportions between categories of states and the overall threshold of just over 70 per cent were confirmed when the EEC was created in 1957 and at each enlargement round afterwards. Newcomers were fitted into the existing scheme (for instance, the UK was given the same number of votes as the three large founding states, and Greece the

---

[94] See Wouters, 'Constitutional Limits of Differentiation: The Principle of Equality', in *ibid.*, 301, at 315–316.

[95] Wouters, *supra* note 94, at 316.

[96] See the analysis of the EEC Treaty negotiations on this point by de l'Ecotais, 'La pondération des voix au Conseil des ministres de la Communauté européenne', *Revue du Marché Commun et de l'Union européenne* [1996] 388.

same number as Belgium and the Netherlands), and new intermediate categories were created for countries situated in between: for instance, Spain was
fitted between the large and the small group, and Denmark and Ireland
between the small and the very small. What did change, of course, was the
overall size of the coalition of states needed to reach a qualified majority. Also,
as there were more small than big countries among the newcomers, the
relative power position of the large states, taken as a group, gradually deteri-
orated. The relative voting power of each individual large state also mathematically diminished with each new accession.[97] This phenomenon became
quite clear with the addition, during the last round, of three smallish
countries, Austria, Finland, and Sweden. The large states took the line, in
the Amsterdam and Nice negotiations, that another semi-automatic adjustment of votes on the occasion of the future eastern enlargement would be
altogether unacceptable and that, instead, an overall reallocation of votes
should take place which would make these more closely proportional to the
population figures of the various groups of countries.

It could hardly be contested that the voting arrangements in the Council
were indeed getting seriously lopsided. The five largest states of the EU,
which together have 80 per cent of the total population, do not jointly possess
a qualified majority. On the other hand, the minimum share of the overall
EU population represented by a possible winning coalition of smaller states is
around 58 per cent (a majority which is not very much 'qualified' in this
respect), and it would, if extrapolated to a Europe of 27, go down to 50 per
cent. The figures are even more striking when looked at from the other end,
namely that of the composition of a 'blocking minority' (that is, the minimum coalition required to prevent the others from assembling a qualified
majority). The minimum share of the population formed by a blocking
minority coalition formed of only small states is now 13 per cent and
would go further down, among the 27, to a mere 10 per cent.[98]

However, one may wonder whether the global *rapport de force* between
small and large states has ever been a genuine political issue. Hayes-Renshaw
and Wallace have argued that there is no systematic cleavage between larger
and smaller states in the operation of the Council, but that winning and
blocking coalitions are typically based on affinities of interests and ideas
related to the specific matter under discussion.[99] Moreover, reallocation of
votes for the benefit of the larger states was not the only possible remedy for

[97] For instructive tables on the history of the weighting of votes and on the changes in the
relative strength of large and small Member States see M. Westlake, *The Council of the
European Union*, rev. edn. (1999), at 96–97.

[98] These figures are drawn from Best, *supra* note 16, at 3.

[99] Hayes-Renshaw and Wallace, *supra* note 40, at 295. See also Wallace, *supra* note 28, at
336: 'there is simply no evidence that the cleavage line often falls between large and small
member states'.

this distorted situation. An easier and more transparent alternative solution was put on the negotiation table, both in Amsterdam and in Nice, and received the backing of a large number of (mainly smaller) Member States. This alternative option was to transform the present weighted-voting system into a system of *dual majority*, in which Council decisions would have to be backed by a simple majority of member countries (eight out of 15 today, 14 out of 27 in a future EU) and also (at the same time) by a number of countries that together form a majority of the European Union population. In this way, the political weight of the larger states would have been duly accounted for, in a straightforward and easily explainable manner, directly derived from accepted principles of democratic representation in divided-power systems. The system could also be applied automatically to any further accession and therefore be stable in time. The fatal flaw of this option was, no doubt, that it would have put an end to the equal influence in Council decision-making which, today, the four major Member States possess. By the increased importance given to actual population figures, the dual majority system would have given Germany more voting power than France, Italy, or the United Kingdom, which seemed politically unacceptable. Therefore, a consensus could only be reached on a generalized re-weighting of actual votes for each present and future Member State (to be effectuated from 2005 onwards), which gives additional voting clout to the larger countries and thereby reduces the collective voting power of the candidate countries (because of the fact that most of them will be small or medium-sized). The Nice compromise took the form of an arithmetical nightmare laid down in a protocol and a declaration to the Nice Treaty.[100] If all happens according to plan, the national delegations in the future Council of the EU-of-27 will together control 345 votes (ranging from 29 votes for each of the four largest countries down to three for Malta), and 258 of these votes will be the minimum threshold for forming a qualified majority.[101] The 12 prospective members will together have 108 votes, which is 31 per cent of the total votes, and this gives them a joint 'blocking minority', but much less than they would have had if the *present* weighting system were extrapolated to a future Europe of 27.[102] 74.8 per cent of the total vote will be required for the

[100] Art. 3 of the Protocol on the enlargement of the European Union; Declaration on the enlargement of the European Union.

[101] For a table summarizing the figures decided in Nice, see Piris, *supra* note 17, at 21. For a description of the full detail of the re-weighting concocted at Nice, see Van Nuffel, *supra* note 17, at 352–359; and Galloway, *supra* note 17, at 76–93. The re-weighting is accompanied by an additional condition for qualified-majority decisions, namely that they must be backed by countries representing together a majority of the Union's population. This added criterion means, in practice, that Germany would obtain a slightly higher blocking power than the other large states.

[102] If the present weighting system were mathematically extended to an EU with 27 Member States, the 12 newcomers would together have 47 out of 134 votes, that is, almost 36 %.

adoption of Council decisions, according to the Nice rules, which is a small increase in the present qualified-majority voting (QMV) percentage—a surprising result for a Treaty reform which was supposed to enhance the EU institutions' capacity to act.[103]

5. CONCLUSION

When embarking on their recent intergovernmental conference of 2000, the Member State governments expressed the conviction that a solution to three narrow and rather technical institutional questions would yield a considerable (or at least, sufficient) improvement of the efficacy of the EU's institutional apparatus in view of enlargement. Some sort of reform was eventually agreed on these three questions of Commission membership and structure, Council voting mode, and allocation of voting weights to each country within the Council. However, on each of these three points the solutions reached at Nice were either very timid or highly questionable. The eventual reduction in the size of the Commission was agreed in principle, but the details still need to be worked out. There was only a modest shift from unanimity to qualified-majority decision-making in the Council, leaving many opportunities for future blackmail by single dissatisfied states. The operation of qualified-majority voting could have been made both simple and democratic by opting for a dual majority system, but instead the weighting system was preserved and the actual allocation was revised in favour of the larger states, but in a way which was not consistent, left bitter feelings among many delegations to the IGC and is almost absurdly obscure. Therefore, the official view, expressed in the Declaration on the future of the Union annexed to the Nice Treaty—that these were successful institutional reforms that have duly prepared the EU for receiving up to 12 new members—is highly questionable. Misgivings about the reform process are compounded by the fact that the Union has not seriously addressed other, particularly daunting, problems of administrative reform relating to the internal functioning of the European institutions and to their day-to-day interaction with national (and regional) levels of government. Finally, the Nice Treaty did not begin to address some of the broader constitutional reform issues.[104]

The forced optimism that was expressed immediately after Nice by the governments and institutions has given way to a more guarded assessment. The European Parliament opined that the Treaty of Nice 'has provided a

[103] See Galloway, *supra* note 17, at 90: 'the final outcome is complex, difficult to explain and undoubtedly runs counter to the general desire at the start of the negotiations not to make Council decision-making more difficult'.

[104] See Wouters, 'Institutional and Constitutional Challenges for the European Union— Some Reflections in the Light of the Treaty of Nice', 26 *ELRev.* (2001) 342.

half-hearted and in some cases inadequate response to the matters encompassed within the already modest Intergovernmental Conference agenda'.[105] In a recent paper, the European Commission stated that, in its view, 'the changes wrought by the Treaty of Nice will not be commensurate, in the medium and long term, with the requirements of the European project in the enlarged Union'.[106] Indeed, the Member State governments themselves have candidly admitted, in their Laeken Declaration, that there must be 'more democracy, transparency and efficiency in the European Union' and that one should move '[t]owards adoption of a Constitution for European citizens'.[107] Taking a pessimistic view, one could say that all previous constitutional reforms were inadequate and that the constitutional implications of enlargement will now have to be faced in the nick of time and under heavy pressure. Taking a more optimistic view, one could say that it is precisely the relentless advance of the enlargement process that has pushed the EU institutions and Member State governments to make the earlier reforms of Amsterdam and Nice and pushes them now to address the future of Europe in openly constitutional terms. In this sense, the enlargement process is not only part of Europe's constitutional problem, but also part of Europe's constitutional solution; it is 'both a threat and challenge to the constitutional integrity of the EU and an opportunity to help secure or deepen that integrity'.[108]

The present Member States are, for the first time, addressing constitutional reform *together* with the candidate countries. The Laeken Declaration states that 'the accession candidate countries will be fully involved in the Convention's proceedings. They will be represented in the same way as the current Member States (one government representative and two national parliament members) and will be able to take part in the proceedings without, however, being able to prevent any consensus which may emerge among the Member States'.[109] The latter restriction seems justified: as long as the candidate countries have not joined the EU, they should not be allowed to veto or restrict its institutional evolution. However, the Convention will be followed, in 2004, by an intergovernmental conference which will take the final decisions on constitutional reforms. By that time, some candidate countries may have become members of the European Union and, if so, will obviously be parties to the revision treaty on an equal footing with (and with the same

---

[105] European Parliament resolution on the Treaty of Nice and the future of the European Union of 31 May 2001, OJ 2002 C 47 E/108, point 2.

[106] Communication from the Commission on the Future of the European Union, *Renewing the Community Method*, COM(2001) 727 of 5 Dec. 2001, at 2.

[107] The quoted words are sub-headings of the Laeken Declaration.

[108] Walker, *supra* note 7.

[109] Laeken Declaration, *supra* note 4.

veto power as) the present Member States. This intergovernmental conference of 2004 will not, even if it leads to a new Treaty revision, formulate the final constitutional settlement for the European Union, if only because enlargement, once it comes into effect, will cause new institutional challenges whose nature will only gradually become apparent and is thus likely to lead towards further constitutional reform debates.

Index